THE *Senior Citizens'* SURVIVAL MANUAL

By Bill Kaysing

PUBLISHED BY

Βellwether
press

5815 Dearborn
Mission, KS 66202

Library of Congress Catalog Card Number 87-72963

ISBN: 0-944136-00-1

Book Design and Typography by: Commtype/Access Publishing
Printed and bound in the United States of America.

Dedication

This book is dedicated to Alan Hopkins Nittler, M.D., a true physician and gentleman who devoted his time, energies and talents to the welfare and benefit of his fellow man.

Acknowledgements

I much appreciate the confidence of my publisher, Bellwether Press, who has made this book possible. Much credit is due to Donna La Brecque, my editor, whose astute revisions have much enhanced the entire presentation. And I thank my friend, Dan Clark, for his many unique ideas which appear throughout. And my very special thanks to Ruth Kaysing who is really the key that unlocked the entire concept.

TABLE OF CONTENTS

PREFACE

This book is the culmination of six decades of research into the field of alternatives. There are many opinions that can be explored to enrich your life as you pursue self-fulfillment. Happiness and contentment are achievable riches, and can be attained without having to buy into the corporate bill of goods.

Until I was about 40, I bought the corporate bill of goods almost 100 percent. Then, in a sudden paradigm shift, my life took on astonishingly new dimensions. I discovered that, as De Chardin said, "There are no limits to our human potential...we are truly partners in creation."

What I discovered was that if you pursued your own dreams instead of what the establishment provided as dreams, you would find something that was rewarding both in monetary and spiritual ways. In my own case, it was writing.

Sure, there were lean times. I can remember not having the rent money and having a check come in from a magazine for an article on the very same day. Close, yes, but at the same time adventurous, risky and exciting.

Of course, there were unforgettable times like when someone asked my daughter if she knew the author of those articles in *Cycle World* magazine, and she replied, with a shake of her curls, "My Dad wrote them." Moments like that went a long way towards filling in the holes in my life.

Now I can see the Western horizon clearly; sometime in the foreseeable future I will, like all seniors, depart this planet. But one thing is definite: by taking the path less traveled, I have seen a different part of the forest, the part with strange and wonderful trees, and not the cardboard image of a what forest is supposed to look like.

Yes, it's been a most entertaining and enlightening journey, one that I invite you to explore with me in the following pages.

And finally, keep in mind that though you are also a senior, it is never too late to start out on a path of your very own.

— B.K.
August 1987

CHAPTER ONE
HEALTH

PROLOGUE

"Strengthen your body with physical labor and eat pure food. Use your knowledge of chemistry and medicine to avoid harmful foodstuffs. Maintain a balanced diet of natural foods for the body can be no better than the building materials which you provide it. The responsibility for its proper nourishment is yours alone. If your body fails you, the Lord cannot use you. Moreover, a sound mind cannot exist in a poor body, nor is a sound body compatible with a distraught mind. Spiritual harmony and advancement demand a vigorous, stable mind and body. Be watchful over your vehicle."

— Essene Brotherhood from the Ultimate Frontier

Placing this chapter first in the book indicates our opinion of its importance to seniors' happiness and well-being. No single aspect of human life is as important, vital and critical as health. If you have it, all things are possible; if not, you are in trouble at any age. As wise old Samuel Johnson once said:

"What can a sick man say but that he is sick."

OVERVIEW

The elements of health and happiness as I have perceived them over the last 65 years are: where you live, what you do, what you think, what you eat, drink and breathe, your social environment (family, friends and associates), exercise, and other miscellaneous considerations.

WHERE YOU LIVE

Most Americans, seniors especially, are crowded into unhealthy cities. About 97 percent of our citizens are crowded onto just three percent of the land, leaving the bulk of our country virtually uninhabited.

To see this in a dramatic way, take a plane trip from San Francisco to New York and see how much of our spacious land is absolutely devoid of development. I recall a trip to Montana during which I drove for miles and miles only to see towering mountains and thousands of square miles of lovely forest and meadow with only a few homes and ranches scattered about.

Then consider the vast and wonderfully warm Sun Belt of the Southwest, where millions of acres of pristine desert await the traveler or settler.

Needless to say, you, whether a senior or not, can have a healthier environment if you live away from an urbania. You can always go into town for a visit, but for lasting health and vigor, try the rural regions. In most cases, you can live for less, as rents and payments are lower and the opportunity to grow your own vegetables is easily viable. Refer to the chapters concerning *Places* and *Food* for more details.

WHAT YOU DO

Many years ago, I was employed as a technical writer for a large aerospace company in the west San Fernando Valley in California. The pay was high, so my family enjoyed a new home, two cars and a generous inventory of recreational vehicles. However, the entire scope of our life was suspended on the rather tenuous and always breakable thread of my own psyche and persona. Stress was heavy and constant; even weekends and vacations did little to alleviate the constant attrition of my somewhat shakey nervous system. I often dreamed of abandoning the entire catastrophe for a more rewarding and relaxing way of life.

The pressure finally built to the point where I either had to leave or suffer physical and mental collapse.

So I departed. As simple as that. Looking back almost a quarter of a century later, I realize it was the wisest move I ever made; my health is good and I enjoy everything I enjoyed when I was 25. I actually feel much better than when I was 25, since I no longer drink, smoke or eat junk food.

What this anecdote proves is that what you do with your life, pre- or post-retirement, is extremely critical to the state of your health. If you have a high-stress lifestyle (and this can exist even after retirement), then you are risking a breakdown. The human body is built to withstand a great deal, but it cannot be continually abused.

What you do with your life is entirely your own business, subject, of course, to the programming that you all received. Be sure, however, that what you choose

doesn't cost you your health. After all, there is nothing in the world, neither gold nor silver, nor 150-foot yachts that is worth your well-being.

WHAT YOU THINK

I recently read an article which compared the human brain to a computer. The point was made that if you put garbage information in, you got garbage information out. The process abbreviated, garbage in, garbage out, is GIGO.

The author made the telling point that if you constantly put negative thoughts into your brain, then your routinely negative thinking would thus only have a negative output. The upcoming chapter on *Philosophy* will make even more sense to you!

For now, remember that your body reflects exactly what your mind is doing. Thinking good thoughts will guarantee good health.

WHAT YOU EAT, DRINK AND BREATHE

Re-read the quotation at the beginning of this chapter; it says it best. And further on in this book we'll discuss the importance of food to health.

Suffice to say that if you eat good food, drink pure water and breathe fresh, unpolluted air, you'll be giving your body what it needs to keep itself in top shape. It is really that unadorned.

YOUR SOCIAL ENVIRONMENT

There is a truism that we often find our worst enemies within the boundaries our own families. How often have we seniors seen a person destroyed by a thoughtless parent, a sibling or a spouse? Dramatic works for the theatre are replete with dreadful tales of destruction and death resulting from strife within the family circle. This is why you should carefully evaluate the real effects of those closest to you. If damage results, you almost always have the option to put a lot of space between you and the person causing the pain.

Friends and associates can be wearing on our psychic defenses as well. It is wise to move periodically so as to evaluate just what a specific person means in terms of your wellness. Unlike in a family situation, it is far easier to put space between you and a false friend or negative associate.

It is interesting to note that Thoreau often found solitude to be more rewarding than associating with most people. He was not necessarily advocating the life of a perpetual hermit, although he did spend a lot of time alone. What he meant, it seems, was that life can be delightful for that senior who has learned to fly solo.

EXERCISE

My friend, Dr. Alan Nittler, told me that every step you took was a friendly boost to your heart, since walking was conducive to improved circulation. So ever since, I have made it a point to walk at least three miles a day no matter where I am or what the circumstances (I even walk around when flying to Europe! After all, those huge planes have plenty of aisles!).

I consider this the king of exercises since there are so many spin-off benefits; you see interesting things and often, the best ideas have come while taking my daily constitutional.

Today there is such a strong emphasis on exercise—gyms and spas are springing up right and left. Also, outdoor exercise opportunities abound; from hang gliding and wind surfing to mountain biking and rock climbing. You can pick from the joyful inventory of healthful exercise, perferably those that are outdoors. With continued implementation, you are destined to enjoy a new body as well as a new outlook!

MISCELLANEOUS

Pick up an alternative lifestyle newspaper and see how many health resources there are—from massage and counseling to wild herbs and hot springs. Notice the abundant inventory of wellness support and take advantage.

In summary, we have tried to make the point that no single element in itself produces the wonderful feeling of total wellness. You need them all. And best of all, they are yours for the taking.

The balance of this chapter consists of selections from various authors and sources of health information that I believe is timely, relevant and important. A final word...

Health is not detached from life...it IS life!

ROBERT MENDELSOHN, M.D.

Dr. Mendelsohn is a pediatrician who followed the precepts of orthodox medicine until it became clear to him that modern medicine was, for the most part, a fraud. Here are some selections from what I consider to be the most damning, perceptive and entertaining book on American medical orthodoxy ever published, *Confessions of a Medical Heretic*. I strongly recommend that you walk to your nearest library and check out a copy. Or better yet, buy a paperback from your nearest bookstore. It has gone into several printings so it should be readily available.

Read it and be amazed:

"I do not believe in Modern Medicine. I am a medical heretic. My aim in this book is to persuade you to become a heretic too.

In medical school I failed to look deeply into a study that was going on around me, of the effects of the hormone DES—because I believed. Who could have suspected that twenty years later we would discover that DES causes vaginal cancer and genital abnormalities in children born to women receiving the drug during pregnancy.

I confess that I failed to be suspicious of oxygen therapy for premature infants, even though the best equipped and most advanced premature nurseries had an incidence of partial or total blindness of around ninety percent of all low-birth-weight infants.

I still believed when I took part in a scientific paper on the use of Terramycin. We claimed there were no side effects. Of course there weren't. We didn't wait long enough to find out that not only didn't Terramycin—or any other antibiotic—do much good for infections, but that it left thousands of children with yellow-green teeth and tetracycline deposits in their bones.

And I believed in the irradiation of tonsils, lymph nodes and the thymus gland. I believed my professors when they said that of course radiation was dangerous, but that the doses we were using were absolutely harmless. Years later, around the time we found out that the "absolutely harmless" radiation done a decade or two before was now reaping a harvest of thyroid tumors. I couldn't help wondering when some of my patients came back with nodules on their thyroids: Why are you coming back to ME? To ME, who did this to you in the first place!

But I no longer believe in Modern Medicine.

I believe that despite all the super technology and elite bedside manner that's supposed to make you feel about as well cared-for as an astronaut on the way to the moon, the greatest danger to your health is the doctor who practices Modern Medicine.

I believe that Modern Medicine's treatments for disease are seldom effective and that they're often more dangerous than the diseases they are designed to treat.

I believe that more than ninety percent of Modern Medicine could disappear from the face of the earth—doctors, hospitals, drugs and equipment—and the effect on our health would be immediate and beneficial."

AUTHOR'S NOTE: A telling case of this occurred when a surgeon's strike at General Hospital in Los Angeles caused a reduction in the death rate. So much for life-saving surgery.

To summarize Mendelsohn's excellent and witty presentation, here are some salient statements...

"The modern medical doctor is a high priest of death."
"The modern hospital is a temple of doom."

Be forewarned. Read the book. Laugh as you are informed about the greatest danger to seniors since WWII.

PERSONAL NOTE: Like Dr. Mendelsohn, I once believed in modern medicine and actually solicited the care of doctors. However, most of my experiences proved to be of no value. About 1952 I decided to go it alone—to be my own doctor. I tossed out all the pills that had been prescribed for me and simply relied on good food, vigorous exercise and the application of my abilities to creative work.

It worked! And I have never felt healthier or more energetic than I do as I write these words. Sure, I could drop dead later in the afternoon, but I would die with a smile; I have enjoyed many fine years of robust health doing everything that I have ever wanted to do—swimming in rushing rivers, climbing mountains, racing motorcycles, flying planes, running boats of all kinds, visiting strange and wonderful places (both primitive and developed) and best of all, meeting lots of fascinating people.

And all of these have been possible not because of having lots of money or possessions because those have always been somewhat scarce. No, it is possible because I HAVE MY HEALTH.

Now, on to another renaissance man—one who changed my life in many ways. And one who can change yours, too.

ALAN HOPKINS NITTLER, M.D.

In my lifetime, I've had the opportunity to meet some truly outstanding people—men and women of drive, courage and accomplishment. In the top ten I would certainly rank Dr. Nittler, or, "Doc" as he liked to be called.

Like Dr. Mendelsohn, Doc once believed in modern medicine. He practiced it for many years. But an incident occured that changed the entire course of his life; it seems that Alan's pet dog became ill and he took it to the vet. Rather than prescribe pills, the vet put the dog on a strict diet of special foods. Within a short time, the dog was chasing around with great vigor.

The demonstration was not lost on Doc Nittler. He began reading up on nutrition and decided to try it in his own practice. Since people who were cured of their diseases recommended Doc to their friends, it wasn't long before he doubled his patient load. In time, Alan became quite well known in the U.S. and was even more famous when he authored the best-selling book, *A New Breed Of Doctor*. Selling in the millions, the book describes how he would prescribe simple foods, a detoxifying diet and other nutritional therapies to his patients.

However, his success did not escape the evil eye of establishment medicine. They were clever and took away Doc's license to practice in California. He still retained his license in his home state of Ohio and could have gone there to practice. However, he chose to remain in the West and instead of an active practice, he began writing about his experiences. The crescendo of his learning appears in a book from which we include some selections. The book is, in my opinion, the most cogent and applicable summary of health problems and solutions in America. What appears is a compendium of Alan's extensive knowledge in brief but specific form. He lists almost all known diseases and then proceeds to give advice on how optimal health can be obtained by keeping the body supplied with the nutrients it needs. This book will be available in the near future, so please write if you are interested in more information.

Here then, are selections from Alan H. Nittler's, *Philosophy of Optimal Health*, a Do-It-Yourself Compendium of Nutritional Expertise.

AUTHOR'S OVERVIEW

Dr. Nittler's magnum opus is presented in manual form. An index of diseases allows an individual to look up his or her ailment and then proceed to be his or her own nutritional advisor.

But preceding the compendium is a well-written dissertation on just why we need to pay attention to what we eat.

"Citizen USA is at the crossroads. He finds himself in a situation where his health care facilities are capable of making him live longer by radical surgical procedures or the use of strong drugs which, when taken long enough, will kill him."

"He faces the prospect of having his doctor tell him that nutrition is not playing a part in his illness even though the doctor does not know the cause of the illness."

"The really sad part of this saga is that organized medicine and government agencies are definitely contrary to individualistic efforts to break the barrier. Trained persons with degrees are threatened with loss of privileges, status and licensure when they delve into basic physiologic, metabolic and nutritional truths regarding health and disease. Of course, this is not a new concept since original thinkers for many centuries have been persecuted, even burned at the stake, when they proposed ideas that were contrary to the establishment."

"We see a society loaded with degenerative diseases involving the heart, blood, bones and joints, respiratory and gastrointestinal systems. Even cancer is rampant. It is estimated that cancer will strike one of three within a few years if the present trend continues."

"How can we account for these figures of gloom? We have thousands of examples of exposure to chemical stresses; dyes, sweeteners, softeners,

acidifiers, alkalizers, hardeners, preservatives, etc., are found abundantly in our foods. It has been speculated that everyone in the U.S. ingests about ten pounds of these chemicals each year."

"Then there are stresses from emotional problems, radiation, microwaves and so on...the net result of all these factors is that our bodies are stressed more than our ancestors."

"The body must do something to counteract the extra stresses imposed on it."

"Man is a total organism living in a total environment who needs total foods to have total metabolism for the total body. Nutrients must be in the form as produced naturally since natural foods contain all the associated synergistic micronutrients which are needed by the body to metabolize that particular food. And natural foods need to be consumed fresh and raw."

Just before Dr. Nittler was attacked by the medical establishment for curing too many people with fresh raw foods and intelligently administered supplements, I had the opportunity to see him in action, as we were co-authoring a book on nutritional self-care. Patients would fly in from distant cities to his Santa Cruz offices barely able to walk a few halting steps into his examination room. Then, in a matter of a week or two, they would bounce into his office, all smiles and happiness. Doc had performed seeming miracles with his astute diagnoses and application of nutritional knowledge. Ruth was one of his patients and to this day adheres to his regimen of pure foods consumed in a balanced dietary program. And at 71, she can out-play, out-hike and out-everything better than many women half her age!

Dr. Nittler's book will be available soon. In the meantime, here are some guidelines:

1. Slowly phase out those artificial drugs you've been taking. That includes the supposedly benign drugs such as aspirin.

2. Go on a juice fast for a several days drinking only pure organic apple juice— about one gallon per day. If you prefer, drink pure organic grape juice diluted 50 percent with pure water.

3. Then try a mono or duo diet eating only one or two kinds of pure, organic, natural fruits and vegetables. My favorite duo diet is bananas and oranges.

4. Gradually add lightly-steamed vegetables, but be sure that at least half of your diet is raw.

5. Exercise, do something constructive and helpful for others, and get out of the urban environment if possible.

These simple measures can often cure or at least alleviate a large percentage of degenerative disease. Try it for a week or so and then write me in care of the publisher as to your experience.

In closing, I want to thank Dr. Nittler, God rest his soul, for his courageous and progressive work in behalf of the health of people everywhere. His dedicated efforts are a lasting inspiration. There is no doubt that history will record him as one of the leaders in the movement to liberate humanity from the bonds of medical ignorance and repression.

FAST FOOD FATS

Heart disease is the leading cause of death in the United States. Much of it is attributable to the excess of fat in the diet. One of the best ways to reduce fat consumption is to eliminate fast foods from your diet.

See *Appendix A* for the facts on the amount of fat in typical fast food offerings by McDonald's, a leading purveyor of what I call "killerburgers." As Nat Pritikin once said, *"McDonald's is doing a great job of killing America."*

PRIME TIMER

Several years ago I wrote a weekly column for a senior newspaper published in Santa Cruz, CA. I loved responding to readers, but knew that sooner or later I would be fired because, as usual, I didn't pull my literary punches, and especially not where the medical establishment was concerned. What we present in *Appendix B* are the actual columns as published without changes or edits.

THE IMMUNE SYSTEM

This book was ready to go to press when the output of news on AIDS made a quantum leap in quantity and scope in all media. Thus, to make this senior guide as timely and relevant as possible, we are presenting a comprehensive abstract of information which will help you avoid AIDS and similar nuisances.

The following is abstracted from a review of the immune system written by Laurence E. Badgley, M.D., a physician in general practice in San Bruno, CA. He specializes in acupuncture, homeopathy, orthomolecular medicine, chelation therapy and nutrition.

> *"The incidence of herpes, AIDS, candida albicans and allergies seems to be rapidly rising. Each of these problems is related to a weakened immune system. There are practical things we can do to fortify ourselves against such problems if we understand how the immune system works. Henceforth, we will refer to the immune system as IS.*
>
> *The IS is a second brain which senses the presence of foreign (non-self)*

materials such as viruses, foods, parasites, bacteria, fungi, toxins, venom, pollens and cancer cells.

Stress can inhibit thymus gland function and depress the IS by increasing adrenal cortisone production. Noise and population density have been related to tumor development in experimental animals. In a study of cancer patients, it was found that common traits included feelings of isolation and despair in youth, a strong adult relationship (person, job or material object) and poor coping skills when the relationship was broken. Others have demonstrated that IS depression occurs after the loss of a spouse, not as a function of stress but as a function of how the survivor perceives and handles the loss.

Individuals become pan-allergic and intolerant to low levels of common foreign materials such as food, perfume, and synthetic gases leaching from carpets, furniture and painted surfaces. Mercury, which is found in most silver dental fillings, has been implicated in injury to the IS.

There are ways to provide natural support to the IS. Experimental evidence has demonstrated the need for vitamins A, B's, pantothenic acid, folic acid, C and E and the minerals manganese, zinc, selenium and iron, all in the proper amounts. A good source for these substances are fresh fruits and vegetables and unprocessed oils. Digestive system function can be measured to evaluate the effective utilization of nutrients. The glandular system must be kept intact and protected from needless surgery. Experiments have demonstrated beneficial effects on the IS from selected glandular products. Indiscriminate use of antibiotics, cortisone (prednisone), hormones (birth control pills), x-rays, and chemical therapies can be injurious to the IS. Limits should be placed on synthetic chemicals in food, water, and air.

Proper mental attitudes of optimism, humor, forgiveness, love, satisfaction, and self-worth all strengthen the IS and can be achieved through attitudinal counseling, biofeedback, autogenic training, meditation.''

IMMUNE SYSTEM DO'S AND DON'T'S

(Reprinted courtesy, Louise Tenney, *Today's Herbal Health*, Woodland Books, P.O. 1422, Provo, UT 84063)

The immune system is the body's main defense against disease. The spleen is the main producer of white blood cells which are the ''police'' of our bodies guarding us against any invading foreign agents or internally produced toxins. Some of these white blood cells are processed by the thymus to become ''detectives.'' They search out, identify and mark the harmful agents in our bodies for destruction by the other white blood cells.

Our cells are fed by the circulating blood system but they are cleansed *by a much larger lymphatic system that acts like an internal vacuum cleaner. It works at sub-atmospheric pressure to suck up the by-products of metabolism at the cellular level. The clear lymph fluid, or plasma, is the liquid media used to transport the toxic wastes away from the cells and to recycle usable products back into the food chain.*

This system can become clogged with excess protein or other dead cells with just a lack of exercise. Since there is no pump to circulate the lymph fluid, we must exercise if we want to maintain the lymphatic highway of our immune system.

The IS can slowly become worn out through years of neglect. Here are the do's and don't's to keep your immune system working at optimum capacity.

IMMUNE SYSTEM DESTROYERS

Alcohol: Overloads the detoxifying organs, liver, kidneys, and the pancreas. Depletes the body of B vitamins.

Caffeine: Puts stress on the body by weakening the heart, nervous system and respiratory tract. Caffeine is a potent diuretic which washes the water soluble vitamins from the system.

Carbonated Beverages: Depletes the amount of digestive enzymes available to digest your food. Undigested food causes an overload on the immune system.

Constipation: Causes a buildup of toxins. When they are not normally eliminated they have to be dealt with by other organs which causes problems in the immune system as toxins are not eliminated properly.

Depression: Depressed people have more viral infections, herpes, candida and cancer.

Food Additives: Such as dyes, flavorings, and antioxidants can be a potent factor in behavioral problems such as learning disabilities and hyperkinesis.

Glutamic Acid: Found in monosodium glutamate (MSG), affects the central nervous system.

High Fat Diets: Prevent the body from producing the intrinsic factor necessary for B12 absorption, as well as many other enzyme reactions for digestion.

High Protein Diets: Excessive protein causes cellular congestion which results in putrification at the cellular level.

Junk Food: Puts a double stress on the body. When junk food is eaten, the appetite for wholesome food is reduced.

Silver Fillings: Increase the number of white blood cells indicating an increased toxic load on the immune system.

Sodium Nitrite: Is found in many foods as a preservative. It is capable of producing seemingly epileptic changes in brain activity.

Sweets, Chocolate and White Flour: Can cause an imbalance in metabolism which lowers immunity.

Stress: Constant stress will cause the weakest part of the system to suffer first.

Tight Clothing: Reduces circulation, the lymph flow is impeded, i.e., lumps in the breast have been eliminated by using bras such as Pennyrich. The lymphatic system is a vital part of the immune system.

IMMUNE SYSTEM FOODS

Acidophilus: Helps to eliminate intestinal putrefaction; provides better digestion and assimilation.

Barley Juice Powder: Dried juice of the barley leaf. Contains SOD, an enzyme that has been found to be a cell protectant against free radicals. It helps the detoxification of poisons in the body.

Flower Pollen: Rich in amino acids. Works with vitamin A to build up the immune system.

Brown Rice: A valuable and natural balanced, nutritious food. Excellent source of the B complex vitamins. It retains the germ, vitamins, minerals, protein, fat, starch and fiber. It is an inexpensive source of fuel for the body. It is a considered a protective food.

Cleansing Diets: Help build up the immune system when used periodically.

Millet: A very nourishing food to use often. It acts as an intestinal lubricant aiding elimination and absorption. It will not leach calcium from the tissues as red meat can. Complete protein alkaline reaction in the body. Rich in lecithin, B complex vitamins, calcium, iron, phosphorus and others.

Vegetables: Eating lots of raw vegetables provides live enzymes, vitamins and minerals as well as providing bulk for a healthy colon.

Whole Grains: Very nourishing especially when sprouted. Use buckwheat and wheat often.

IMMUNE SYSTEM FOOD SUPPLEMENTS *(SPECIAL DIETARY HELPS)*

Vitamin A: Contains anti-viral properties. Use with zinc and protein (sunflower seeds). Increases immunity, especially against air pollution. Beta-carotene converts into vitamin A inside the body. The liver stores vitamin A and when stress or disease develop and increase the need for vitamin A, the liver will release enough vitamin A to keep the blood level up.

B Complex Vitamins: Need to be replaced daily. Brewer's yeast, bee pollen, rice, polishings, grains.

Vitamin C: Helps the body to produce natural interferon to protect the immune system. Vitamin C is a potent anti-oxidant that protects us against cancer. It helps to block the formation of nitrite compounds that weaken the IS.

Calcium: Healing to the body, prevents many disorders in the body, bone loss, nervous problems, works with magnesium, phosphorus.

Vitamin E: Helps to repair cell damage, builds up immunity along with selenium. Vitamin E prevents the oxidized state that cancer cells thrive in and it deactivates the free radicals that promote cellular damage leading to malignancy.

Iron: For healthy blood. Yellow dock and dandelion are both very rich in organic iron and other minerals.

Folic Acid: Along with B12 are involved in maintaining a healthy IS. They are both deficient in the typical American diet.

Food Enzymes: Deficiency in enzymes can inhibit proper digestion and cause toxins to weaken the IS.

Lysine: An amino acid; helps calcium absorption; helps to control herpes infections and along with the right diet, helps inhibit its growth.

Selenium: Strengthens the immune system and helps clean up free radicals. Improves antibody production.

Tryptophan: An essential amino acid soothing for the nerves. Taken at first sign of an attack of herpes II has helped many people.

Zinc: Speeds up the healing process and helps balance minerals. Builds up the immune system. 70 enzymes in the body depend on zinc.

IMMUNE SYSTEM HERBS FOR CLEANSING AND FEEDING

Black Walnut: High in organic iodine for killing germs; very healing.

Echinacea: Increases the immunity levels and contains properties which elevate the white blood count to absorb and eliminate harmful bacteria. Contains essential fatty acids which are involved in the proper function of the immune system.

Evening Primrose Oil: Stimulates the T-cells of the IS. Experiments done in test tubes show that it reverts cancer cells back to normal cells. PGE is a vitamin-like compound involved in the proper function of the immune system. A shortage of PGE is believed to cause abnormal and harmful immune response and is required for T-cells of the IS to attack cancer. T-cells are the main mechanisms of the IS to protect the body from foreign cells, viruses, bacteria, fungi and allergens. Evening Primrose contains high amounts of PGE.

Garlic: Considered to be nature's penicillin. Contains antibiotic properties.

Hops: Rich in B complex vitamins and calming for the nerves. Relaxes the body and builds up the nervous system to protect the IS from damage.

Myrrh: Strengthens and builds up the immune system; contains antiseptic properties to combat staph and other infections.

Pau D'Arco: Contains anti-fungal properties. Strengthens the immune system. Need to simmer 30 minutes to steep out the active ingredients.

Red Raspberry: Contains anti-fungal properties, rich in calcium and other vital vitamins and minerals. A good herbal tea to build up the immune system.

Sage: Contains anti-fungal properties.

Scullcap: A weakened-immune system is related to stress and puts a strain on the nerves. Scullcap feeds and strengthens the nerves and helps in emotional problems.

Thyme: Strengthens the immune system and has antiseptic and antifungal properties.

Watercress: A prevention herb rich in iodine good for the thyroid and all the endocrine glands.

Wheatgrass: Especially the wheatgrass juice which builds the immune system.
Yarrow: Contains tranquilizing properties, builds up the central nervous system.

WILD BILL'S WESTERN HEALTH CEREAL

Several years ago I met Dr. Joseph Walters, an M.D. who advocated the use of healthful foods rather than mediocre foods and supplements. He sold a line of foods composed of dates, raisins, dried fruits, nuts and so forth and claimed that by eating these natural foods, you would gain the advantage of all the peripheral nutrients that accompanied vitamins and minerals.

This line of reasoning made a lot of sense to me; I began to depend more on the foods that I ate rather than on tablets from a bottle. Now, I am not knocking vitamin and mineral supplements, but if you can get all you need from plain natural foods, why not?

So, among my favorite real foods is a cereal that is made very quickly and easily from a few basic items. Just mix the following items:

4 cups organic rolled oats

1/4 cup each of: dates, raisins, peanuts, sunflower seeds, pumpkin seeds, chopped dried apples, granular lecithin, dried skim milk powder

2 tablespoons brewer's yeast

If you place these items in a container with a tightly-fitting lid, they will keep for a long time. To eat, just pour a portion into a bowl and add fluid skim milk or fruit juice. Let soak for a few minutes and enjoy.

The advantage of this cereal is that it needs no refrigeration and can be taken anywhere to provide a healthy, energy-filled breakfast or snack.

BEYOND NUTRITION

A remarkable book that summarizes the on-going transformation in health is *The Aquarian Conspiracy* by Marilyn Ferguson.

She has sifted an abundance of data and extracted the pure gold. Her chapter on health is, in my opinion, the most astute and discerning analysis of just what is happening in the field of human well-being.

Be sure to buy a copy of this storehouse of insightful information, or check one out from the library. You may end up reading it, as I have, five times over. Each time was more enjoyable and informative than the last.

"Complete health and awakening are really the same."
— *Tarthang Tulku*

*"Something we were withholding made us weak
until we found it was ourselves."*

— Robert Frost

(The above quotes are from Chapter 8, *Healing Ourselves*)

(Below are pure Ferguson:)

"The hope for real social transformation need not rest on circumstantial evidence. One major arena, health care, has already begun to experience wrenching change. The impending transformation of medicine is a window to the transformation of all our institutions. Here we can see what happens when consumers begin to withdraw legitimacy from an authoritarian institution. We see the rise of the autonomous health seeker, the transformation of a profession by leadership, the impact of new models from science, the way decentralized networks are effecting wide geographic change."

AUTHOR'S NOTE: The following quotes summarize the intent of this entire book—to show that senior survival is truly a matter of transforming one's entire lifestyle, from the lifestyle that corporations programmed us for, to one that is highly individualistic and independent.

"Holistic refers to a qualitatively different approach, one that respects the interaction of mind, body and environment.

Beyond the allopathic approach of treating the disease and symptoms of disease, it seeks to correct the underlying disharmony causing the problem. A holistic approach may include a variety of diagnostic tools and treatments, some orthodox, some not. For example, the old medicine assumed that the direction to be taken was the treatment of symptoms while under the holistic view there is a search for patterns and causes..."

"Health is a governing harmony, just as the moon governs the tides."

"Well-being cannot be infused intravenously or ladled in by prescription. It comes from a matrix: the bodymind. It reflects psychological and somatic harmony. In a sense, we always know there is a doctor in the house."

"(Health) originates in an attitude: an acceptance of life's uncertainties, a willingness to accept responsibility for habits, a way of perceiving and dealing with stress, more satisfying human relationships, a sense of purpose."

AUTHORS NOTE: It is interesting to note how much of what Marilyn says is corroborated by great philosophers and by the most advanced medical minds. For example, 2,000 years ago, Marcus Aurelius said that nothing is neither good nor bad, it is thinking that makes it so. Certainly this is an ancient yet modern way of "perceiving and dealing with stress." And the wise old Doc Nittler said, "The body has memory," thus substantiating the precept that there is "always a doctor in the house!"

I would also like to comment on "a sense of purpose." In *Passages*, Carol Sheehy says that an older person needs what she calls "generativity" or the ability to use your creative powers for a good purpose. Again, substantiation of a basic truth. We seniors don't need any more advice on how to go live in a Sun City and play shuffleboard and fiddle with knitting needles and jigsaws. What we need is to motivate ourselves to be all we can possibly be, REGARDLESS OF AGE. That is the true source of real health and energy whether you are ten or a hundred.

> *"Stimulation in the environment affects the growth and connections of the human brain from its earliest days to its last..its weight, nutrients, and number of cells. Even in the elderly, the physical brain does not lose a measurable number of cells if the environment is stimulating."*

In my opinion, this is the most important statement in the entire chapter; Marilyn is telling us seniors that we can enjoy clear minds and creative thoughts to the very end *if* we are willing to live in an atmosphere of challenge and risk. No wonder so many professionals—doctors, musicians, sportsmen—live long and productive lives; they never give up trying to improve themselves. To these victors in the game of life, there is no such thing as retirement!

Ms. Ferguson quotes the feisty Maggie Kuhn of the Gray Panthers:

> *"Let's not pit ourselves against the young. Together we can devise health centers, to challenge and change, to point the way. We can be coalition builders. And we can experiment. Those of us who are old can afford to live dangerously. We have less to lose."*

> *"Old people don't grow senile if they maintain an interest in life."*

> *"Surely historians will marvel at the heresy we fell into, the recent decades in which we disregarded the spirit in our efforts to cure the body. Now, in finding health, we find ourselves."*

AUTHOR'S NOTE: Again, to learn about what is happening to all of us in these "best and worst of times," read Ms. Ferguson's landmark summation.

JACK SCHWARZ

One of the remarkable men mentioned by Marilyn Ferguson in her book is Jack Schwarz, an author, healer, philosopher—a true renaissance man. He has written three books: *The Path of Action*, *Voluntary Controls* and *Human Energy Systems*.

Jack has an uncanny way of presenting what we recognize as the truth in a most outspoken, forthright manner. Here are some quotes from an interview originally published in *Whole Life Monthly*, April, 1987:

"We are hoarding potentials so great they are unimaginable."

"Everyone says, 'don't be so emotional'
and yet emotion is energy in motion (e motion)."

"The key to healthy utilization of energy is creative expression."

AUTHOR'S NOTE: Observe the similarities between this and Ferguson's and Sheehy's comments.

"The whole art of life is to find joy even when negative conditions
lead us to believe it can't be found."

"We have to get away from the idea that spirit is something different from
pure, undiluted, unadulterated energy. Because that's what spirit is."

Mr. Schwarz was a member of the Dutch underground during WWII and suffered from many adverse experiences. However, he was able to practice his own preachments and emerged from hard times with an unshakable faith in the human potential. He now teaches at his *Aletheia Dynamic Health Training Center* in Ashland, Oregon. I strongly recommend you obtain literature and then decide for yourself. I know that I am now planning to go to Ashland for some lessons from this most remarkable, perceptive and highly energized man.

THE CANCER STORY

One of the most trying experiences all seniors face is the possibility of contracting cancer. Most of us have experienced this nightmare vicariously. I know that I have watched with frustration and horror as my friends and relatives have died from this, the most dreaded of diseases.

At one time in my life I believed that there were only three possible cures for cancer: surgery, radiation and chemotherapy. All were sanctioned by the American Medical Association (AMA), the U.S. government and other authoritarian entities. All are invasive, costly and for most people, lethal.

It is interesting to note that the establishment or "straight press" fosters the myth that these modalities are the only ones that have any efficacy in the fight against cancer. But if you delve into what I call the alternative press, you will find references to such interesting organizations as the *Cancer Control Society*.

Here you find a group of highly motivated, totally dedicated and courageous Americans who believe that there are alternatives to "cut, burn and poison," as the three accepted therapies have come to be called. What follows are annotated selections from their literature package.

DIRECTORY OF NUTRITION–MINDED DOCTORS IN THE LOS ANGELES AREA

Cancer Control Society
and other nutritionally related diseases
2043 No. Berendo Street • Los Angeles, CA 90027
(213) 663-7801

(CANCER PATIENTS SEE GREEN SHEET)

April 1987

● NUTRITION MEDICAL DOCTORS

Bio Med Health Services
11311 Camarillo St., Suite 103
North Hollywood, CA 91602
818-985-1103
(Chelation, Hypoglycemia &
Nutrition)

James Braly, M.D.
West Valley Medical Center
5363 Balboa Blvd., Ste. 536
Encino, CA 91316
818-990-4442
(Allergy & Clinical Ecology)

Metabolic Medical Group
301 E. Colorado Blvd.,Suite 810
Pasadena, CA 91101
818-578-0531
(Hypoglycemia & Nutrition)

James Privitera, M.D.
105 N. Grandview
Covina, CA 91723
818-966-1618
(Allergies & Chelation)

Glen Mahoney, M.D.
Health Resource Center
2223 Main St., Suite 44
Huntington Beach, CA 92648
714-969-5255
(Nutrition & Chelation)

Ecology Health Center
Laurence Reich, M.D.
2243 E. Washington Blvd.
Pasadena, CA 91104
213-684-6328
(Allergy, Hypoglycemia &
Body Chemistry)

Virginia Flanagan, M.D.
13320 Riverside Dr., Suite 112
Sherman Oaks, CA 91423
818-995-4233
(Preventive Nutrition &
Psychiatry)

Paul Fleiss, M.D.
1824 Hillhurst Ave.
Los Angeles, CA 90027
213-664-1977
(Pediatrics)

Arnold Fox, M.D.
9903 Santa Monica Blvd.,Ste.128
Beverly Hills, CA 90212
213-278-6447
(Preventive Medicine)

James J. Julian, M.D.
1654 N. Cahuenga Blvd.
Hollywood, CA 90028
213-466-0126
(Preventive Medicine,
Chelation & Nutrition)

Arthur Kaslow, M.D.
795 Alamo Pintado
Solvang, CA 93463
805-688-5519
805-969-3237 (Montecito)
714-662-0108 (Santa Ana)
(MS & Nutrition, Acupressure)

Leonard Klepp, M.D.
16311 Ventura Blvd., Ste. 725
Encino, CA 91436
818-981-5511
(Nutrition & Chelation)

Gershon Lesser, M.D.
6200 Wilshire Blvd.Suite 1509
Los Angeles, CA 90048
213-937-4144
(Cardiology & Nutrition)

Emil Levin, M.D.
450 S. Beverly Dr.
Beverly Hills, CA 90212
213-556-2091
(Preventive Medicine-Chelation)

Bruce Halstead, M.D.
Rancho Mediterranea
11155 Mtn. View Ave., Ste. 101
Loma Linda, CA 92354
714-824-1750
(Preventive Medicine & Chelation)

Frank Varese, M.D.
24953 Paseo De Valencia, 7-C
Laguna Hills, CA 92653
714-837-1510
(Preventive Med.& Nutrition)

The Bresler Center
2901 Wilshire Blvd, Ste. 345
Santa Monica, CA 90403
213-828-6471
(Bio-Feedback & Pain)

Harvey Ross, M.D.
7080 Hollywood Blvd., #1015
Los Angeles, CA 90028
213-466-8330
(Psychiatry & Nutrition)

Robert Scott, M.D.
11600 Wilshire Blvd., #424
Los Angeles, CA 90025
213-477-7555
(Obstetrics & Gynecology)

Robert Gold, D.O.
Southcoast Medical Group
1905 N. College Ave., B-2
Santa Ana, CA 92706
714-541-4080
(Chelation, Cardiovascular
& Allergy)

Ronald Wempen, M.D.
3620 S. Bristol St., Ste. 306
Santa Ana, CA 92704
714-546-4325
(Metabolic Medicine)

Phillip Taylor, M.D.
325 S. Moorpark Rd.
Thousand Oaks, CA 91360
805-497-3839
(Orthomolecular
Medicine & Psychiatry)

● NUTRITION DENTISTS

Jack Alpan, D.D.S.
2440 West 3rd St.
Los Angeles, CA 90057
213-383-3833

Constantine B. Aronis, D.D.S.
3875 Wilshire Blvd., Suite 707
Los Angeles, CA 90010
213-385-2029

Mark Hulet, D.D.S.
21948 Hwy. 18
Apple Valley, CA 92307
619-247-6491
(Mercury Toxicity)

Isadore Imber, D.D.S.
19231 Victory Blvd.,Suite 205
Reseda, CA 91335
818-345-6100

Jarvis & Helyn Luechauer, D.D.S.
3169 Barbara Court
Hollywood, CA 90068
213-876-6440

Roy Smudde, D.D.S.
11311 Camarillo St., Suite 211
North Hollywood, CA 91602
818-506-0047

Harold Stone, D.D.S.
111 No. Euclid St.
La Habra, CA 90631
213-697-1229

● NUTRITION CHIROPRACTORS

Joseph Stadish, D.C.
160 Lasky Drive
Beverly Hills, CA 90212
213-859-8500

Albert Hertz, D.C.
247 N. Larchmont
Los Angeles, CA 90004
213-461-9373

Frederick Levenston, D.C.
105 E. Tamarack Ave.
Inglewood, CA 90301
213-677-7002

Carol Port, D.C.
Wholistic Health Institute
4524 Saugus Ave.
Sherman Oaks, CA 91403
818-905-5755

● NUTRITIONAL CONSULTANT

Paul Cinaman, B.S.
8330 Laurel Canyon, Suite 105
Sun Valley, CA 91352
818-504-0129
(Allergies & Psycho-Nutrition)

Esther Thaler, R.N., C.M.T.
(Body Chemistry Balancing)
Los Angeles, CA
213-552-2677 - 707-579-9355

● HEALTH CASSETTE TAPES

Ray Womack
14314 Anola St.
Whittier, CA 90604
213-944-1908

● NUTRITION SCHOOLS

Donsbach University
Kurt Donsbach, Ph.D., President
P.O. Box 5550
20800 Beach Blvd., Suite B
Huntington Beach, CA 92648
714-969-5664
(also Nutrient Deficiency Test)

● HEALTH RESORTS

Rancho La Puerta
Tecate, CA 92080
619-478-5341

● VISION TRAINING

Cataract Research Fdt.
Stuart Kemeny, M.D.
3340 W. Ball Rd., Ste. A
Anaheim, CA 92804
714-827-4350

Diana Deimel
Author "Vision Victory"
32880 Olive Ave.
Winchester, CA 92396
714-926-2555

Don Getz, O.D.
7136 Haskell Ave., Suite 125
Van Nuys, CA 91406
818-997-7888

Edgar Lucidi, M.D.
Nutritional Ophthalmology
410 W. Central, Ste. 101
Brea, CA 92621
213-691-2279/714-879-9500

● ORGANICALLY GROWN
FRUITS & VEGETABLES

(Composting & Food
Growing Classes)

Bio-Dynamic Association
Peter Dukish, Instructor
17106 Sunderland Dr.
Granada Hills, CA 91344
818-368-6848

Dr. Tom's Vegetable Gardening
(Installation & Maintenance)
1440 Veteran Ave., #359
Los Angeles, CA 90024
213-473-7901

(OVER)

CANCER CONTROL SOCIETY • TREE OF LIFE

NON-TOXIC THERAPIES & DIAGNOSTIC TESTS DIRECTORY

Cancer Control Society
2043 No. Berendo Street • Los Angeles, CA 90027
(213) 663-7801

"Frequently a combination of more than one non-toxic therapy renders a more complete approach for a given individual, and thus offers a greater protection and range of benefits."

April 1987   Listed by States & Countries

● LAETRILE THERAPY
(also known as Vit. B-17 or Amygdalin)

Vera Allison, N.M.D.
4600 Kietzke Lane,
Bldg. B, Suite 112
Reno, NV 89502
702-826-8207

* * * * * * * *

Hans Nieper, M.D.
21 Sedanstrasse
3000 Hanover, W. Germany
011-49-511-348-0808
(2-4 p.m. office)
011-49-511-733-031
(9-11 a.m. hospital)
For more information call the
Hans Nieper Fdt. 714-240-3775

Hans Moolenburgh, M.D.
Oranjeplein II
Haarlem, Holland
023-316818

Manner Clinic
Harold Manner, Ph.D., Director
Apartado 3437
Tijuana, B.C., Mexico
706-680-4422
(U.S. Contact) P.O. Box 4290
San Ysidro, CA 92073
706-680-4222 (reservations)
800-433-4962
305-454-8969

Ernesto Contreras, M.D.
Centro Medico Del Mar
Paseo De Tijuana 1-A
Playas De Tijuana, Mexico
706-680-1203/4 or 1222
(U.S. Contact) P.O. Box 1561
Chula Vista, CA 92012
619-428-6438   (9:00-3:00 M-F)

Rosarita Beach Clinic
(Tijuana, Mexico)
P.O. Box 5982
Chula Vista, CA 92012
706-689-4465 Mexico
619-426-2002

American Biologics Hosp. Mexico
Tijuana Mexico
Rodrigo Rodriguez, M.D.
118U Walnut Ave.
Chula Vista, CA 92011
619-429-8200
800-227-4458

Manuel Navarro, M.D.
3553 Sining Morningside Terr.
Santa Mesa, Manila 2806
Philippines
2070-21 Loc. 391-47-21-51-55

Jan de Vries, Ph.N.D.
Auchenkyle Southwoods
Monkton, Ayrshire, Scotland
Troon 311414 (0292)

● METABOLIC THERAPY

Metabolics
Nita A. Wolf, Director
P.O. Box 416
Wheatridge, CO 80033
303-233-1811/237-9006

Ronald Schmid, N.D.
2420 Main St.
Stratford, CT 06497
203-375-8752/377-7606

W.W. Mittelstadt, D.O.
4001 N. Ocean Dr., #305
Ft. Lauderdale, FL 33308
305-491-4656

American Int'l. Hospital
Oscar Rasmussen, Ph.D.
Dir. Nutritional Services
Shiloh Blvd./Emmaus Ave.
Zion, Il 60099
312-872-4561
800-367-4357

Paul Beals, M.D.
9101 Cherry Lane, Suite 205
Laurel, MD 20708
301-490-9911

Ahmad Shamim, M.D.
200 Fort Meade Rd.
Laurel, MD 20707
301-776-3700

W. Douglas Brodie, M.D.
3670 Grand
Reno, NV 89509
702-825-2282

Michael Schachter, M.D.
Mountainview Med. Assoc.
Mountainview Ave.
Nyack, NY 10960
914-358-6800

Brian Briggs, M.D.
718 6th St., S.W.
Minot, ND 58701
701-838-6011

Jack Slingluff, D.O.
5850 Fulton Rd., N.W.
Canton, OH 44718
216-494-8641

Bob Gibson, M.D.
215 N. 3rd St.
Ponca City, OK 74601
405-765-4414
405-762-5746 (patient info.)

Donald Mantell, M.D.
Preventive Medicine & Nutrition
6505 Mars Rd.
Evans City, PA 16033
412-776-5610

Carol Morrison, M.D.
P.O. Box 422
Martins Creek, PA 18063
215-253-3852

P. Jayalakshmi, M.D.
6366 Sherwood Rd.
Philadelphia, PA 19151
215-473-4226

Dan Dotson, M.D.
921 4th St.
Graham, TX 76046
817-549-3663

Owen Robins, M.D.
6565 De Moss, Ste. 202
Houston, TX 77074
713-981-7500

John Sessions, D.O.
1609 S. Margaret St.
Kirbyville, TX 75956
409-423-2166

Irving Miller, N.D.
2613 N. Stevens
Tacoma, WA 98407
206-752-2555 / 457-1515

William Faber, D.O.
6529 W. Fond du Lac Ave.
Milwaukee, WI 53218
414-464-7680

* * * * * * * * *

Preventive Medical Services
P.O. Box 82
Strathfield 2135
Sydney, Australia / 02-764-4144

Seiichi Kawachi, M.D.
7-3-8 Ginza Chuo-ku,
Tokyo, 104 Japan / 03-572-5455

Salvadore Rubio, M.D.
(Tijuana, Mexico)
P.O. Box 1044-0180
San Ysidro, CA 92073
706-684-0948

● FOR LAETRILE (B-17), DMSO,
Hydrazine Sulfate, Orotates, Digestive Enzymes (Pancreatic & Bromalin) or Vit. B-15, etc
WRITE OR CALL . . .

American Biologics
1180 Walnut Ave.
Chula Vista, CA 92011
619-429-8200
800-227-4473

Great Expectations
P.O. Box 4744
Laguna Beach, CA 92652
714-497-7080

Kem, S.A. Laboratories
P.O. Box 1561
Chula Vista, CA 92012
011-526-680-1850 thru 1855

Vita Chem Int'l
241 Hazel Ave.
Redwood City, CA 94061
415-365-6692

L & S Pharma Specialties
P.O. Box 724
Hammond, IN 46320
219-932-8860

Henderson's Pharmacy
7401 Harford Rd.
Baltimore, MD 21234
800-638-0142 (Toll Free)
301-444-5100

A.O. Supply Co.
P.O. Box 275
Millersport, OH 43046
614-467-2190

Imu, Inc.
(Colostrum Products)
P.O. Box 368
Toronto, SD 57268
605-794-8551

● APRICOT KERNELS

Health World
P.O. Box 4228
Thousand Oaks, CA 91359
805-497-1308

Rainbow Acres
13208 Washington Blvd.
Los Angeles, CA 90066
213-306-8330

O-V-E-R

Your response to the doctor and/or clinic is invited.

* * * * * * * * * * *

Pharma - Export
Falkenstrasse 87
D-7292 Baiersbronn,
West Germany

C.P.W.Rahlstedt GMBH (LTD)
P.O. Box 73 05 27
D-2000 Hamburg 73, Germany
011-49-40-677-00-37

(For those who wish to do a "double check" with comparative tests)

CANCER TESTS (Immuno Diagnostic Urine & Blood)

Emile Schandl, Ph.D.
CA Laboratory
1818 Sheridan St.
Hollywood, FL 33020
305-929-4814

* * * * * * * * * *

Neunhoeffer Test
Bio-Medical Center
P.O. Box 3654
San Ysidro, CA 92073
706-685-0967/688-1679 Eves.

Institute of Regeneration
Calle Ensenada, #393
Tijuana, B.C. Mexico
706-688-0526

Manuel Navarro, M.D.
3553 Sining,Morningside Terr.
Santa Mesa, Manila 2806
Philippines

LAETRILE RESEARCH

Ernst T. Krebs, Jr., D.Sc.
John Beard Memorial Foundation
P.O. Box 685
San Francisco, CA 94101
415-824-1067

Andrew McNaughton
McNaughton Foundation
P.O. Box B 17
San Ysidro, CA 92073

Dean Burk, Ph.D.
Dean Burk Foundation
4719 44th St.
Washington, D.C. 20016

Harold Manner, Ph.D.
(Doctor Information)
Pres. Metabolic Research Fdn.
P.O Box 4290
San Ysidro, CA 92073
706-680-4222 (reservations)
501-675-4962
305-454-8969

Robert Bradford
Research Institute
1180 Walnut Ave.
Chula Vista, CA 92011
619-429-8200
800-277-4458

CELLULAR THERAPY

Hospital Santa Monica
Kurt Donsbach, Ph.D.
Carlos Soria, M.D.
Rosarita Beach, Mexico
714-964-1535
011-526-612-1330

Wolfram Kühnau, M.D.
American Biologics Hosp. Mexico
Tijuana Mexico
1180 Walnut Ave.
Chula Vista, CA 92011
619-429-8200
800-227-4458

Genesis West
Clinic in Mexico
241 Hazel Ave.
Redwood City, CA 94061
415-365-6692

NUTRITION PROGRAM
Diet considered excellent for nutritional support as to Laetrile patients

Michael Cessna, D.C.
504 N. 13th St.
Rogers, AR 72756
501-636-1178

James Privitera, M.D.
105 N. Grandview
Covina, CA 91723
818-966-1618

Vega Macrobiotic Center
1511 Robinson St.
Oroville, CA 95965
916-533-7702

Jewell Warren, D.C.
5121 Evangeline St.
Baton Rouge, LA 70805
504-355-3741

Ray Beach, D.C.
300 W. 23rd St.
Freemont, NE 68025
402-721-1190

Ruth Yale Long, Ph.D.
3647 Glen Haven
Houston, TX 77025
713-665-2946

The Int'l Health Institute
William D. Kelley, D.D.S.
P.O. Box 802536
Dallas, TX 75380
214-233-6830

* * * * * * * * * *

Ruth Cilento, M.D.
1 Trackson St.
Alderley, Brisbane, 4051
Australia
07-352-6634

Dorothea Snook, N.D.
Radiant Health Centre
Private Hospital
Doctor's Hill
Northam, West Australia

Lauri Campbell, N.D.
12027 Arbour St.
Windsor, Ont. N8N 1N7, Canada
(near Detroit, MI)
519-735-1384

John Cosh, M.D.
Cancer Help Centre
Grove House, Cornwallis Grove,
Clifton, Bristol BS8 4PG, England
0272 743216

GERSON THERAPY

Gerson Institute
Charlotte Gerson, Pres.
P.O. Box 430
Bonita, CA 92002
619-267-1150

HOXSEY THERAPY (Herbal)
Considered compatible w/Laetrile

Bio-Medical Center
P.O. Box 727
615 General Ferreira
(Colonia Juarez)
Tijuana, B.C., Mexico
706-684-9011/9132 Eves.

IMMUNOLOGY (B.C.G. Vaccines & Nutrition)

Virginia Livingston, M.D.
3232 Duke St.
San Diego, CA 92110
619-224-3515

Steenblock Medical Clinic
22821 Lake Forest Dr., Ste. 114
El Toro, CA 92630
714-770-9616

* * * * * * * * * *

Lawrence Burton, Ph.D.
Immunology Researching Center
P.O. Box F 2689
Freeport, Grand Bahamas Island
809-352-7455/6

Yolanda Fraire, M.D.
(Tijuana, Mexico)
P.O. Box 484
Coronado, CA 92118
619-488-4706
706-685-4665

WHEAT GRASS THERAPY

Health Institute of San Diego
6970 Central Ave.
Lemon Grove, CA 92045
619-464-3346

Hippocrates Health Institute
Educator-Victor Molinari
(Living Foods Specialist)
Montebello, CA
213-723-1994

Hippocrates Health Institute
1443 Palmdale Ct.
West Palm Beach, FL 33411
305-471-8876

Creative Health Institute
918 Union City Rd.
Union City, MI 49094
517-278-6260/5837

OTHER THERAPIES

Linus Pauling Institute
440 Page Mill Rd.
Palo Alto, CA 94306
415-327-4064

St. Jude's International
Jimmy Keller, Adm.
Tijuana, Mexico
706-685-4434 (10 a.m.-2 p.m.)
706-681-3026 (evenings)

Institute of Regeneration
Arthritis & Other Diseases
Calle Ensenada, #393
Tijuana, B.C., Mexico
706-688-0526

INSURANCE COORDINATORS

North American Health
Insurance Coordinators, Inc.
5847 San Felipe Rd., Suite 4250
Houston, TX 77057-3011
713-953-0906
800-223-6688

TRAVEL

CCS Cancer Clinic Tours & Travel Service
P.O. Box 4651
Modesto, CA 95352
209-529-4697

Private Cancer Clinic Tours
6512 Vista del Mar
Playa del Rey, CA 90293
818-570-4136
213-821-1975

LOCAL HOTELS

Int'l Motor Inn/RV Park
(Formerly Motel 8)
190 E. Calle Primera
San Ysidro, CA 92073
619-428-4486

Los Girasoles Motel
Ave. Paseo De Tijuana No. 4
Playas De Tijuana, Mexico
011-526-680-2271/1854, 1855

LITERATURE

Cancer Book House
2043 N. Berendo St.
Los Angeles, CA 90027
213-663-7801

PSYCHOTHERAPISTS

Cancer Care Center
Jordan Weiss, M.D.
11770 E. Warner Ave., Suite 110
Fountain Valley, CA 92708
714-966-0384

Simonton Method
Robert Price, Ph.D.
205 W. Walnut Ave.
San Diego, CA 92103
619-425-0369

NOTICE: Most non-toxic independent cancer therapies are in limited supply. Persons seeking unorthodox and orthodox help for cancer are urged to investigate carefully the doctor, the product and the price before deciding on a course of action. Please remember the C.C.S. does not recommend or endorse in this instance, nor does it assume any responsibility. Because of many requests this information has been offered.

For more information, Patient List, Cancer Book House List, and membership application to Cancer Control Journal Contact the CANCER CONTROL SOCIETY. Memberships start at $25.00.

If you, or any of your relatives and friends have cancer, the time is NOW to investigate some reasonable options. Write:

Cancer Control Society at 2043 N. Berendo St., Los Angeles, CA 90027.

DMSO (OR THE STORY OF THE HOOKER, THE KILLER AND WILD BILL)

In the spring of 1980 I found myself in the southern Nevada desert wondering what adventures I might have next. I checked in with the cosmic guides and expressed a preference for something that would be helpful to the many sick people who were lying around waiting for something fortunate to happen.

The very next day I was in Las Vegas bottling a rather strange solvent known as dimethyl sulfoxide or, DMSO, for short. The bottles were intended for sale to those afflicted with arthritis, those who had heard about the healing properties of DMSO on the network TV show, *60 Minutes*.

With a few ads in a local paper, it became evident that there was a tremendous demand for this pain-reliever. But after a few days of runaway sales, I was asked by the Las Vegas Police Department to take my DMSO and leave town before something unpleasant happened.

At about this time, a friend of mine who had shot and killed about 500 human beings while on duty in Vietnam got in touch with me and asked for a ride out of town. And oddly, a hooker that I had come to know through a mutual friend phoned me and said that she had decided to go straight and "could I find her a job in some other town?"

And so a strange cargo left Sin City in my trusty GMC camper—50 gallons of DMSO, one expert killer and a young woman of about 28 who had experienced the indescribable life of a prostitute for 11 years.

It was a pleasure leaving both the thermal and police heat of Vegas behind to enjoy the truest blessings of a benevolent God—cool breezes off a deep blue ocean. The town we chose to resume the DMSO sales was Santa Barbara. Within a short time, we experienced the same flak as we had in Vegas. But the killer and the hooker were rather tough birds and agreed to stand and fight rather than turn tail and run away.

We had some rather close escapes as the armed agents of the local DA tried to find and arrest us. But my killer friend had developed an uncanny sense of the presence of danger— no doubt responsible for his survival in 'Nam. Time after time, he was able to move us to another location before the DA's men struck.

We sold and gave away a lot of DMSO, the hooker got a job as a bartender while the killer continued to function as the best watchman I have ever known. Thanks to the killer we were never caught and arrested, although we were tried in absentia and fined 200,000 dollars.

Today, the excitement of distributing DMSO has vanished and it is available in many stores. It is always sold as a solvent because it has never been approved by the FDA except for a couple of obscure diseases. But it is effective, as these testimonials prove:

DMSO, The Wonder Healer

By Edward L. Carl. N.D., D.O.

A liquid derived from trees is becoming the wonder healer of this century.

Dimethyl sulfoxide, nicknamed DMSO, is the leading liquid made from wood. To date DMSO has been found to have marvelous healing effects in an unbelieveable variety of conditions including arthritis, bursitis, strokes, varicose veins, mental retardation, senility, mongolism, cancer, nerve blindness, cataracts, sinusitis, asthma, emphysema, burns, baldness, gangrene, fungus infections, virus infections, ulcers, gout, lupus, Parkinson's disease, back problems including ruptured disc, frostbite, shingles, cystitis, gum infections, cold sores, schizophrenia, quadriplegia, traumatic paraplegia, kidney stones, athletic injuries, sprains, phlebitis, poor ciculation, enlarged prostate, radiation damage, retinitis pigmentosa, arteriosclerosis, multple scherosis, scar tissue, heart conditions, and the list is still growing.

As you would expect, anything so beneficial to mankind, with practically no toxicity, and in direct competition with the hundreds of expensive and very toxic drugs, is being violently opposed and obstructed by none other but the FDA, that great enemy of vitamins, laetrile, and other non-toxic therapies and friend of most every toxic drug and insecticide, herbicide, birth control drugs, etc.

Dr. Stanley Jacob of the University of Oregon Medical School has been the world's pioneer investigator of DMSO therapy and for this reason the FDA has tried hard to smear and crucify him. For the incredible story of DMSO and the FDA opposition read THE PERSECUTED DRUG, THE STORY OF DMSO by Pat McGrády, Doubleday & Co.

The FDA purports to base its opposition to DMSO on an exeriment in which animals were immersed in the liquid for long periods of time, thus receiving hundreds of times the

dosage used for humans. Still the only bad effect resulting was some change in the lens of the eyes. In thousands of human applications to adults and children, some in massive doses, in the USA, Germany, and many other countries, this bad effect has never been observed. On the contrary doctors have repeatedly applied DMSO dilutions directly into the eyes with benefit for various conditions including nerve blindness. About the worst effect sometimes resulting from DMSO application is some slight temporary skin irritation. I myself have applied this wonder healing liquid undiluted to my skin, drank it, injected into my muscles and applied it directly into my eyes, nose, and mouth in 50 per cent dilution as part of my own investigation.

Here at Port of Health we have been using DMSO as a supplement to other non-toxic therapies. For example, in arthritis, varicose veins, bursitis, gout, and circulation problems a natural food cleansing diet program plus natural vitamin-mineral supplements, herbs, deep nerve massage, and colon detoxification are basic. But all of these necessary natural therapies do their wonderful healing work slowly over a period of days, weeks and months. Now with DMSO we can often bring the patient blessed relief from suffering within a few minutes and greatly accelerate the entire natural healing process in these and other conditions. Naturally this also is a great psychological inspiration to the patient to follow through with his complete natural healing program as the DMSO helps him over the often difficult rough spots.

In Santiago, Chile, Dr. Nicolas Weinstein, president of Laboratorios Recaline, S.A. has combined DMSO with Gamma-amino-butyric acid and gamma-amino-eta-hydroxy-butyric acid. DMSO allows the transportation of these amino acids to the brain where they liberate glutamic acid and other elements to directly stimulate cerebral function thus correcting

many neurological syndromes found in mental retardation, loss of memory, senility, depression and anguish in children, adults, and old persons. I have seen Dr. Weinstein's impressive booklet showing before and after pictures and intelligence tests of retarded and mongoloid children with the resulting dramatic improvements. In particular I hope to visit Dr. Weinstein in the near future to obtain supply of this medicine for use with my own mentally retarded son who is tremendously improved by years of other natural therapies. I am hoping that this medicine will bring him still closer to normal.

In the USA the FDA has now finally released DMSO for some animal treatment only. Thus you might be able to obtain some for a sick dog or horse, but not for a suffering human patient. For this reason many Americans are slipping through the FDA iron curtain into Mexico, Germany, Chile, and other countries where DMSO, Laetrile, and other non-toxic therapies are not suppressed, persecuted and forbidden.

No doubt in this matter as in all others good will eventually triumph, but the length of time and the amount of suffering between now and the hour of victory depends in a large part upon how hard all of us fight against the FDA tyrant and his cohorts.

As a start for your part in this battle you can join the National Health Federation today, or if you are already a member you can help by recruiting one or two other new members.

PORT OF HEALTH
Apdo 270
Chapala, Jal. México
Tel. 5-22-13 Chapala

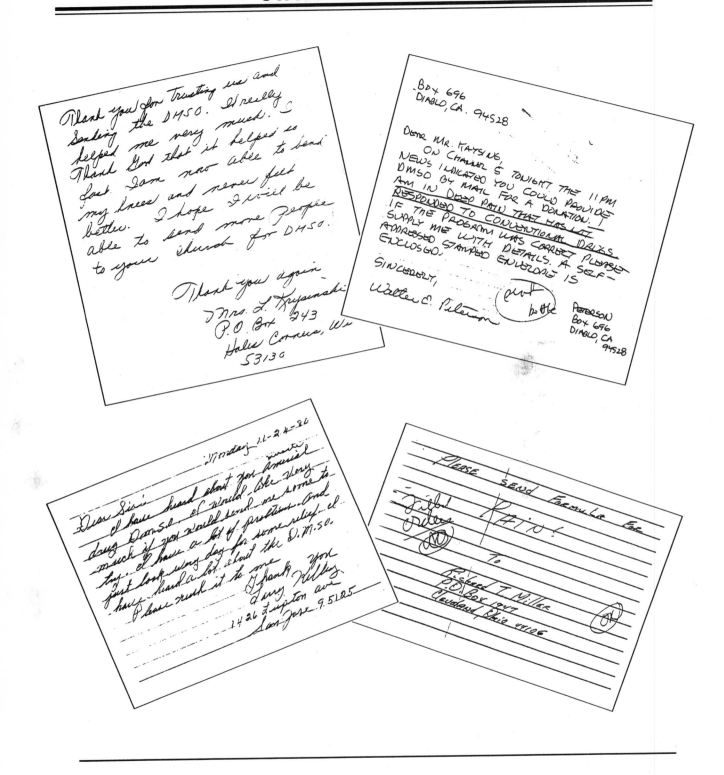

If you don't find it in your neighborhood, write to: *Clinic Supply, 26620 Dartmouth, Hemet, CA.* They'll send you a wholesale price list and you can not only buy what you need, but start a little home business helping the sick. Nothing else provides such great rewards, as Dr. Nittler once said about doing good works, "it returns riches of the soul."

Incidentally, I have written a booklet on DMSO which describes its many beneficial properties. For more information on how to obtain a copy, write to:

Bellwether Productions, 321 Hampton, Venice, CA, 90291.

AUTHOR'S NOTE: Instruction on senior exercising for health is an important topic that Life Management Group provides. We recommend that you contact them at *Life Management Group, PO 3287, La Jolla, CA 92038, (619) 459-5554* for more information on this important aspect of senior health. They are providers of health data to many organizations such as *Blue Cross* and *Blue Shield Associations of America.*

EXERCISE

As a devotee of a daily walk, I totally agree with what my good friend, Dr. Paul Ash, of the *Life Management Group* advocates. Exercise is absolutely vital in my opinion to over-all senior health. And best of all, it is really so cost-free and easy that there is no excuse for not taking advantage of joyful exercise. I know that you will feel better almost immediately. Incidentally, I have always used exercise as a stress-reduction tool. When I worked for a large corporation, I found that regular walks were beneficial in reducing desk-bound stress attacks. Often I would invite my boss for a stroll through the scenic test facility that was my work assignment. We were both much more relaxed in discussing work problems while ambling amongst the Simi Hills.

Try exercise now and enjoy the good feelings of wellness tomorrow.

COOL DOWN

Many sports-type injuries during exercise are caused by forgetting to cool down after strenuous exercise. These injuries range from minor to serious. It is extremely important to follow your vigorous exercise with some relaxing and milder activity that reduces the heart rate slowly. These cool-down exercises should, for example, include some stretching after running or a slow stroll.

NUTRITION

Obviously, you need to accompany your exercise regimen with good nutrition so that your body has the fuel it needs to perform. This is, of course, information available in the *Food* chapter.

PREVENT DISEASE WITH THIS PREVENTION DIET

Here is one of the best summaries of nutrition information to be found. It's reprinted courtesy of the *National Health Federation, Claremont, CA.*

BASIC INSTRUCTIONS

1. Cook only in stainless steel, corning or enamel-ware or glass. Do not use aluminum or pressure cookers.

2. Use butter instead of substitutes. A spread high in unsaturated fats; blend ½ pound of sweet cream butter with ½ cup sesame oil.

3. Use drinking water liberally, preferably well or spring water. Use soups often.

4. Use a natural sea-salt sparingly and watch labels for hidden salts in foods.

5. Use a variety of herbs and spices in cooking—thyme, rosemary,sage, nutmeg, cinnamon, etc.—for food interest and for stimulating the appetite and gastric juices.

6. The use of apple cider vinegar aids in maintaining good gastric acidity.

Do:

1. Eat natural foods and eat them raw if possible.

2. Eat only foods that will spoil and eat them before they do.

3. See that 30 percent of your calories are proteins, 20 percent are fats and 50 percent unrefined carbohydrates.

4. Use naturally raised meat, including fish, seafood, poultry, beef and lamb.

5. Use variety meats one to two times a week, such as liver, heart, sweetbreads, giblets, kidney and others.

6. Use organically grown fruits and vegetables if at all possible. Can you grow your own?

7. Obtain good fresh produce in season and freeze for later use. Sprout seeds and use daily.

8. Use fertile eggs as they provide more nutrients and are less likely to contain antibiotics, sprays.

9. Make your own bread and bakery products. Buy a flour mill and make your own flour.

10. For shortening in baked goods, use soya, sesame, peanut or safflower oil made by cold process with no preservatives.

11. Use sesame or safflower oil for frying as they have the highest smoke point of good oils.

12. Use carob for chocolate-like flavor which carries its own sweetner.

13. Make your own ice cream, yogurt and cottage cheese.

14. Drink certified raw milk where available.

15. Drink herb teas and coffee substitutes.

16. Drink spring water, milk, natural unsweetened juices in place of other beverages.

17. Shop in a natural foods store and wisely in a supermarket. Be a label reader and detective.

Don't:

1. Don't eat highly processed foods such as sugar, white bread, cookies, crackers, TV dinners, etc.

2. Don't eat foods containing chemical preservatives, dyes, artificial colors and flavors, etc.

3. Don't use "foodless" snacks. Plan for proper balance.

4. Don't eat commercial meat that has DES (stilbestrol) or other chemicals or from animals that have been inhumanely raised.

5. Don't constantly use the muscle meats which are the least nutritious part of the animal.

6. Don't use fruits and vegetables which have been sprayed, fumigated, dyed, waxed.

7. Don't use canned fruits and vegetables. Most fruits are over-sweetened and many vegetables are overcooked.

8. Don't use eggs produced by hens in small cages, force fattened, and sprayed with insecticides.

9. Don't eat commercial white bread or other bakery products.

10. Don't use hydrogenated shortenings and heat-treated oils with preservatives.

11. Don't use deep fat frying as fatty acids break down at high temperatures. Avoid fried foods.

12. Don't use chocolate as it interferes with mineral utilization; is highly allergenic.

13. Don't use commercial milk products which contain artificial coloring, flavoring, emulsifiers, sweeteners, etc.

14. Don't drink soft drinks with or without sugar; avoid stimulating drinks which exhaust the adrenals and pancreas.

15. Don't drink instant coffee.

16. Don't use processed milk like pasteurized, homogenized, dried, canned.

17. Don't buy junk foods in a supermarket.

CONCLUSIONS

I hope you have enjoyed reading this chapter. It was rewritten several times to achieve a balance of personal anecdotes, selections from great books on health and some of the best information I can offer on how to obtain and maintain good health. Someone once said that health is balance...balance of our physical, mental, emotional and spiritual components. Becoming balanced, centered and adjusted is not an easy task, but it can be accomplished with dedication and perseverance.

Believe it, it is worth the effort.

Super-senior Eric de Reynier at 81.

CHAPTER TWO
HYPE IN AMERICA

Recently, a book titled *Trading With the Enemy* was published to a dead silent response by the establishment. When you read it, you'll understand why the corporate state which runs America did not even acknowledge the book. In it, the author gives documented evidence that all during WWII, it was business as usual with allies and enemies alike! The United States was actually involved in business deals with our enemies, especially the Germans.

For example, during the fiercest battles in the air over Germany, Standard Oil of New Jersey arranged to have its petroleum shipped in Spanish tankers to Spain for eventual use by the Luftwaffe. I can offer corroboration for this; my old U.S. Navy buddy, Jack Keefe, whom I have known for 50 years, was on an Atlantic-seaboard patrol vessel. They were told to leave Spanish tankers alone! Higham, the author, cites many other instances of how the American armed forces and the public were duped about what really happened before, during, and after WWII. I would like to add a true story of my own based on my WWII experiences aboard a destroyer that had been converted to a radar research, training and picket vessel.

Little was released in the press about the problems of racial prejudice that existed in the U.S. Naval forces. White sailors from the deep south did not want to associate with blacks—especially in close contact where they had to share the same crews' quarters. Often, ten men had to eat and sleep in a space not larger than a closet. On board my ship, we had a token black who was assigned to my watch in the after fireroom. My chief petty officer told me to "watch him closely and don't trust him, don't even turn your back on him." Some southern sailors intimated that they might toss the black over the side some dark night while far at sea. Incidentally, fragging was not invented in Vietnam—many unpleasant naval personnel, including officers, disappeared over the sides of navy ships throughout WWII. As any Navy vet knows, it was dangerous to stop at sea because a submarine could then torpedo a ship like a sitting duck.

This was an uneasy time aboard our ship, but finally the black sailor was transferred. Where he went became clear later as we saw that certain vessels, like yard oilers, had all-black crews with a single white officer in command. In this way, most, if not all conflicts were eliminated. There was no integration of white and black, other than the proximity of a white commissioned officer and black petty officers. This, however, always entailed physical separation. The white captain had his own quarters and was served by his black stewards just as though the Civil War had never been fought!

Despite this situation, which extended to the Army, Marines and Air Corps (in the latter, blacks were formed into their own, all-black squadrons) all during WWII and in subsequent wars, our films, books, and papers are full of pure hype about how black and white fought side by side to vanquish the enemy. In many films there is the obligatory mixture of races to prove that Americans lose their prejudices when threatened by outsiders.

The above is just once of many instances wherein the truth is distorted for the purpose of creating false images. These images are ones that have become cultural imprints on our entire society and have, for their *raison d'etres*, the manipulation of people's minds. We are told only what those in control want us to know. Let's take a look at America as viewed by some of our writers.

HYPE AS VIEWED BY SOME AMERICAN WRITERS

A number of perceptive, thoughtful and philosophical writers have presented a picture of the U.S. that is contradictory to what the corporate-controlled media espouses. Here are selections from some of my own favorites:

ELIA KAZAN

Elia Kazan is best known as a film director of such stunning movies as *On the Waterfront* and *Network*. When he was 58 years old, he wrote a powerful novel called *The Arrangement*. It tells the story of a Los Angeles advertising executive who is confronted by a series of dilemmas in his personal and business life. Dilemma is defined as a situation requiring a choice between two evils; that is exactly what Kazan's protagonist, Eddie Anderson, faces. For example, he can continue his work as a huckster for cigarettes in smog-ridden L.A. or leave and lose his large income. He can stay with his mind-constricting wife, a total shrike, or run off over the horizon with a spaced-out young mistress who recognizes him for what he really is—a man seething with inner rage and frustration.

Throughout the book, Kazan presents cogent comments on our modern social structure. Here are selections:

> I was on the street. I didn't know exactly where. It was hot. Above me the sun was shining. There was one place in the cover of smog brighter than the rest. My eyes smarted. I could smell the industrial waste. I could taste it. There was something malignant in the air.

> In some cities you go in to a bar to comfort yourself against the cold. In L.A. you go into a bar to get out of the hot lard that people live in and breathe.

> I had to be at a fixed place, at a fixed time, leave my pug mark and then pass on to the next checkpoint. I had often said that the use of money was the liberty it bought. But money had only made it necessary for me and then pass on to the next checkpoint. I had often said that the us

money was the liberty it bought. But money had only made it necessary for me to be in certain places at certain times with certain people, and most often with people I didn't really want to be with. And in places I really loathed. What possible excuse was there for any man to live in New York City or Los Angeles? They were not fit habitations for men.

All this talk about Christian civilization. We have a business civilization. The idea is not to love your brother but to get the better of him and do it so there won't be any blood to wash off your hands in public. Everybody knows that's the way it is. But we live in pretense. The pretense and the facts and the gulf between is getting bigger every year. Well, I've stopped pretending, and you'd be amazed how much that eliminates of what a person usually does all day.

I thought, this society is insane. I mean all of it, the customs, the clothes, the work, the hours devoted to work, the way people spoke to each other without looking, the homes they lived in, the streets they walked, the air, the noise, the filth, the bread—all the basics. But the real thing that bothered me was that this country, despite all the talk about happiness—was in some pervasive way anti-pleasure. Oh, I know we're always stuffing something into our mouths—a drink, a piece of nickel candy. And we're forever riding here and there. There's music everywhere, even in the elevators and you can see old movies day and night on TV. But, where do you go to really have a good time in this city?

JAMIE KELSO

Jamie is a real person; he speaks in the outstanding book, *The Class of 1965.*

So I enrolled at UCLA. The intellectual disintegration was unbelievable. All the professors were using drugs and it was an incredible, zombie, Alice-in-Wonderland world of irrational spinning people. I refused to do my papers and I got F's. Then I left, I quit.

I got a job as a lineman for General Telephone and I brought home $135 every two weeks. I was risking my life up those poles and crawling down in sewers and shit. I felt I was not cut out to be a lineman. I went back to school because I learned that the world of jobs was more horrible than the world of school.

In the eyes of the ruling classes, I am insane. So be it. I may have a hallucination now and then but I do not commit genocide, I do not starve and exploit whole continents, I do not sell bombs and war planes to corrupt dictatorships, I do not make killing and oppression 'legal', I do not imprison anybody and I do not seek to be judged sane by a secret government of liberal facists.

I do expect that truth will prevail. Inside of 20 years I will live on a planet where communism, socialism, big brotherism, collectivism, fascism and all variant systems of terrorizing free men will repose on the scrap heap of history. But whether we win or lose the battle, all of those who have figured out the game for themselves have already won the ultimate victory. That victory is individual freedom, five minutes of which easily outweighs a thousand lifetimes of a mind enslaved.

GAIL SHEEHY

Gail writes with great enthusiasm and style, often emphasizing her points with lively conversation. Her classic work, *Passages* was first published in 1974. Here are some salient passages:

"What's it all about?" DeLorean asked himself. "Why are you doing all this? You're just like one of the machines. Suddenly you'll be obsolete and worn out and they'll scrap you. Does that make sense?"

"Here I was, spending my life bending the fenders a little differently to try to convince the public they were getting a new and dramatically different product. What gross excesses! It was ridiculous. There's got to be more to life than this. Am I doing the thing that God would have me do here on earth?"

"Corporate life is a security blanket. Sure, I could have coasted along for 17 more years at $750,000 a year without trying too hard, but coasting along is not my style. I wanted to make a contribution. Most people wait until retirement age and all of a sudden they don't have the drive and zest and zeal left. As long as I am going to change the direction of my life, this would be a good time to stake out a year and do some of the things I've been talking about."

DeLorean's experiences with the hype of corporate life continued with the dreadful battle to defeat a drug sting, a battle which he surprisingly won. Today, he is assuredly a much wiser man, a veteran of the hype wars who can vouch for the intensity of hype and its power to confound and confuse.

Today, more and more people are seeing the naked Emperor—Iranscam, exposure of the TV evangelists and AIDS to name a few. We are not as easily fooled any longer; skepticism is the rule for any new age hype. Lincoln was right.

My own rules regarding hype may be of interest to you:

1. If you lie, at least don't lie to yourself.

2. If you don't like something, whatever it may be, don't pretend otherwise. For example, if you don't like a child, he or she will pick up on it—children are

very intuitive. As much as you might want to hang clothes on your emperor, it won't hide the nakedness in a child's view.

3. The way to continue a relationship that you enjoy is to be totally honest, warts and all. Hidden facts are like gangrene...they fester and finally kill the good as well.

I'm sure you get the picture—it's best expressed in the old and timeless phrase:

"The truth will make you free."

AN EXERCISE IN HYPE DETECTION

Here is a fun project for seniors. First read some selections from a book by Dr. David Reuben; it is so devastating to the American food industry that they ran Dave out of the country with death threats. He now lives in Costa Rica. Once you read these cogent truths, you'll never feel the same way about a supermarket or restaurant.

Selections from Reuben's *Everything You Wanted to Know About Nutrition*:

"Every qualified scientist agrees that human diseases can be caused by synthetic chemicals. The people of the U.S. are the biggest eaters of cancer-causing synthetic chemicals in the world. And our rate of cancer incidence is increasing every year. At the same time that chemicals were added to our food (now about ten pound per year), the cancer death rate went up 400 percent!"

"You be the judge. Would you ask your children to sit down to the dinner table tonight and choke down ten pounds of chemicals with names like dodecalactone, carvacryl ether, hydratropaldehyde, dimethyl acetal, hexylacetoxyte-trahydrofuan, nonanoyl-4-dihydroxy-3-methoxybenzylamide. Over 5,000 compounds, such as those listed above, are dumped into the American processed food supply. Two things are wrong with this situation. First you are eating these chemicals to make life easier and bank accounts fatter for the food industry and second, you are running a terrifying risk of giving yourself and your loved ones fatal cancer."

"How can you prevent getting cancer? Just stop eating food that contains anything that has an ingredient that even sounds like it came from a laboratory instead of a kitchen. If you don't understand what it is, don't buy it. And don't be fooled by some sucker labels that say "BHA and BHT added to preserve freshness." That's the new tactic of food processors to sell you alibis with their chemicals. If they can't get it to you fresh without artificial-synthetic chemicals, you don't want it. And you don't want chemicals with an explanation—you just don't want chemicals in your food at all."

Now after that learned review of the situation, notice what McDonald's has in their food. No wonder Pritikin said that McDonald's was doing a great job of killing Americans.

See *Appendix A* for the pages from a booklet published by McDonald's, one of the leading fast food chains.

As an exercise in detecting hype, read these pages carefully and see if you can pick out all the half-truths, distortions of facts and outright lies. You'll be greatly aided if you have a copy of Reuben's book next to you. It just might be in your library. Like many books of its kind, it is often hard to find, but keep trying. It is worth the effort since it is truly a matter of your life and your death.

THE AARP

They are very subtle as the Establishment most often is—just enough truth to shield all the lies and misrepresentations and complete hype.

Yes, this organization, the *American Association of Retired Persons* is a Big Brother clone brought to you by the same people that told you that smoking was harmless, that Roosevelt was surprised by Pearl Harbor and that we should all work until we are 65 and then draw social security for two years (the average lifespan of an American male).

They publish a slick, color magazine called *Modern Maturity* which you can have delivered for just five dollars year. A bargain?

Well, it all depends on what you define as a bargain. There are a lot of ads for AARP-sponsored enterprises like insurance, investment plans, travel and so forth. In effect, the magazine is really a catalogue of things that AARP and their cohorts would like to sell you. Now that is suspect, but not as bad as their advertising of a lot of drugs which may do more harm than good. Take, for example, Lopressor by Geigy. Get out your magnifying glass and be prepared for some shocking, "fine-print" information regarding the side effects of this popular prescription drug.

The conclusion that I have drawn is that a gift horse should be carefully checked. A nice magazine for just five dollars which includes a membership in the AARP? Must be a catch-22, and in my book, there is.

VANILLIN

Try this experiment. Go to any store selling chocolate and try to find a chocolate bar or other chocolate candy without the artificial flavoring vanillin, a known carcinogenic. I have noticed that even the fine chocolate items from Europe have this dangerous chemical in them.

Now what conclusions do you draw from this? I would appreciate reader-feedback, especially from people who have had experience in either investigative journalism or chemistry or both. I think that research on why vanillin is in just about ALL chocolate products tells us something important about how the world is structured and controlled on an international basis.

Lopressor®
metoprolol tartrate USP

Tablets
Ampuls
Prefilled Syringes

BRIEF SUMMARY
(FOR FULL PRESCRIBING INFORMATION, SEE PACKAGE INSERT)

INDICATIONS AND USAGE
Hypertension
Lopressor tablets are indicated for the treatment of hypertension. They may be used alone or in combination with other antihypertensive agents.
Angina Pectoris
Lopressor is indicated in the long-term treatment of angina pectoris.
Myocardial Infarction
Lopressor ampuls, prefilled syringes, and tablets are indicated in the treatment of hemodynamically stable patients with definite or suspected acute myocardial infarction to reduce cardiovascular mortality. Treatment with intravenous Lopressor can be initiated as soon as the patient's clinical condition allows (see DOSAGE AND ADMINISTRATION, CONTRAINDICATIONS, and WARNINGS). Alternatively, treatment can begin within 3 to 10 days of the acute event (see DOSAGE AND ADMINISTRATION).

CONTRAINDICATIONS
Hypertension and Angina
Lopressor is contraindicated in sinus bradycardia, heart block greater than first degree, cardiogenic shock, and overt cardiac failure (see WARNINGS).
Myocardial Infarction
Lopressor is contraindicated in patients with a heart rate < 45 beats/min; second- and third-degree heart block; significant first-degree heart block (P-R interval ≥ 0.24 sec); systolic blood pressure < 100 mmHg; or moderate-to-severe cardiac failure (see WARNINGS).

WARNINGS
Hypertension and Angina
Cardiac Failure: Sympathetic stimulation is a vital component supporting circulatory function in congestive heart failure, and beta blockade carries the potential hazard of further depressing myocardial contractility and precipitating more severe failure. In hypertensive and angina patients who have congestive heart failure controlled by digitalis and diuretics, Lopressor should be administered cautiously. Both digitalis and Lopressor slow AV conduction.

In Patients Without a History of Cardiac Failure: Continued depression of the myocardium with beta-blocking agents over a period of time can, in some cases, lead to cardiac failure. At the first sign or symptom of impending cardiac failure, patients should be fully digitalized and/or given a diuretic. The response should be observed closely. If cardiac failure continues, despite adequate digitalization and diuretic therapy, Lopressor should be withdrawn.

Ischemic Heart Disease: Following abrupt cessation of therapy with certain beta-blocking agents, exacerbations of angina pectoris and, in some cases, myocardial infarction have occurred. When discontinuing chronically administered Lopressor, particularly in patients with ischemic heart disease, the dosage should be gradually reduced over a period of 1-2 weeks and the patient should be carefully monitored. If angina markedly worsens or acute coronary insufficiency develops, Lopressor administration should be reinstated promptly, at least temporarily, and other measures appropriate for the management of unstable angina should be taken. Patients should be warned against interruption or discontinuation of therapy without the physician's advice. Because coronary artery disease is common and may be unrecognized, it may be prudent not to discontinue Lopressor therapy abruptly even in patients treated only for hypertension.

Bronchospastic Diseases: PATIENTS WITH BRONCHO-SPASTIC DISEASES SHOULD, IN GENERAL, NOT RECEIVE BETA BLOCKERS. Because of its relative beta₁ selectivity, however, Lopressor may be used with caution in patients with bronchospastic disease who do not respond to, or cannot tolerate, other antihypertensive treatment. Since beta₁ selectivity is not absolute, a beta₂-stimulating agent should be administered concomitantly, and the lowest possible dose of Lopressor should be used. In these circumstances it would be prudent initially to administer Lopressor in smaller doses three times daily, instead of larger doses two times daily, to avoid the higher plasma levels associated with the longer dosing interval. (See DOSAGE AND ADMINISTRATION.)

Major Surgery: The necessity or desirability of withdrawing beta-blocking therapy prior to major surgery is controversial; the impaired ability of the heart to respond to reflex adrenergic stimuli may augment the risks of general anesthesia and surgical procedures.

Lopressor, like other beta blockers, is a competitive inhibitor of beta-receptor agonists, and its effects can be reversed by administration of such agents, e.g., dobutamine or isoproterenol. However, such patients may be subject to protracted severe hypotension. Difficulty in restarting and maintaining the heart beat has also been reported with beta blockers.

Diabetes and Hypoglycemia: Lopressor should be used with caution in diabetic patients if a beta-blocking agent is required. Beta blockers may mask tachycardia occurring with hypoglycemia, but other manifestations such as dizziness and sweating may not be significantly affected.

Thyrotoxicosis: Beta-adrenergic blockade may mask certain clinical signs (e.g., tachycardia) of hyperthyroidism. Patients suspected of developing thyrotoxicosis should be managed carefully to avoid abrupt withdrawal of beta blockade, which might precipitate a thyroid storm.
Myocardial Infarction
Cardiac Failure: Sympathetic stimulation is a vital component supporting circulatory function, and beta blockade carries the potential hazard of depressing myocardial contractility and precipitating or exacerbating minimal cardiac failure.

During treatment with Lopressor, the hemodynamic status of the patient should be carefully monitored. If heart failure occurs or persists despite appropriate treatment, Lopressor should be discontinued.

Bradycardia: Lopressor produces a decrease in sinus heart rate in most patients; this decrease is greatest among patients with high initial heart rates and least among patients with low initial heart rates. Acute myocardial infarction (particularly inferior infarction) may in itself produce significant lowering of the sinus rate. If the sinus rate decreases to < 40 beats/min, particularly if associated with evidence of lowered cardiac output, atropine (0.25-0.5 mg) should be administered intravenously. If treatment with atropine is not successful, Lopressor should be discontinued, and cautious administration of isoproterenol or installation of a cardiac pacemaker should be considered.

AV Block: Lopressor slows AV conduction and may produce significant first- (P-R interval ≥0.26 sec), second-, or third-degree heart block. Acute myocardial infarction also produces heart block.

If heart block occurs, Lopressor should be discontinued and atropine (0.25-0.5 mg) should be administered intravenously. If treatment with atropine is not successful, cautious administration of isoproterenol or installation of a cardiac pacemaker should be considered.

Hypotension: If hypotension (systolic blood pressure ≤ 90 mmHg) occurs, Lopressor should be discontinued, and the hemodynamic status of the patient and the extent of myocardial damage carefully assessed. Invasive monitoring of central venous, pulmonary capillary wedge, and arterial pressures may be required. Appropriate therapy with fluids, positive inotropic agents, balloon counterpulsation, or other treatment modalities should be instituted. If hypotension is associated with sinus bradycardia or AV block, treatment should be directed at reversing these (see above).

Bronchospastic Diseases: PATIENTS WITH BRONCHO-SPASTIC DISEASES SHOULD, IN GENERAL, NOT RECEIVE BETA BLOCKERS. Because of its relative beta₁ selectivity, Lopressor may be used with extreme caution in patients with bronchospastic disease. Because it is unknown to what extent beta₂-stimulating agents may exacerbate myocardial ischemia and the extent of infarction, these agents should *not* be used prophylactically. If bronchospasm not related to congestive heart failure occurs, Lopressor should be discontinued. A theophylline derivative or a beta₂ agonist may be administered cautiously, depending on the clinical condition of the patient. Both theophylline derivatives and beta₂ agonists may produce serious cardiac arrhythmias.

PRECAUTIONS
General
Lopressor should be used with caution in patients with impaired hepatic function.
Information for Patients
Patients should be advised to take Lopressor regularly and continuously, as directed, with or immediately following meals. If a dose should be missed, the patient should take only the next scheduled dose (without doubling it). Patients should not discontinue Lopressor without consulting the physician.

Patients should be advised (1) to avoid operating automobiles and machinery or engaging in other tasks requiring alertness until the patient's response to therapy with Lopressor has been determined; (2) to contact the physician if any difficulty in breathing occurs; (3) to inform the physician or dentist before any type of surgery that he or she is taking Lopressor.
Laboratory Tests
Clinical laboratory findings may include elevated levels of serum transaminase, alkaline phosphatase, and lactate dehydrogenase.
Drug Interactions
Catecholamine-depleting drugs (e.g., reserpine) may have an additive effect when given with beta-blocking agents. Patients treated with Lopressor plus a catecholamine depletor should therefore be closely observed for evidence of hypotension or marked bradycardia, which may produce vertigo, syncope, or postural hypotension.
Carcinogenesis, Mutagenesis, Impairment of Fertility
Long-term studies in animals have been conducted to evaluate carcinogenic potential. In 2-year studies in rats at three oral dosage levels of up to 800 mg/kg per day, there was no increase in the development of spontaneously occurring benign or malignant neoplasms of any type. The only histologic changes that appeared to be drug related were an increased incidence of generally mild focal accumulation of foamy macrophages in pulmonary alveoli and a slight increase in biliary hyperplasia. Neither finding represents symptoms of a known disease entity in man. In a 21-month study in Swiss albino mice at three oral dosage levels of up to 750 mg/kg per day, benign lung tumors (small adenomas) occurred more frequently in female mice receiving the highest dose than in untreated control animals. There was no increase in malignant or total (benign plus malignant) lung tumors, nor in the overall incidence of tumors or malignant tumors. This 21-month study was repeated in CD-1 mice, and no statistically or biologically significant differences were observed between treated and control mice of either sex for any type of tumor.

All mutagenicity tests performed (a dominant lethal study in mice, chromosome studies in somatic cells, a Salmonella/mammalian-microsome mutagenicity test, and a nucleus anomaly test in somatic interphase nuclei) were negative.

No evidence of impaired fertility due to Lopressor was observed in a study performed in rats at doses up to 55.5 times the maximum daily human dose of 450 mg.
Pregnancy Category C
Lopressor has been shown to increase postimplantation loss and decrease neonatal survival in rats at doses up to 55.5 times the maximum daily human dose of 450 mg. Distribution studies in mice confirm exposure of the fetus when Lopressor is administered to the pregnant animal. These studies have revealed no evidence of impaired fertility or teratogenicity. There are no adequate and well-controlled studies in pregnant women. Because animal reproduction studies are not always predictive of human response, this drug should be used during pregnancy only if clearly needed.
Nursing Mothers
Lopressor is excreted in breast milk in very small quantity. An infant consuming 1 liter of breast milk daily would receive a dose of less than 1 mg of the drug. Caution should be exercised when Lopressor is administered to a nursing woman.
Pediatric Use
Safety and effectiveness in children have not been established.
ADVERSE REACTIONS
Hypertension and Angina
Most adverse effects have been mild and transient.

Central Nervous System: Tiredness and dizziness have occurred in about 10 of 100 patients. Depression has been reported in about 5 of 100 patients. Mental confusion and short-term memory loss have been reported. Headache, nightmares, and insomnia have also been reported.

Cardiovascular: Shortness of breath and bradycardia have occurred in approximately 3 of 100 patients. Cold extremities; arterial insufficiency, usually of the Raynaud type; palpitations; congestive heart failure; peripheral edema; and hypotension have been reported in about 1 of 100 patients. (See CONTRAINDICATIONS, WARNINGS, and PRECAUTIONS.)

Respiratory: Wheezing (bronchospasm) and dyspnea have been reported in about 1 of 100 patients (see WARNINGS).

Gastrointestinal: Diarrhea has occurred in about 5 of 100 patients. Nausea, dry mouth, gastric pain, constipation, flatulence, and heartburn have been reported in about 1 of 100 patients.

Hypersensitive Reactions: Pruritus or rash have occurred in about 5 of 100 patients. Worsening of psoriasis has also been reported.

Miscellaneous: Peyronie's disease has been reported in fewer than 1 of 100,000 patients. Musculoskeletal pain, blurred vision, and tinnitus have also been reported.

There have been rare reports of reversible alopecia, agranulocytosis, and dry eyes. Discontinuation of the drug should be considered if any such reaction is not otherwise explicable.

The oculomucocutaneous syndrome associated with the beta blocker practolol has not been reported with Lopressor.
Myocardial Infarction
Central Nervous System: Tiredness has been reported in about 1 of 100 patients. Vertigo, sleep disturbances, hallucinations, headache, dizziness, visual disturbances, confusion, and reduced libido have also been reported, but a drug relationship is not clear.

Cardiovascular: In the randomized comparison of Lopressor and placebo described in the CLINICAL PHARMACOLOGY section, the following adverse reactions were reported:

	Lopressor	Placebo
Hypotension (systolic BP < 90 mmHg)	27.4%	23.2%
Bradycardia (heart rate < 40 beats/min)	15.9%	6.7%
Second- or third-degree heart block	4.7%	4.7%
First-degree heart block (P-R ≥ 0.26 sec)	5.3%	1.9%
Heart failure	27.5%	29.6%

Respiratory: Dyspnea of pulmonary origin has been reported in fewer than 1 of 100 patients.

Gastrointestinal: Nausea and abdominal pain have been reported in fewer than 1 of 100 patients.

Dermatologic: Rash and worsened psoriasis have been reported, but a drug relationship is not clear.

Miscellaneous: Unstable diabetes and claudication have been reported, but a drug relationship is not clear.
Potential Adverse Reactions
A variety of adverse reactions not listed above have been reported with other beta-adrenergic blocking agents and should be considered potential adverse reactions to Lopressor.

Central Nervous System: Reversible mental depression progressing to catatonia; an acute reversible syndrome characterized by disorientation for time and place, short-term memory loss, emotional lability, slightly clouded sensorium, and decreased performance on neuropsychometrics.

Cardiovascular: Intensification of AV block (see CONTRAINDICATIONS).

Hematologic: Agranulocytosis, nonthrombocytopenic purpura, thrombocytopenic purpura.

Hypersensitive Reactions: Fever combined with aching and sore throat, laryngospasm, and respiratory distress.

Geigy
C86-36 (Rev. 6/86)

GEIGY Pharmaceuticals
Division of CIBA-GEIGY Corporation
Ardsley, New York 10502

© 1986, Geigy.

CHAPTER TWO

Following are excerpts from *"The Crippling of America,"* an article written by Gary Null. Published in *Penthouse* magazine, February 1987, Volume 18, No. 6.
(Copyright 1987 by Penthouse Publications International, Ltd. Reprinted with the permission of the copyright owner.)

"The Arthritis Foundation, which collects millions of dollars every year, has repeatedly refused to seriously consider an inexpensive method of controlling this disease."

"...At a time when the guardians of medical orthodoxy are stepping up repression against dissidents, a new phenomenon is beginning to emerge. Suddenly, serious criticism of accepted, long-established medical practices is blossoming from within the medical establishment.

For years, the alternative health movement has charged that conventional medicine deals inadequately with the issue of prevention, supresses information about alternative treatments, and refuses to take responsibility for iatrogenic illnesses—those caused by medical treatment itself.

This position has been supported by occasional lone voices from within the establishment: Cardiologist Thomas Preston, M.D., who criticized coronary-bypass surgery in the *Atlantic Monthly:* pediatrician Robert Mendelsohn, whose series of best-selling books, including *Confessions of a Medical Heretic*, criticize traditional practices and trace their origins to material interests; and obstetrician Tom Brewer, who crusaded single-handedly for many years against low-salt, low-calorie diets for pregnant women.

But now—just when the American Medical Association is pushing for legislation against so-called quackery; when medical societies are pursuing chelation therapists in ethics hearings and in courts all over the country; when pioneering cancer researchers like Dr. Emanuel Revici face persecution and loss of their licenses; when, in short, the medical establishment is desperately trying to close the door on alternative therapies and treatment modalities—a loud chorus of critical voices is arising from within the establishment itself. The situation is no longer that of the occasional disillusioned medic blowing the whistle on an out-moded traditional practice. The number of well-credentialed people speaking out is now greater than at any other time. At last, the public is being given an opportunity to find out exactly what kind of trouble medicine is in."

"...Traditional rheumatologists deny that allergy has anything to do with arthritis, yet they themselves admit that the immune system—which is intimately involved with allergies—is related to arthritis. They are willing to poison people's bodies with potent toxic drugs, such as cyclophosphamide, also known as Cytoxan, a synthetic anticancer drug related to the nitrogen mustards, or with azathioprine, also known as Imuran, which surpresses the immune system and carries with it the risk of inducing cancer and lowering the patient's resistance to infection."

"...This first article is based on the controversial arthritis treatment advocated by Marshall Mandel, M.D., an establishment-trained allergist who has turned to clinical ecology.

The Arthritis Foundation proclaims that arthritis is incurable and loudly denounces any physician who practices clinical ecology, metabolic nutrition, orthomolecular medicine, or who prescribes food supplements, detoxification programs, or rotary diets to uncover food allergies.

One could accept the argument that such therapies are questionable if there were no established criteria for measuring changes in arthritic joints, or if the therapists were unqualified. But what can be said of a board-certified specialist with impeccable academic and clinical credentials who has taught, published, and presented information to his peers for a quarter-century; who has cumulative experience treating tens of thousands of patients by these methods; and whose field includes hundreds of medical professionals with similar credentials?

To deny the individual and collective experience of these scientists is itself unscientific. Such denials can be understood only by considering the following argument: For the arthritis establishment to acknowledge that diet or food sensitivities might play a role in causing or treating arthritis would establish a precedent, allowing a forum for the theory to be demonstrated as fact.

There are over a hundred forms of arthritis, as the Arthritis Foundation is quick to point out—a smoke screen behind which they hide the inadequacies of the traditional methods of treatment.

Rheumatoid arthritis and osteoarthritis are the most common forms. Six to eight million people in this country suffer from it. The disorder is a lifelong course of pain and progressive disability. Around ten to 20 percent are bedridden.

About half of rheumatoid arthritis cases can be controlled by symptom-suppressing drugs, but that doesn't eliminate the disease. During the course of the illness, there are periods in which it quiets down. The traditional physician calls these remissions. Rheumatologists and the Arthritis Foundation offer no explanation for remission—or for flare-ups—except to say that these are characteristic of the illness.

In contrast, there is no question that clinical ecologists can turn rheumatoid arthritis around, slow it down, and "cure" it by identifying and manipulating the underlying factors that trigger it.

The other common form of arthritis, osteoarthritis, isn't actually an inflammation, as the word arthritis suggests; rather, it's a degenerative illness involving a breakdown of the internal structure of joints through use and other factors, known and unknown. We know that allergies and nutrition play an important role. People who have osteoarthritis can greatly benefit from an investigation of dietary and environmental factors, including air pollutants and chemicals that contaminate our food and water supply...by using pure spring water in place of ordinary tap water, a person can eliminate chlorine, fluorides, pesticides, and industrial waste from his [or her] diet. The next method is control of the patient's domestic environment. Chemical pollution of indoor air is prevented by prohibiting the use of waxes, polishes, and disinfectants in maintaining the hospital room or the home. The patient is protected against these and other indoor pollutants, such as insecticide sprays, laundry detergents, chlorine bleach, and toxic glues, that we have come to accept as our normal way of living. Paints, gasoline, and lawn and garden chemicals, which are frequently stored in garages, can affect people sleeping in adjacent rooms. Building materials also present a hazard, especially those that contain formaldehyde, which is found in plywood and particle board and is used extensively for paneling and carpeting. If we can protect a person for four to six days from these chemicals, the number of ailments that can be ameliorated or completely cleared up is amazing. These simple ecological measures have been termed "comprehensive environmental control" by Dr. Theron G. Randolph of Chicago."

"...The Arthritis Foundation has ignored several studies that document the efficacy of clinical ecology...the foundation describes arthritis as an incurable disease of unknown cause. It suggests psychological treatment to help arthritis adjust to lifelong suffering, and says that through drugs and supervison by an arthritis specialist the disease can be controlled. It has been shown that arthritis sufferers can be helped without risking the serious side effects of drug therapy.

We can only speculate on the motives of the Arthritis Foundation. Perhaps it's afraid its fund-raising would be affected if it could be shown that arthritis sufferers do not need new drugs but comprehensive investigation of their diet, eating habits, nutritional status, and overall environment. The foundation would certainly lose the financial support of the pharmaceutical sponsors."

CONCLUSIONS

I am delighted to report that there are now some large gaps in the once seamless facade of solid hype. More and more people are listening to the pioneering voices; men like Alan H. Nittler, M.D., John Richardson, M.D., and to alternative publishers like Bellwether, Eden Press and Loompanics. Also, there are networks of people who are circulating the truth about food, health and the general subjects that affect us all. And computer links are beginning to show some promise as a means of quickly disseminating valuable verities.

This suggests, fellow seniors, that you arise and challenge hype wherever it appears. Do what is the best thing I've ever found to do in life...

QUESTION AUTHORITY

CHAPTER THREE
FOOD

We were only jesting; after all, you shell the corn before you grind it.

I am sure you get the picture—preparing your own food from the basics is the way of good health and savings.

In this chapter, you'll learn how to bypass the food processors and in so doing, how to bypass a lot of unhealthy chemicals and avoid paying absurd prices.

To introduce this chapter, we present a series of newspaper columns which describe the concept in just a few words. Most of the material in this chapter is from our two books, *Eat Well on a Dollar a Day* and the sequel, *The Dollar a Day Cookbook*.

SUNFLOWERS

For many years, the Russians have been steadily increasing their harvest of sunflower seeds. Do they know something we don't know? I think so.

Read this fact sheet on sunflowers published by the *National Garden Bureau* and see what you think. Incidentally, write to them at *628 Executive Drive, Willowbrook, IL 60521,* for more information on sunflower seeds and related subjects. They are a great organization and a wonderful ally of seniors.

1986 YEAR OF THE Sunflower

FACT SHEET
Published by: National Garden Bureau

INTRODUCTION

The National Garden Bureau focuses this year on the significance of the sunflower. A native American plant, Helianthus species have adapted to growing in each state of the continental U.S. The sunflower family is a true native wild flower and deserves recognition for its wild and cultivated forms.

Any gardener would marvel at the diversity of the Helianthus family. Some wild subspecies look more like cosmos or creeping zinnia (sanvitalia) than our vision of a stately sunflower. There are creamy white, red, bronze and bicolor flowers of cultivated varieties that any gardener could grow. We hope this information encourages gardeners to learn more about our native sunflower. ◊

HISTORY

The sunflower would appear to be one of America's unsung heroes. One of the few cultivated plants native to North America, it is believed that wild sunflowers covered thousands of square miles of land that is now the western United States.

Sunflower remains have been found in North American archaeological sites, reports the National Garden Bureau, as early as 3,000 B.C. The center of origin for wild sunflowers is considered to be the Western Plains of North America but the ancestors of the cultivated type have been traced to the Southwest or the Missouri-Mississippi River valley areas. The first breeders of sunflowers appear to be the Ozark Bluff dwellers who selected plants and seed for cultivation.

The sunflower and American Indians shared the land and had close contact in early American history. For most Indians, the primary use of the sunflower was as food. They were lightly roasted then ground into flour and used in breads or with other vegetables. The ingenuity of the American Indians found other uses for the seed, as well as other parts of the plant. Some medicinal uses include: The Zunis used it

as a cure for rattlesnake bites. The Dakotas, and other tribes made an infusion from the sunflower head to relieve chest pain. The Cochite extracted the juice from the stem for cuts and wounds believing it helped in a quick recovery without infection. The extracted oil was also used to annoint the hair and as a base for paint pigments. A yellow dye was extracted from the ray flowers, and a purple dye was made from soaked purple seeds which were used to make color baskets and to decorate the skin.

Spanish explorers, while looking for gold and treasures, collected many of the new world's flora, introducing the sunflower to Europe for its ornamental qualities. It was grown as a curiosity; the herbalists of the time found no virtues in sunflowers. The first published record of the sunflower was in 1568 by the famous Belgian herbalist

Rembert Dodoens. By 1616, the sunflower was common in England's gardens.

It is not known for sure when the rediscovery of the food value of the sunflower seed happened. Some had experimented with eating and preparing different parts of the sunflower as food and even found the buds to be quite good. In 1699 John Evlyn wrote of making macaroons out of a flour made from ground seeds — but he found the flavor to be similar to turpentine. However, Charles Bryant, in 1783, wrote that "the seeds have as agreeable flavor as almonds and are excellent food for domestic poultry." He also noted the high content of oil stored in the seeds and how easy it was to extract.

The sunflower spread quickly throughout most of Europe but it was grown more for its ornamental value than anything else.

NGB Photo 86-1-1 Shelled (on left) and unshelled sunflower seeds. The unshelled seeds came from the flower head in the foreground.

-1-

LAUREL

Her book, *Laurel's Kitchen*, was a runaway best seller despite the fact that there are more books on cooking than any other category. Here is her story; it not only relates to good food, but also to a changing world. Read it and see if you don't agree: (Reprinted courtesy of *Whole Life Times*)

WHOLE LIFE PERSON

Laurel Robertson: Home Is Where the Hearth Is

By Clara Silverstein and Kimberly French

With her brunette hair swept back, highlighting her rosy cheeks and sparkling blue eyes, Laurel Robertson is a walking advertisement for the principles of good health that she espouses in *Laurel's Kitchen* (Petaluma, California: Nilgiri Press, 1976), which has sold more than 800,000 copies.

Since the publication of *The Laurel's Kitchen Bread Book* (New York: Random House, 1984) in August, Laurel has been traveling around the country spreading her newest message: that nearly everyone can learn to bake whole-grain bread at home and make it a central part of the diet.

Her manner reflects her books' down-to-earth tone. During an interview, she shares bites of her lunch, apologizes to the waitress for not being able to finish her side order of bread, and offers advice for cleaning a coffee spot off a dress.

Recounting some of the stories and ideas behind the bread book, she is as relaxed and chatty as a next-door neighbor.

"I have a fairy tale about bread," she confides. "It's a series of events, all caused by people who begin to bake their own bread. They enjoy baking, so they decide to stay home more. Then they see that they like making their own food, so they decide to plant a vegetable garden. Soon, they realize that they really don't need the supermarket to feed themselves. Their neighbors see that they are happy, and soon others are baking and eating simply too . . . and there is no more hunger, because there is enough for everyone who eats this way!"

Laurel's real life parallels the early stages of this tale. Fifteen years ago she and 18 other members of her meditation group, many of whom were faculty members or students at the University of California at Berkeley, bought 250 acres together in Marin County at the suggestion of their teacher, Eknath Easwaran. Today the group numbers about 40, with every age from infant to 70.

Members of the group work as a cooperative—"not a commune," Laurel says—set up as a non-profit corporation called The Blue Mountain Center of Meditation Inc. Everyone pays rent, sharing household and outdoor tasks, and cooks and eats together while living separately as families or single people. Many of the adults work as doctors, nurses, computer specialists, and other professionals. Laurel's husband Ed Robertson has a graphic-arts business in town.

"We all became vegetarians in the mid-'60s," Laurel, now 40, says. "And with about 20 people rotating as the head cook each night, we came up with some pretty neat recipes.

"Many people then didn't know how to be vegetarians. There were no vegetarian cookbooks except the Seventh-day Adventists', and they don't use milk and also have the idea that if you give up hamburger you have to eat something that looks like hamburger. That didn't appeal to us. Other people we knew through meditation asked how we did it, so Carol [Flinders, one of the co-authors] and I put together a booklet."

Bronwen Godfrey, who became the third co-author, looked at the manuscript and felt it should be more comprehensive, Laurel relates. So the community's cooks spent a year and a half testing every recipe and researching with George Briggs, a nutrition professor at Berkeley.

©Terrence K. Morrison

They learned so much in the process that they changed some of their ideas about diet. "We learned you don't have to balance protein; in fact, you don't have to worry much about it at all [see "Breaking the Protein Myth," *Whole Life Times*, July/August 1984]. We cut back on fats and threw out about half the dessert section, to everyone's extreme dismay. We started eating more whole foods."

Laurel says it still embarrasses her that her name was the one to appear on the title. "It wasn't my idea," she says, "although the kitchen was always my main job; I have an affinity for that. Or maybe it's just because my mother gave me a nice name, and we all liked the way 'Laurel's Kitchen' sounded."

Before the book was published, the community's kitchen was in the big, old Victorian house on the land, but the royalty money enabled the group to build a beautiful, larger kitchen and dining room. They plan to use the money from the *Bread Book* to build more housing. Several of the group live in the farmhouse and three geodesic domes on the land, but some still live in trailers.

The barn has been transformed into a print shop and bindery, where the community first printed *Laurel's Kitchen*. The group also printed and contributed to Easwaran's book *Gandhi the Man* (Petaluma, California: Nilgiri Press, 1978) and two other meditation guides based on the *Bhagavad Gita*, the classic Hindu spiritual text.

The group's philosophical ideas underpin the kitchen work and vice versa.

"If you're eating a [meat-based] diet that you know is not possible for everyone else to eat, at some level you feel guilty, and that make you feel desperate," Laurel says. "But when you start eating pretty much what everyone all over the world is eating—grains, legumes, and vegetables—it gives you the ability to be hopeful.

"The best example is how they're burning the rain forests in Brazil to graze cattle for our hamburgers," she continues. "Those rain forests are so important to world climate. It's been shown there's a connection between them and the rhythm of the monsoons in India—when they fall on the ocean, when they fall on land. Changing your diet may seem like a small thing, but when you pull on a teeny bit of the problem, you see how it's connected to everything in the world."

Laurel, Carol, and Bronwen also connect bread-baking with self-reliance, just as Gandhi did with spinning cotton cloth. "What Gandhi was insisting upon with that spinning wheel was the absolutely vital importance of how we accomplish the most mundane things in life: the putting of clothes on our backs and food on our tables," Carol writes in *The Bread Book*. "There is always a simpler way to meet these needs, he taught, and a more self-reliant one—always an adjustment to make that will foster better health and

draw you into more richly interdependent relationships with others."

"When people bake bread," Laurel adds, "they rediscover that home is a wonderful place. But you have to make it happen. You have to stop looking for entertainment outside the home, and rediscover the people around you. This also relieves pressure on the environment, when you stop buying all the artificial junk people make at the expense of the environment."

After the excitement generated by *The Bread Book* wanes a bit, Laurel foresees herself educating people more about nutrition issues—like inventive ways to prepare "the ninth recipe for kale this month." Always modest, she acknowledges "all the pioneers out there on the cutting edge who are doing the fine research about nutrition, like Frankie

Lappe [director of the Institute for Food and Development Policy in San Francisco; see "Frances Moore Lappe's Recipe for a Whole Planet," *Whole Life Times*, July/August 1984] and the macrobiotics."

She tilts her head to the side, pauses a moment, and then admits, "I'm just in the position of getting the good word out."

To Learn More

Notes from Laurel's Kitchen Newsletter
P.O. Box 477
Petaluma, CA 94943
(707) 878-2369

Clara Silverstein is a free-lance writer in Boston who frequently contributes to *Whole Life Times*.
Kimberly French is editor of *Whole Life Times*.

National Garden Bureau Brochures

An organization devoted to current health food and nutritional trends.

I find these releases to be chock-full of invaluable information. Highly recommended.

The following recipes are straight from my book, *Dollar a Day Cookbook*, the sequel to *Eat Well on a Dollar a Day*. Both books sold well and appear in many libraries coast to coast.

There are current plans to reprint both books, but for now we hope this generous sampling of recipes enjoys you many culinary delights, and healthy, no less! They are easy to prepare while traveling, and even more so in the comforts of your home and garden.

Basic Foods

Here's a list of basic bulk foods that will give you the foundation for many, many low-cost meals. The total cost, calculated recently at good natural food stores, came to about $46. To this basic larder, we would add fresh fruits, vegetables, and dairy products as available. The foods are listed roughly in the order of their importance, though we'd hate to have to get along without any of them. We've also included some notes to give you a general idea of how we use them. You'll find specific recipes in abundance in the chapters that follow.

Whole Wheat: *This is the anchor of our diet. By sprouting it, we have a fresh vegetable. By cooking it whole, we have a bean substitute, and by grinding it, we can enjoy fresh cereal, breads, biscuits, and a wide variety of delicious desserts. As of this writing, the bulk price of wheat has gone down due to bumper crops. Even if it goes up slightly, it's still a bargain. Cost: $8.00 for 100 pounds.*

Whole Corn: *We love this stuff! It's useful in so many ways (see Chapter 4) that we couldn't be without it. One of the best methods is to grind it in your blender, boil it up, and use it as a breakfast cereal, or chilled with added fruits or meats as scrapple. Corn slumped in price too last year. Cost: $4.00 for 50 pounds.*

Alfalfa Seed: *Why do we list this third? Simply because sprouted seeds can provide you with almost all the vitamins you need. Not only that, you can sprout them anytime, under almost any circumstances. Cost: $1.65 for 1 pound.*

Non-Instant Powdered Milk: *Surprise! We do use this for cooking and drinking, but we use it even more for making yogurt. With the nutritional changes that take place during this process, you gain tremendously on your investment. Powdered buttermilk is a delightful variation that's great for making pancakes and other recipes where dry milk is specified. Cost: $1.80 for 2 pounds.*

Brewer's Yeast: *One of the best natural sources of vitamins and minerals. Brewer's yeast can be added to drinks, pancake batter, or just eaten plain by the spoonful, if you can stand the taste! Cost: $1.81 for 1 pound.*

Brown Rice: *Rice is a universal food, useful in dozens of ways. Just be sure that it's brown and not white, since the latter has no real food value beyond carbohydrates. Cost: $3.50 for 10 pounds.*

Soybeans: *Another great staple, loaded with protein, vitamins, and iron. Cost: $2.50 for 10 pounds.*

Pinto Beans: *We saw these on special for just 20 cents a pound because they were split. This is no disadvantage; in fact, they'll cook faster this way. With beans and corn in the cupboard, no Mexican feels deprived. One can make countless tasty dishes from this combination. Actually, you might pay even less if you bought 50 or 100 pounds. Cost: $2.00 for 10 pounds.*

Potatoes: *One of the most useful foods in anyone's larder, and delicious too. The Irish lived on a potato diet for many decades and worked up enough energy to migrate to the U.S.! Cost $1.60 for 20 pounds.*

Mung Beans: *Get these for the same reason: they make delicious, giant-sized sprouts even in the dead of winter. Cost: $1.20 for 2 pounds.*

Onions: *If you buy them at the right time of year and store them carefully, they'll last a long time. Added to any diet, onions spell good flavor and nutritional value. In fact, they're the basic flavoring for most peasant dishes. Cost: $2.00 for 20 pounds.*

Assorted Nuts: *A useful source of protein. Nuts can be used in main dishes or for healthful snacks anytime. Cost: $7.00 for 10 pounds.*

Safflower Oil: *We use this for cooking, frying, and salad dressings. Stay with the cold-pressed oils—safflower, soy, olive, and sesame are good ones. Use them sparingly, since they're expensive. Cost: $2.50 for 2 quarts.*

Raisins: *Raisins are expensive but provide good food value. A few added to many a recipe adds flavor and interest. Cost: $1.30 for 1 pound.*

Dates: *If you buy the dry variety, they are often relatively cheap. Cost: $2.00 for 5 pounds.*

Soy Sauce: *A seasoning that's vital to the success of your Chinese dishes. Buy it in a Chinese market if possible to get the real thing at low cost. Cost: 90 cents for 1 quart.*

Sea Salt: *An important staple; a little goes a long way. If it's from the sea, you get the trace minerals free. Cost: 10 cents for 1 pound.*

Honey: *The best sweetener you can buy, and it contains more food value than any other natural sugar. Cost: $1.20 for 2 pounds.*

Assorted Spices: *A mixture of cumin, paprika, pepper, curry powder, and others. (We like to grow our herbs at home, or gather them wild.) Cost: $2.00 for ½ pound.*

Ways with Wheat

Wheat is a staple food for billions of people, and no wonder—it's tasty, nutritious, versatile, and cheap! As of this writing, whole grain wheat is selling for $8 per 100-pound sack in Santa Cruz, California. This is certainly a great bargain for such a valuable food, so invest now. If you can't store 100 pounds, share it with a neighbor or friend.

Once you have a big sack or barrel of wheat in your pantry, you'll be tempted to experiment with it. Everybody enjoys ground wheat in cereals, breads, cookies, and so on, but many people don't know how good plain whole grain wheat can be. It makes a delicious cereal at breakfast or rice substitute at dinnertime. Just remember to presoak it in water to cut down on the cooking time.

Overnight Cereal

Soak a cup of whole grain wheat overnight in water to cover. In the morning, just barely bring it to a boil. Then add dates, nuts, raisins, honey, milk, or even a bit of cream if you feel economically daring. What a delicious cereal, with plenty of body and chewiness! Try it once, and you'll have it often. Serves 2 generously.

Here are some combinations to try at dinnertime:

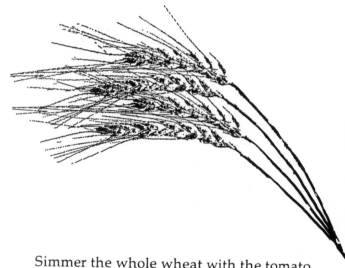

Tasty Tomato Wheat

* ☆ 1 cup whole grain wheat, soaked overnight
* ☆ 3 cups thin tomato purée
* ☆ 1 onion, chopped
* ☆ 2 cloves garlic, minced
* ☆ 1 cup chopped celery
* ☆ ¼ cup soy sauce
* ☆ 1 teaspoon sea salt
* ☆ 1 bay leaf, crumbled
* ☆ 1 teaspoon basil or oregano
* ☆ ½ cup grated cheese

Simmer the whole wheat with the tomato purée until the wheat is tender, replenishing the liquid if necessary. Add all the remaining ingredients except the cheese.

Simmer until well blended. Pour into a buttered casserole dish, cover with grated cheese, and bake uncovered at 350° for 10 or 15 minutes, or until the cheese is bubbly. Serves 4.

Wheat Sprouts

Simply soak any desired quantity of wheat overnight in a jar, drain it, and then rinse and drain the grains twice a day until they send out leaves and roots. The resultant sprouts may be eaten plain, chopped up and added to bread dough, tossed into casseroles, or used in salad.

Alternatively, sprinkle the wheat on a damp towel and let it sprout there. When the sprouts are a couple of inches high, cut them off with scissors. For more information on sprouts of all kinds, see Chapter 3.

Chili with Beans and Wheat

☆ 2¼ cups pinto beans
☆ 7 cups boiling water
☆ 3½ cups cooked tomatoes
☆ 1 cup chopped onions, sautéed
☆ ½ cup chopped green chilies, sautéed
☆ 2 tablespoons oil
☆ 1 tablespoon honey
☆ 1 cup cooked whole wheat
☆ ½ teaspoon cumin
☆ ½ teaspoon oregano
☆ ½ teaspoon basil
☆ ¼ teaspoon garlic powder
☆ ½ tablespoon sea salt

Cover the beans with the water and bring them to a boil. Turn off the heat and let them stand 1 hour. Then bring them to a boil again, turn down the heat, and simmer 1 more hour or until tender. Add the remaining ingredients and simmer until thick. Serves 6-8.

Use More Millet

Long a staple in southern China, Russia, Manchuria, Japan, and India, millet is still rarely found on most American tables. Yet this remarkable birdseed-like food is well worth discovering. While most grains lack two or more of the eight amino acids essential for a complete protein, millet lacks only one, lysine. Since lysine is found in abundance in seafood, dairy products, legumes, and most vegetables, just add any one of these to millet and voila! You have a healthy diet.

So go to your nearest grain supplier or natural food store, pick up a pound or two of millet, and experiment with some of the following recipes. Millet is rather bland by itself, but you can learn to combine it with a wide variety of other foods and seasonings with excellent results.

Morning Millet

Brown 1 cup of millet in a little oil and combine with 1 cup of sesame seed meal (grind your own seeds in the blender) and 5 cups of water. Cook until thick (approximately 20 minutes), pour into a pan, and chill. When cold, it can be sliced and fried in oil with a slice of jack or other cheese on top of each portion, making a great breakfast (or even lunch or dinner). Serves 4.

Savory Millet

☆ 4 cups seasoned stock
☆ 1 cup millet
☆ 2 tablespoons oil
☆ ½ green pepper, chopped
☆ 1 small onion, chopped
☆ 1 clove garlic, minced
☆ 3 tablespoons chopped parsley
☆ 1 tablespoon sweet basil
☆ dash cayenne pepper
☆ salt to taste

Put the stock in the top of a double boiler, set it over direct heat, and bring it to a boil. Add the millet, stir, cover, and boil a few minutes. Meanwhile, bring some water to a boil in the bottom of the double boiler. Set the top over the bottom and let the millet continue to cook gently.

In a frying pan sauté the pepper, onion, and garlic in the oil. Stir in the parsley, basil, cayenne, and salt. Then add the vegetable mixture to the millet and cook until all the liquid is absorbed and the millet is tender. Serves 4.

How to Sprout Any Seed

1. Be sure the seeds are not coated with anything. Many seeds intended for planting have fungicide on them, and this would be harmful to eat.

2. Wash them anyway.

3. Pour a small quantity in a large jar, leaving plenty of room for expansion, and soak them overnight.

4. Drain them thoroughly and rinse them at least twice a day; three times is even better. Keep them moist but not soggy. If they are too wet, they will rot.

5. To make it easy to rinse the seeds, put a piece of porous cloth—an old but clean nylon stocking works fine—over the top of the jar and hold it in place with a rubber band.

6. Store the sprouting seeds in a dark, fairly warm place. After all, you are simulating the environment of a seed sprouting in damp soil on a warm spring day.

7. In a few days, or less for small seeds, you will be pleased to observe developing roots and tops. You can eat the sprouts at any stage, raw or cooked, but they're more nutritious raw.

8. If you wish, you may increase the chlorophyll content of your sprouts by placing them in indirect sunlight for a few hours. Then store them in the refrigerator just like any other fresh vegetable.

Once you start this routine, you'll want to have a batch of sprouts going all the time. If you start some every couple of days, you will never be without a crunchy, nutritious supply.

Dollar-a-Day Chop Suey

First make up 6 cups of mung bean sprouts yourself. They will only cost about 30 cents. Then cook in a wok or frying pan:

* ☆ 2 large onions, chopped rather coarsely
* ☆ 1 medium stalk of celery, tops and all, sliced
* ☆ a few mushrooms, sliced
* ☆ 6 cloves of garlic, minced

You can steam them with a bit of water in the bottom or add a teaspoon of sesame oil to prevent sticking and add flavor. Cook until tender. Now add the 6 cups of drained sprouts and cook only until they're warm and delicately tender. Serve with chopsticks and plenty of soy sauce—the authentic kind bought from a Chinese grocery. Serves 4, at a cost per serving of about 17 cents for a most generous dish.

Incidentally, this is a great party dish. People love it, and it's inexpensive and quite simple to make. If you want to dress it up, add a few slivers of cooked pork or beef just before serving.

Popcorn

Take advantage of this inexpensive food often. Buy it in bulk, pop it in an iron skillet with a little peanut or soy oil, and add anything you like to the result. Salt and butter are standard, but it's fun to experiment with such deluxe touches as chopped almonds and honey, cashews and maple syrup, hazel nuts and date sugar, or peanuts and molasses.

Ground up in your blender or food mill, popcorn becomes a fabulous cereal which can be cooked and served with milk, dried fruits, or whatever you fancy. Once you try your own popcorn treats, you won't be tempted to pay 69 cents for a package of ready-made ones in the supermarket. In fact, you'll pass them up with a righteous sneer.

Since we've gotten started on describing how you can make your own snack foods, here are a few more.

Corn Crackers

These are much better for you than any store-bought crackers, and certainly much cheaper.

* ☆ 1½ cups freshly ground corn meal
* ☆ 1 cup whole wheat flour
* ☆ ½ cup wheat germ
* ☆ ½ teaspoon sea salt
* ☆ 1 teaspoon honey
* ☆ ½ cup water
* ☆ ⅓ cup oil

Mix the dry ingredients. Beat the honey, water, and oil together, and add them slowly to the dry mixture. Mix and knead lightly. Roll out the dough with a rolling pin as thinly as possible. If desired, sprinkle it with salt. Cut the dough into whatever size and shape you want, and place the crackers on a well-greased cookie sheet.

Bake them for 1 minute at 400°; then reduce the heat to 300° and bake for 25 minutes more. Remove them from the cookie sheet to cool, and try to keep from eating all of them at once.

Homemade Corn Chips

Put fresh corn tortillas in a 300° oven and bake them until they're crisp. Cool, break into bite-sized pieces, and store in an airtight jar. For a fraction of what you would pay for the oil-fried kind, you have a convenient chip for dips. (Thanks to our good friend Dan Clark for this dandy method.)

Oatmeal-Date Muffins

* ☆ 2 cups rolled oats
* ☆ 1½ cups sour milk or buttermilk
* ☆ 2 tablespoons honey
* ☆ 1 egg
* ☆ 2 tablespoons oil
* ☆ 1 cup whole wheat flour
* ☆ 1 teaspoon baking soda
* ☆ 1 teaspoon sea salt
* ☆ ½ cup chopped dates

Add the oats to the sour milk or buttermilk and let them stand an hour or so. Beat in the honey, egg, and oil. Blend the flour, baking soda, and salt, and add them all at once, stirring only until the flour disappears. Fold the dates in last.

Bake in greased muffin pans for 30 to 35 minutes in a 400° oven. Makes about 2 dozen.

Date-Rice Pudding

* ☆ 2 cups chopped dates
* ☆ 1½ cups raw brown rice
* ☆ 2½ cups milk made from powder
* ☆ ½ cup honey
* ☆ 1 egg, beaten
* ☆ 1 teaspoon cinnamon
* ☆ ½ teaspoon nutmeg
* ☆ ¼ teaspoon ground ginger
* ☆ 1 cup homemade yogurt

Cook the dates in water to cover until soft; drain. Cook the rice in the milk until tender. Stir in the honey, egg, and spices. Spread half of the rice into an oiled 1-quart casserole. Cover it with half of the cooked dates. Repeat the two layers.

Bake at 350° for 25 minutes. Remove and cool. Spread the yogurt over the top and chill before serving. Serves 6-8.

Date-Coconut Chews

* ☆ 1 cup water mixed with ½ cup milk powder
* ☆ 1 cup dates, pitted and chopped
* ☆ 1 cup shredded coconut
* ☆ ½ cup chopped walnuts
* ☆ ½ cup whole wheat flour
* ☆ 2 teaspoons vanilla
* ☆ ⅛ teaspoon sea salt

Mix all the ingredients thoroughly with a fork. Then form the dough into small balls, place them on an oiled cookie sheet, and bake them at 325° for 12 minutes or until lightly browned. Makes 18-20 chews.

The other day we bought an entire lug box of beautiful fresh dates for just $6, or less than 30 cents a pound. There was a catch to the deal. The dates had been nibbled on by birds while they were on the tree. But my reasoning was this: the birds, free to sample any date, would choose the sweetest ones! And here's what we made with some of this big bargain.

Cracked Wheat Raisin-Apple Bread

* 2 packages active dry yeast
* ½ cup lukewarm water
* 1 cup milk
* 3 tablespoons honey
* 1 tablespoon salt
* 1 egg, beaten
* ½ cup cracked wheat
* 1 cup raisins
* 1 cup chopped tart apple
* 3 cups whole wheat flour
* 1 egg yolk
* 1 teaspoon milk

Dissolve the yeast in the water. Scald the milk, add the honey and salt, and cool to lukewarm. Add the yeast mixture and the beaten egg. Stir in all but a tablespoon of the cracked wheat, the raisins, the apples, and 2 cups of the flour. Knead in the remaining flour.

Let the dough rise for 1 hour. Punch it down and form it into a loaf. Put it in a buttered loaf pan and let it rise again for about 45 minutes. Beat the egg yolk with the milk and brush it on top of the loaf. Sprinkle the top with the remaining cracked wheat. Bake for 45 minutes in a 375° oven. Remove from the pan and cool on a rack. Makes one 2-pound loaf.

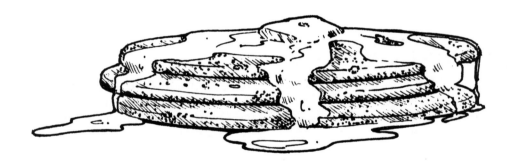

Pantry Pancakes

* ½ cup whole wheat flour
* ½ cup corn meal
* ½ cup rye flour
* ¼ cup wheat germ
* ¼ cup soy flour
* 4 eggs
* 1½ cups buttermilk or sour milk
* 1 teaspoon soda
* ⅓ cup oil
* 1 tablespoon honey or molasses

Blend all the ingredients well and fry on a hot greased griddle. More liquid may be added if a thinner pancake is desired. This batter may also be baked in a waffle iron. For a lighter waffle, separate the eggs, folding in the stiffly beaten egg whites last. Serves 4.

Hearty Oatmeal Cookies

- ☆ 3 eggs
- ☆ ¾ cup honey (you can use part molasses)
- ☆ ¾ cup oil
- ☆ 1 teaspoon vanilla
- ☆ ½ teaspoon baking powder
- ☆ ¼ cup milk
- ☆ 2 cups flour (use a mixture of whole wheat, soy, bran, or wheat germ if you like)
- ☆ 2 cups oatmeal
- ☆ 1 cup chopped dried fruit (raisins, dates, prunes, apricots)
- ☆ 1 cup chopped walnuts
- ☆ ½ cup sesame seeds
- ☆ ½ cup sunflower seeds

Everyone has a recipe for oatmeal cookies like the one that comes on the box of rolled oats using 1 cup of white sugar, 1 cup of brown sugar, and 1 cup of white flour. Once you've tried the next recipe using wholesome ingredients, you'll throw your old one away. They're wonderful in your child's lunchbox, in a picnic basket, or as a snack. This is a large recipe, but they store well.

Mix the ingredients in the order given and drop by spoonfuls on a greased cookie sheet. Bake at 350° for 15 minutes or until light brown. Makes about 8 dozen!

Oatmeal Croquettes

Oats for dinner!

- ☆ 1 cup rolled oats
- ☆ ¾ cup hot water or milk
- ☆ 1 egg, beaten
- ☆ 1 large onion, chopped
- ☆ 1 teaspoon salt
- ☆ ⅛ teaspoon pepper
- ☆ ¼ cup oil

Soak the oats in water or milk for about an hour. Add the rest of the ingredients and drop by spoonfuls into the hot oil in a skillet. Brown on each side, drain on paper towels, and serve as an accompaniment to any vegetable dish. Serves 4.

Barley — A Coffee Alternative

As of this writing, the price of coffee has soared beyond belief. Here's a way to continue enjoying that unique coffee flavor without having to eliminate some more nutritious item from your food budget. Roast half a pound of barley in the oven at 350° for about 30 minutes until deep brown. Mix with a pound of coffee beans. Grind it in your blender or coffee grinder as desired and brew in your favorite fashion. With coffee beans at $4 a pound and barley costing only 10 cents a pound, you have now cut the price of your coffee almost in half. And the flavor? Not bad at all . . . try it!

Italian Tomato Sauce

* 2 large onions, chopped
* 4 or 5 cloves garlic, minced
* ½ cup oil (olive, if you can afford it)
* basil, oregano, thyme, bay leaf
* 4 cups tomato purée
* sea salt and pepper
* 1 teaspoon honey
* ½ cup sliced mushrooms

Sauté the onions and garlic in the oil, sprinkling the herbs on top to simmer at the same time. Then add the tomato purée, salt and pepper, and honey. Sauté the mushrooms in oil separately and add them last. As with any good Italian sauce, the longer you simmer it, the better. Makes about 4 cups.

A tomato sauce like this is the classic accompaniment to spaghetti, of course. And it's always delicious. But for a welcome change, spaghetti can go with more delicate sauces too.

Spaghetti alla Toscana

* 1 medium cauliflower
* ½ pound soy spaghetti
* 2 cups Whole Wheat Cream Sauce (see p. 122)
* ½ cup grated cheese
* 1 pound fresh peas, cooked
* salt and pepper
* 2 teaspoons chopped chives

Steam the cauliflower and the peas until tender and cook the spaghetti in boiling water. Heat the cream sauce and add the cheese. Place the cauliflower in a serving dish and surround it with the peas and the spaghetti, seasoned with salt and pepper. Pour the hot cream sauce over all and top with the chives. Serves 4.

Navy Bean Soup

If you've never tried bay leaves in your soup, here's your chance to find out what a nice subtle flavor they can add.

* 1 cup navy beans
* 3 medium onions
* 2 carrots
* 2 cups chopped celery and leaves
* 1 clove garlic
* 2 tablespoons oil
* 2 or 3 bay leaves
* sea salt and pepper to taste
* 3 tablespoons miso
* ⅔ cup raw brown rice

Soak the beans in water overnight; then cook them until tender. Mash them slightly with a fork. Sauté the chopped onions, carrots, celery, and garlic in the oil until tender. Add the seasonings. Dissolve the miso in some of the hot stock from the cooked beans. Add the beans and liquid along with the rice to the cooked vegetables, using a large 4-quart pot. Add more water or stock to cover and simmer until the rice is cooked. Serves 6.

Homemade Bulgur

Boil a cup or two of whole grain wheat, dry it in the sun or your oven, and grind it briefly in a blender. As an alternative to grinding it, you can toast it in a pan until it's golden-brown. Then you'll have an Indian-type snack that can be carried on hikes or picnics. Children love its crunchiness, and it's far better for them than any sugar-coated cereal you could buy.

Rattatweetle

We couldn't resist giving our own nickname to the classic Ratatouille.

* 1 large eggplant
* 1 green pepper, chopped
* 1 large onion, chopped
* 2 cloves garlic, minced
* 2 tablespoons olive oil
* bay leaf, thyme, oregano, basil
* sea salt, pepper
* 3-4 tomatoes, chopped
* 2 medium zucchini, sliced

Peel the eggplant and cut it into cubes. Parboil them for 3 minutes in boiling water. Sauté the green pepper, onion, and garlic in the oil and add the herbs and seasonings. Add the eggplant, tomatoes, and zucchini, and simmer covered for 20 minutes, stirring occasionally until well blended. This can be eaten hot or cold, and is always better the second day. Serves 6-8.

This is one of the most delicious and nutritious vegetable dishes we know of. People who say they hate vegetables come back for more every time, and best of all, it fits in perfectly with the dollar-a-day concept.

Don't hesitate to experiment with this recipe yourself. We recently encountered a version in which everything was green. The cook, Ann Johnson of Santa Barbara, California, decided that she was going to try a monochromatic Ratatouille just for fun. It turned out to be the most delicious version we've ever tasted. With her permission we're going to give away the culinary secret of the century: she added some green chilies that lent just the right amount of Mexican heat to make the dish literally sing!

Marvelous Mushrooms

Too expensive? Just get yourself some mushroom spore (check any gardening magazine for ads), find a nice, cool, dark place, combine the spore with a rich bed of cool earth and manure, and hang easy. The mushrooms know exactly what to do under the right conditions.

Homegrown or storebought, mushrooms have excellent nutritional value and few calories. Also, they usually haven't been processed in any way. Fry them in a little butter for a side dish. Pop them into the next pot of soup you make just before it's ready to take from the fire, leaving them in just long enough to warm up. Overcooking destroys their delicate flavor and some of their nutritional value. Another excellent use is in salads: just slice them and toss them with your greens and dressing.

Remember, too, that when the price is low, you can buy large quantities of mushrooms and dry them. They'll add an elegant touch to your dollar-a-day diet.

Mushroom-Spinach Salad

* ☆ 2 bunches fresh spinach, thoroughly washed and patted dry
* ☆ 1 cup bean sprouts
* ☆ ¼ pound raw mushrooms
* ☆ 5 ounces canned water chestnuts, sliced (optional)
* ☆ 1 cup oil
* ☆ ⅓ cup vinegar
* ☆ ⅓ cup catsup
* ☆ 1 minced onion
* ☆ salt and pepper to taste

Combine the spinach, sprouts, mushrooms, and water chestnuts. Whirl the remaining ingredients in your blender to make the dressing, and toss all together. Serves 6.

Red and Green Salad

Last Christmas we tried this combination, and not only were the colors right for the occasion, but it was surprisingly tasty.

* ☆ 2 cups grated raw broccoli
* ☆ 2 cups chopped fresh tomatoes
* ☆ mayonnaise
* ☆ lettuce

Combine the broccoli and tomatoes with sufficient mayonnaise to moisten and serve on lettuce leaves. Serves 6.

Salad with Fresh Herbs

* ☆ 4 tomatoes, sliced
* ☆ 1 green pepper, sliced in strips
* ☆ 1 large cucumber, diced
* ☆ 1 Bermuda onion, slivered
* ☆ 2 stalks celery, sliced
* ☆ 2 tablespoons minced fresh herbs, such as tarragon, basil, mint, chervil, or chives

Combine all ingredients and toss with Ruth's French Dressing (see p. 125). Serve on lettuce leaves. Serves 6.

Sage Hen Sauté

Out in sagebrush country the controversy has raged for years over how to cook a wild sage hen so it won't taste like a wild sage hen. Some suggest soaking it overnight in vinegar. Others maintain that soaking it in lye is the only way. Old timers have their own favorite recipe that goes like this:

Soak the sage hen 2 days and nights in salt water to which a can of kerosene has been added. Sauté for 6 hours in a hot frying pan. Then boil for 3 days. Pour off the water. Then fill the frying pan with grease and put the bird back for another day. Then throw the bird into the brush and eat the frying pan.

Cabbage with Caraway Seeds

Cooked cabbage is ordinarily very bland. But add some caraway seeds and a few drops of lemon juice, and voila! You have a tasty companion for your main dish.

* ☆ 1 medium head green cabbage
* ☆ 4 tablespoons butter
* ☆ 2 teaspoons caraway seeds
* ☆ juice of half a lemon

Cut the cabbage in quarters and boil for 8 minutes in salted water. Melt the butter and add the caraway seeds and lemon juice. Drain the cabbage, place it in a serving dish, and pour the sauce over it. Serves 4.

Stuffed Cabbage Rolls

A delightful vegetarian version that still has plenty of protein for a main dish.

* ☆ 1 head cabbage
* ☆ ½ cup cooked garbanzo beans
* ☆ ½ cup yogurt
* ☆ ¾ cup cooked brown rice
* ☆ 2 tablespoons chopped parsley
* ☆ 2 tablespoons chopped chives
* ☆ ½ teaspoon crushed celery seeds
* ☆ ½ teaspoon oregano
* ☆ 1 tablespoon soy sauce
* ☆ ⅓ cup chopped celery
* ☆ ⅓ cup grated cheese
* ☆ ⅔ cup chopped mushrooms
* ☆ 1 teaspoon sea salt
* ☆ 3 fresh tomatoes, chopped

Core the cabbage and steam it over hot water for 5 minutes or until the leaves can be separated. Blend the cooked garbanzo beans and yogurt in a blender, and then place them in a mixing bowl. Add all the remaining ingredients except the tomatoes. Blend well. Stuff each cabbage leaf with a couple of tablespoonfuls of the mixture and fold over the edges, fastening with a toothpick.

Place in an oiled casserole dish, cover with the chopped tomatoes, and bake covered at 350° for about 30 minutes. Serves 4-6.

One-Pot Turkey-Noodle Dinner

Great for that leftover turkey!

* ☆ 1 medium onion, chopped
* ☆ ½ cup sliced carrots
* ☆ ½ cup sliced celery
* ☆ 2 tablespoons butter, oil, or rendered turkey fat
* ☆ 2¾ cups water or stock
* ☆ 2 cups diced turkey
* ☆ 8 oz. whole wheat noodles
* ☆ 1 cup turkey gravy
* ☆ 1 teaspoon sea salt
* ☆ ½ teaspoon basil
* ☆ pepper to taste

In a heavy skillet, sauté the onion, carrots, and celery until tender. Add the remaining ingredients, bring to a boil, reduce heat and cover. Simmer for 10 minutes or until the noodles are tender, stirring frequently. Serves 4.

Honey-Glazed Chicken

* A 3-pound frying chicken, cut into serving pieces
* salt and pepper
* ¼ cup oil
* ¼ cup honey
* ¼ cup lemon juice
* ¼ teaspoon paprika
* ½ teaspoon dry mustard

Wash and dry the chicken pieces, and season them with the salt and pepper. Heat the oil in the skillet and sauté the chicken, turning once to brown on both sides. Cover and cook over medium heat for 15 minutes. Blend the remaining ingredients and pour them over the chicken. Cook uncovered another 20 minutes, basting frequently. The chicken is done when a fork may be inserted easily. Serves 4-6.

This dish may also be baked in the oven. Arrange the chicken pieces, skin side down, in a shallow greased baking dish. Brush them with the marinade, cover the pan with foil, and bake 30 minutes at 350°. Remove the foil, turn the chicken, and brush it with the marinade. Increase the temperature to 400° and bake 15 or 20 minutes more, or until the chicken is golden-brown and tender.

Island Chicken

* A 3½-pound chicken, cut into serving pieces
* ⅓ cup soy sauce
* 2 tablespoons lemon juice
* 1 teaspoon sage
* 1 teaspoon salt
* ½ teaspoon pepper
* 1 teaspoon ginger
* ½ cup whole wheat flour
* ¼ cup oil
* 1 cup boiling water
* 1 large onion, cut in chunks

Place the washed chicken pieces in a bowl and pour over them the soy sauce, lemon juice, sage, salt, pepper, and ginger. Marinate for 1 hour or longer.

Lift the chicken pieces out and roll them in the flour. Heat the oil in a skillet and fry the chicken until it's deep gold. Transfer it to a casserole or shallow pan, pour the boiling water in at the side, and arrange the onion chunks around. Pour the marinade over the chicken, cover, and bake at 350° for 1 hour. Serves 4-6.

Pumpkin-Cheese Pie

* 1½ cups cooked pumpkin
* 1½ cups cottage cheese
* ½ cup honey
* ¼ cup orange juice
* 1 teaspoon grated orange rind
* 3 eggs
* 1 teaspoon cinnamon
* ½ teaspoon each ginger, allspice, and cloves

Whirl all ingredients in a blender and pour them into a whole wheat pie crust. Bake at 350° for 1 hour. Makes 1 pie.

Pumpkin Pudding

* 1½ cups puréed cooked pumpkin
* 1½ cups milk made with dry milk powder
* 2 tablespoons honey
* 2 tablespoons molasses
* 2 eggs, beaten
* 1 teaspoon each cinnamon and allspice
* ½ teaspoon ginger

Combine all ingredients in a mixer or blender and beat until thoroughly mixed. Pour into a buttered 1½-quart casserole and bake at 325° for 1 hour. Serves 6-8.

Acorn Squash Dinner

* 1 large acorn squash
* 1 onion, chopped
* ⅓ cup green pepper, chopped
* 1 tablespoon oil
* 1 cup brown rice, cooked
* 1 tablespoon soy sauce
* sea salt and pepper
* 1 tablespoon chopped parsley
* ⅔ cup grated cheese

Cut the squash in half and remove the seeds. Set the two halves upside down in a small amount of water in a flat baking pan, and bake at 325° for about 45 minutes.

Meanwhile, sauté the onion and green pepper in the oil and mix them with the cooked brown rice, soy sauce, and salt and pepper. Mound the rice mixture in the center of the squash, sprinkle with parsley, and top with grated cheese. Melt the cheese slowly in a warm oven. Serves 4.

Zucchini-Corn Pudding

* 1 onion, chopped
* 1 clove garlic, minced
* ½ green pepper, chopped
* 2 tablespoons butter or oil
* 1 pound zucchini, cooked and chopped fine
* 1 cup cooked corn, cut off the cob
* ½ cup grated cheddar cheese
* 3 eggs, separated
* sea salt to taste

Sauté the onion, garlic, and green pepper in the oil. Remove from the heat and add the zucchini, corn, cheese, and beaten egg yolks. Season with salt. Fold in the stiffly beaten egg whites. Spoon the mixture into a greased casserole and bake at 350° for 1 hour. Serves 4.

Gussied Up Beans & Rice

Here is that basic, complete-protein combination of beans and rice, gussied up a bit to make a hearty meal.

- ✩ 1 onion, chopped
- ✩ 1 clove garlic
- ✩ 2 tablespoons oil
- ✩ 2 cups cooked red beans
- ✩ 2 cups cooked brown rice
- ✩ ½ cup chopped parsley
- ✩ 1 teaspoon sea salt
- ✩ ¼ cup grated cheese
- ✩ 1 egg
- ✩ 1 cup milk

Sauté the onion and garlic in the oil and blend with the beans and rice. Add the parsley, salt, and cheese. Beat the egg and milk together and add to the bean-rice mixture. Bake in a casserole for 30 minutes at 350° Serves 4-6.

Puffy Tuna-Rice Casserole

- ✩ ⅓ cup vegetable oil
- ✩ ¼ cup whole wheat flour
- ✩ ½ teaspoon salt
- ✩ 1½ cups milk
- ✩ 3 eggs, separated
- ✩ 1 can tuna or ¾ cup cooked fish, flaked
- ✩ 2 tablespoons grated onion
- ✩ 1 tablespoon lemon juice
- ✩ 2 cups cooked brown rice
- ✩ 2 slices cheese

Make a white sauce by blending the oil, flour, salt, and milk in a blender, then heating the mixture in a saucepan, stirring constantly. When thickened, beat the egg yolks, add a little sauce to them, and then add the yolks to the sauce in the pan. Cook for about 2 minutes over low heat while continuing to stir. Remove from heat and fold in tuna, onion, lemon juice, and rice. Beat the egg whites until stiff and fold them into the tuna mixture. Pour into a 1½-quart casserole.

Cut the cheese slices in half diagonally and arrange them around the top. Set the casserole in a pan of hot water. Bake at 350° for about 40 minutes or until firm. Serves 4.

Rice Ranchero

- ✩ 1 quart homemade tomato soup seasoned with 1 tablespoon chili powder
- ✩ ¾ cup finely chopped onions
- ✩ 3 cups cooked brown rice
- ✩ 1½ cups crushed homemade corn chips
- ✩ ¾ cup grated cheese

Mix the soup and onions, and heat until boiling. Add the rice and mix well. Pour into a 2-quart casserole. Top with crushed corn chips and cheese. Bake at 375° for 25 to 30 minutes. Serves 6.

Oven French Fries

Things fried in hot oil or fat aren't supposed to be good for us, so if you crave French fries, try this oven method.

☆ 4 medium potatoes
☆ ¼ cup melted butter
☆ sea salt, paprika
☆ ¼ cup grated Parmesan cheese

Pare the potatoes and cut them into strips. Soak them in cold water for 30 minutes. Drain and dry well. Place them on a well-greased cookie sheet and brush with melted butter. Sprinkle salt and paprika over them and bake in a 450° oven for 25 to 30 minutes. Sprinkle with the Parmesan cheese when you take them out of the oven. Serves 4.

Potato Volcano with Cheese

Here's a recipe you might want to prepare as a conversation piece for guests. It's not only fun but nutritious.

☆ 3 cups mashed potatoes
☆ ⅓ cup melted butter
☆ 2 egg yolks
☆ 4 tablespoons grated cheese
☆ sea salt, paprika
☆ ½ cup bread crumbs

Shape the potatoes into a large mound in a greased baking dish, making a hollow at the top the depth of a teacup. Pour part of the melted butter mixed with the egg yolks, cheese, and seasonings into this hollow. Reserve about 2 tablespoons of butter to drizzle around the outside of the mound. Coat the mound with bread crumbs. Brown in the oven at 350° for about 15 minutes. Individual volcanoes for each guest could also be made. Serves 4-6.

Potato Pancakes

No section of potato recipes would be complete without a recipe for potato pancakes, the kind that begins with raw grated potatoes.

☆ 4 large potatoes
☆ 1 small onion
☆ ½ cup milk
☆ 1 teaspoon salt
☆ 1 egg, beaten
☆ 2 tablespoons whole wheat flour
☆ oil for frying
☆ salt, paprika, pepper
☆ favorite herbs (optional)

Scrub the potatoes well and grate them along with the onion into the milk. Add the remaining ingredients and drop by tablespoons into a skillet with hot oil (safflower does fine). Season well with salt, paprika, pepper and maybe a sprinkling of your favorite herbs. Serves 6.

Garbanzo, or Chick Pea

Anyone who likes Italian minestrone soup is already acquainted with garbanzos, or chick peas. They are the round camel-colored beans found in the bottom of every bowl. Garbanzos are also extremely popular in the Middle East, where they're used in the tasty falafels now finding their way into American craft fairs as well as small ethnic and vegetarian restaurants. For those who would like to make their own, here's how.

Falafels

- ☆ 2 cups dried garbanzo beans
- ☆ ½ cup water
- ☆ 1 clove garlic
- ☆ 2 tablespoons parsley
- ☆ ¼ teaspoon cumin
- ☆ 1 teaspoon salt
- ☆ 1 cup bread crumbs

Wash the garbanzos and soak them overnight in the refrigerator. Grind 1⅓ cups of the soaked garbanzos in a meat grinder or chop them in a blender without water. Blend the remaining ⅔ cup of garbanzos with ½ cup cold water until ground fine. Add the garlic, parsley, cumin, and salt, and combine with the ground garbanzos. Drop spoonfuls of the mixture into a bowl of bread crumbs and turn them to coat, forming a small ball with your fingers if necessary.

Put them on an ungreased baking pan, cover with foil, and bake at 350° for 15 minutes. Then turn them over and bake for 10 minutes uncovered. Serve hot on pita bread with tahini sauce (see below), chopped cucumbers, tomato, lettuce, and green onion. Makes 2 dozen.

Pita

A Middle Eastern flatbread, to serve with falafels.

- ☆ 1 tablespoon dry yeast
- ☆ ¼ cup warm water
- ☆ 1 teaspoon salt
- ☆ ¾ cup warm water
- ☆ about 2½ cups whole wheat flour

Dissolve the yeast in ¼ cup water; then add the salt and ¾ cup water. Add the flour. Turn the dough out on a floured board and knead it until smooth and elastic.

Let it rise in a warm place until double in bulk, turn it out on a floured board, and form it into 12 balls. Roll each into a circle ¼ inch thick; place them on a greased baking sheet and let them rise for 15 minutes. Then bake at 500° for 10 minutes. Make sure they don't brown too much. Makes 12.

Sesame, Sunflower & Co.

Among the many edible seeds, there are two we use most often—sesame and sunflower. These can be valuable sources of protein, particularly when you combine them with beans or dairy products.

Available in any well-stocked natural food store, sesame seeds are useful and tasty. Sprinkle a thin layer on a cookie sheet and toast them at low heat in the oven. They are then delicious eaten just plain or sprinkled on hot cereals, on rolls before baking, on soups or stews, or practically anyplace where you need more flavor and nutritional value.

You can make your own tahini sauce, too (see our recipe in Chapter 4). Tahini's not only perfect for your falafels; it can be used as a spread for sandwiches, as a flavoring for dishes such as stews and soups, as a dressing for soyburgers, or anyplace where you want some really fine flavor to spark up an otherwise bland dish. Another easy way to use sesame seeds is simply to toss a handful into your blender when you are making smoothies or health drinks. They will add just that little touch of crunchiness that tastes so good in a malt-like drink, plus extra protein.

Our other favorite eating seed, the sunflower seed, is an important crop for the Russians, who plant millions of acres every year. Their acreage, as well as ours, is increasing as more and more people become acquainted with this valuable food. Sunflower seeds can be purchased hulled or unhulled. In the hulled state, they're ready to add to any dish or simply to eat out of your hand. Keep them and any other shelled seeds in the refrigerator. In the unhulled state, you have a good time-passer while you're waiting for the Second Coming!

An interesting fact about sunflowers is that they face toward the sun all day long and then turn back to dawn position during the night. (I haven't stayed up all night to watch them do it but I know it's true because if they didn't, they would wring their own green necks.)

We'd like just to mention some other seeds you might want to experiment with:

★ pumpkin or squash (toast them—they're great snack food)

★ poppy, caraway, anise, celery, dill (all for seasoning)

★ fenugreek (makes a wonderful tea, better still with a few drops of honey).

Now for some favorite recipes using our favorite seeds.

Sunflower-Oat Waffles

☆ 1 cup rolled oats
☆ 2 cups hot water
☆ 1 cup whole wheat flour
☆ ½ cup milk powder
☆ 1 egg, beaten
☆ 2 tablespoons oil
☆ 2 tablespoons honey
☆ 2 teaspoons baking powder
☆ ½ teaspoon sea salt
☆ ⅔ cup sunflower seeds

Pour the hot water over the oats and let them stand until softened. Add the remaining ingredients, blending well, and bake in a hot waffle iron.

These can be topped with homemade applesauce sweetened with honey and flavored with cinnamon. Molasses and honey are also good toppings. Makes about 6 waffles.

Your Own Yogurt

One of the best arguments for making your own yogurt is that the commercial varieties contain many unnecessary additives that you are better off without. These can include emulsifiers, starches, carrageenan, guar gum, cellulose, and worst of all, sugar and artificial flavorings. When you make yogurt yourself, you know exactly what went into it; and all you really need is milk and a starter.

The latter can be from a good-quality yogurt you purchased at a natural food store or some left over from your last batch. Here are the proportions:

* 1 cup whole milk
* 2 tablespoons starter
* 1 cup warm water
* 1 cup non-instant milk powder
* 2 cups warm water

Put the first 3 ingredients into your blender and whirl. Gradually add the non-instant milk powder and the remaining warm water. Pour into several small glass jars or one large glass container, cover, and keep at 110° for several hours until you have yogurt. The time it takes varies according to the weather.

Makes about 1 quart.

There are various methods you can use to maintain the proper temperature. A regular yogurt maker is of course ideal. You can also set the jars on a food warmer or hot tray, most markets—just another big argument in ket, or set them inside a down-filled sleeping bag. You can set your oven at its lowest possible setting, below 200°, and turn it off if it gets too warm. Or simply set the yogurt mixture in small jars inside a larger container and fill this with warm water, adding more hot water from time to time. Other naturally warm areas such as radiators, pilot lights on stove tops, and hot water heaters will work as well.

The longer it sets, the tarter your yogurt will become. Once it's firm, refrigerate it and plan to use it within a week, at which time you can start a fresh batch.

You can flavor your own yogurt with honey, fresh fruits, carob, or molasses, or dried fruits, nuts, and seeds. Yogurt made with the above ingredients will cost you only 16 cents a pint, whereas plain commercial yogurt sells for around 60 cents or more in more markets—just another big argument in favor of the do-it-yourself policy.

Your Own Cottage Cheese

This is so simple, you'll wonder why you never tried it before.

* 1 quart whole milk
* 2 tablespoons lemon juice

Heat the milk just to scalding; do not boil. Remove from the heat and add the lemon juice. Cover and let it sit on the sink for several hours at room temperature. Now pour the mixture through a strainer or colander which has been lined with two thicknesses of cheesecloth and placed over a bowl.

You may refrigerate the liquid or whey which drips through and use it to mix with non-instant milk powder for making yogurt. Allow the cheese mixture to drain for several hours or until it's dry.

If you want to make a harder cheese, put the mixture between two boards and apply pressure. The combination of squeezing and drying will give you a more characteristic cheese. You can add some sea salt if you wish and then refrigerate. Could anything be easier?

Last year we were in Mendocino County, California, where we met a charming couple, the Sinclairs of Little River. Judy makes her own goat's milk cheese, and what they don't eat, she sells. It's so simple and yet so good. The method is the same as for cottage cheese, above, except that you only need about a teaspoonful of lemon juice to each quart of scalded goat's milk.

One of Judy's great inventions is green onion cheese. All you do is chop up some green onions or scallions and add them to the curdled milk just before you squeeze it out.

Everyone has a hankering for something sweet now and then. Fortunately there are many ways to satisfy that sweet tooth without resorting to refined white sugar, which is nutritionally worthless and even damaging to your health. One alternative, of course, is honey, a natural sugar which contains healthful minerals and vitamins. Others are date sugar, molasses, and maple syrup. And there's a wide variety of dried fruits that can be eaten by themselves or added to various desserts.

Honey is the most logical substitute for sugar in most recipes, but bear in mind that because of its sweetness you won't need to use as much. If a recipe calls for ¾ cup sugar, substitute ½ cup honey. Since any kind of sugar is harmful if used to excess, we hesitate to recommend even honey too strongly. It's a fine condiment, but use it sparingly. Honey keeps extremely well. If you are setting some foods by for later use, include a gallon or two of honey. While it may crystallize, it won't spoil.

Incidentally, as of this writing, it's been selling pretty steadily for 50 cents a pound at one of our local natural food stores. (Bring your own container!)

Chocolate is one of the most universally beloved flavors of all time. How unfortunate that it's so unhealthy! It's full of oxalic acid, which prevents the body from absorbing calcium. It contains caffeine and other harmful substances. Because of its bitterness large amounts of sugar must be used along with it. Many people are even allergic to it.

Luckily we have an alternative in carob, a food which tastes very much like chocolate but has none of its bad qualities. In fact, carob has over twice as much calcium as chocolate, with only half as many calories and 1 percent as much fat. It contains 26 percent natural sugar and a generous amount of vitamins and minerals. Try some of the following recipes. You may get hooked on carob and find it easy to ignore the next candy counter you pass. Oh, and check the price . . . carob powder in bulk at natural food stores is $1.50 a pound; cocoa powder at the local supermarket is $2.00, plus the cost of the additional sweetener it requires.

Carob Energy Balls

* ½ cup each carob powder, honey, peanut butter, sunflower seeds, and sesame seeds
* ¼ cup each wheat germ and sifted soy flour
* ½ cup chopped peanuts or shredded unsweetened coconut

Combine the carob powder and honey in the top of a double boiler and cook them over hot water for a few minutes. Remove from the heat and blend in the rest of the ingredients, adding a few tablespoons of cold water if needed. Roll the dough into balls and coat them with the peanuts or coconut. Makes 20-25 balls.

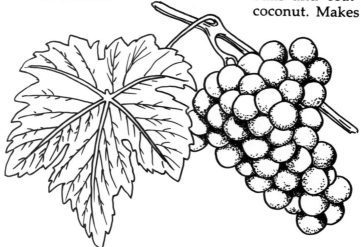

Apples, Apricots, Bananas...

Now, the first step to enjoying fruit on a dollar a day is getting it fresh, ripe, and natural at a low, low cost. As usual, the supermarket is the worst bet, even though prices may drop dramatically at the height of the season. What are your alternatives?

★ *If you've got some yard space available, how about growing some dwarf fruit trees?*

★ *Look around your neighborhood; you might find a volunteer fruit tree or two growing on an abandoned piece of property. Last year we harvested several boxes of apples and figs from trees that apparently belonged to no one.*

★ *Local growers will often let you pick your own at a big discount. Even better, sometimes you can pick your own for free. Once, while driving from Stockton, California, to a village in the Sierra foothills, I passed a cherry orchard alive with*

pickers. I stopped to watch and discovered that all the cherries that had fallen to the ground were free to anyone who wanted them. Apparently the law says that if they touch the ground, they can't go to market. So I promptly got out my trusty burlap bag (I always keep one in the trunk of my car) and proceeded to pick 5 or 6 pounds of the ripest, sweetest cherries you've ever eaten. All they needed was a quick rinse and they were ready for the fruit bowl, cherry cobbler, or preserves.

★ *Always keep an eye peeled for good bargains at roadside stands. Then eat a lot, dry a lot, and can what you can.*

The best recipe for fruits is to simply eat them fresh as soon as they're ripe, without any cooking, coating, processing, or fumbling by the corporate state. But it's fun to play around with them too and here are some good ways to do it.

Apple Flannel Cakes

☆ 2 eggs
☆ 1½ cups sour milk
☆ 2 tablespoons melted butter, margarine, or oil
☆ 1 cup whole wheat pastry flour
☆ 2 tablespoons date sugar
☆ 1 teaspoon vanilla
☆ ½ teaspoon cinnamon
☆ ¼ teaspoon soda
☆ 2 apples, peeled, cored, and quartered

Put all the ingredients in a blender and whirl for 1 minute. Heat a griddle until fairly hot, pour on the batter, and tilt the griddle from side to side to spread the batter out thinner. Continue cooking as any pancake.

These may be served with honey, maple syrup, or blackstrap molasses. But try them plain first, and you may decide they don't need any embellishment at all. That's how we feel about them. Makes 6 to 8 pancakes.

Johnny Appleseed's Special

This delectable dessert requires no cooking at all.

* 4 apples
* 1 tablespoon honey
* 1 tablespoon lemon juice
* ½ cup chopped dates
* 1 cup homemade yogurt
* 4 tablespoon chopped almonds or other nuts

Core the apples and shred them, skins and all, into a large bowl. Sprinkle them with the honey, lemon juice, and dates. Add a dollop of yogurt, and top them with the nuts for garnish. Serves 4.

Apple Whip

* 2 cups applesauce
* 2 envelopes plain gelatin
* 2 tablespoons honey
* 2 teaspoons lemon juice
* 2 egg whites
* nutmeg and cinnamon

Place 1 cup of the applesauce in a double boiler over boiling water. Add the gelatin, stir, and let it dissolve. Remove it from the heat and add the honey, lemon juice, and remaining cup of applesauce.

Let it cool, and refrigerate until it's almost set. Beat the egg whites until they're stiff and fold them into the apple mixture. Return it to the refrigerator until set. Scoop into serving glasses and top with nutmeg and cinnamon. Mmmmm. Serves 4-6.

Apple Crisp

A worldwide favorite that appears in the culinary records of many cultures. Try it this way.

* 8 large apples
* ¼ cup honey
* 2 tablespoons lemon juice
* ½ teaspoon cinnamon
* ½ cup rolled oats
* ½ cup wheat germ
* ⅓ cup fresh bran
* ¼ cup brown rice flour
* ¼ cup ground dried dates
* ¼ cup safflower oil or melted butter

Wash, core, and slice 8 large apples. Mix the honey, lemon juice, and cinnamon, and add them to the apples. Toss to mix and coat. Place the mixture in a buttered baking dish and add a topping made of the remaining ingredients, mixed well and sprinkled over the apples to cover.

Bake in a preheated oven at about 325° for 35 to 45 minutes, or until the apples are tender. Remove and see how much cooling time you can allow before it's totally devoured by apple bandits. Serves 6 normal people, or 2 apple bandits!

WHOLE GRAINS (AND THEIR USE IN A SENIOR KITCHEN)

Everything I intend to say about wheat, corn, rice, barley and other whole grains is beautifully presented in this new catalogue from one of the best suppliers of such commodities.

You can reach *Arrowhead Mills* at *P.O. Box 2059, Hereford, TX 79045*, and although they do not sell directly, they can tell you where you can buy their fine products. If you are not near one of the stores they list, ask your local natural food store to special order the products for you. I have used these products for many years and can vouch for their purity and quality. I have no connection with them— merely a tie of integrity.

GRANOLAS

Maple Nut Granola

Maple Nut Granola is a wholesome, nutritious alternative to over-processed, sugar-coated cereals.

Instead of containing grains with most of the goodness milled away and refined sugar, it is made from natural whole grains and a natural sweetener.

This granola is made from oat flakes, wheat flakes, soybean flakes, rye flakes, triticale flakes, raisins, sunflower seeds, filberts, almonds and sesame seeds. It is sweetened with pure maple syrup and real vanilla.

Apple Amaranth Granola

Apple Amaranth Granola is a combination of amaranth, whole grain flakes, almonds, dried applies, sunflower seeds and other natural ingredients.

When amaranth, a whole grain rich in protein and fiber, is combined with other grains like oats and wheat, the mixture becomes a balanced, complete protein. To this complete protein we add the nutty flavor of roasted grains, nuts and seeds. Then we enhance the already delicious flavor with apple juice concentrate and a touch of cinnamon. Just the right sweetness comes from honey, maple syrup and barley malt syrup.

For a granola that's better than homemade, try ours!

CEREALS

Oat Flake Banana Bread

Yield: 1 loaf

1 cup oat flakes
½ cup hot milk
3 very ripe bananas, mashed
¾ cup honey
½ cup unrefined safflower oil

2 eggs
2 cups whole-wheat pastry flour
4 teaspoons low-sodium baking powder
½ teaspoon sea salt, optional
½ teaspoon ground cinnamon

Mix hot milk and oat flakes together and let them stand until mixture is cooled. Add the 3 mashed bananas. Cream together the honey, oil and eggs until very smooth. Beat the oat flake and banana mixture and the remaining ingredients into the creamed mixture. Pour into greased and floured loaf pan. Bake for 1 hour and 15 minutes at 375° F. or until a wooden pick inserted in the center comes out clean. Cool in the pan 10 minutes; loosen edges with metal spatula. Remove from pan; cool completely on wire racks. (This is great for wrapping and freezing for sudden party needs or for gift ideas.)

Oat Flakes

Oat flakes are similar to quick rolled oats, but are not exposed to such high temperatures and thus retain most of their original nutritive value.

Oat flakes take a little longer to cook than rolled oats. They may be used as oatmeal or are good for adding to breads. They give a moist sweetness to breads, pancakes, biscuits and other doughs.

Oats contain natural antioxidants which extend the keeping quality of any food to which they are added.

Oats are high in protein, B-vitamins, vitamin E, phosphorous, iron and copper. They are very good for digestion and can act as a mild laxative. Oat flakes are easily digestible.

Wheat Germ Nutri-Loaf

1 bunch spinach or chard
3 tbsp. vegetable oil
1 onion, diced
¼ cup fresh parsley, chopped
1 tsp. garlic powder
4 mushrooms, chopped
1 tsp. oregano

½ tsp. basil
2 cups tofu, mashed
¾ cup cracked wheat cereal, cooked
¾ cup wheat germ, lightly toasted
½ cup tomato sauce (plus additional sauce for top)
1 tbsp. Tamari Soy Sauce
1 tbsp. nutritional yeast (optional) or parmesan cheese

Saute spinach until tender; add vegetables and herbs and continue to saute. Remove from heat. Combine all ingredients (except nutritional yeast and additional sauce). Shape into a loaf. Spread extra sauce and sprinkle with yeast. Bake at 350° F. for 30-45 minutes.

Wheat Germ

Wheat germ is the embryo or the life force of the wheat kernel. It is responsible for carrying the spark of life to the next generation of wheat.

Even though both provide fiber in the diet, wheat germ should not be confused with wheat bran, or the outer, brown layer of the wheat berry. Since the germ contains the oil of the grain, you want to make sure it's purchased fresh and kept refrigerated when you get it home.

Wheat germ is a very nutritious addition to bread doughs, cereals (sprinkle it on top of cooked or cold cereals), casseroles, salads, or main dishes. It is a veritable bonanza of nutrients, containing exceptional amounts of high quality protein.

It has good quantities of polyunsaturated oil for healthy skin and circulation. A generous amount of vitamin E is present to protect the oil, retard damaging oxidation throughout the body and help circulation.

Nearly the entire B vitamin complex is present, much to the benefit of the heart, blood, nerves and mental health. A lot of iron, a wealth of magnesium and plenty of zinc are all present in wheat germ.

Fiber

Fiber is an essential ingredient in the well-balanced diet. It provides the bulk that helps our bodies to function properly.

However, with the abundance of refined foods on the market today, fiber is severely lacking in the diet of most Americans.

At Arrowhead Mills we understand the important role of fiber in the diet. That's why our products are unrefined -- high in nutrition and natural fiber content.

To add fiber to your diet try Arrowhead Mills Unprocessed Wheat Bran. The outer layer of the whole wheat kernel is an economical and dependable source of dietary fiber that is also rich in vitamins.

Known as "the poor man's rice," millet is another grain that is high in fiber and nutrition. Use millet in soups and stews as well as for a breakfast cereal.

With the cost of food these days, eating inexpensively and well is not always easy to do. But good natural foods can help.

Perhaps the biggest bargain in natural foods is the line of Arrowhead Mills flakes -- wheat, rye, oat, barley, triticale, rice and soy. Keeping a variety of these grain flakes on hand is like having a health food store right in your kitchen.

All the nutrition of the original whole grain is still there in our flakes because all of the original whole grain is still there. Nothing is added.

Flakes are an inexpensive way to stretch your casseroles, soups, breads and granolas and put more food on your table for less money.

Bulgur Soy Grit "Sausage" Patties

2 cups cooked bulgur soy grits
1 egg
¼ cup whole wheat flour
¾ teaspoon black pepper, optional
1 tablespoon crushed basil leaves

¾ teaspoon saga
¾ teaspoon poultry seasoning
sea salt to taste
whole wheat flour
unrefined safflower oil

Mix the bulgur soy grits, egg, whole wheat flour, pepper, basil, sage, poultry seasoning and salt together. Form into patties and roll in whole wheat flour. Fry in a small amount of oil until lightly browned. These may be wrapped in individual packages and reheated.

Variation: Form into cocktail size balls and serve with sweet and sour sauce.
Note: 1. ¾ cup grated cheddar cheese can be added.
2. Mixture forms better when slightly chilled.

Bulgur Soy Grits

Bulgur Soy Grits are one of the tastiest and most versatile of all the Arrowhead Mills products.

A blend of bulgur wheat and soy flakes, they form a well-balanced protein. They can be used in place of potatoes or rice, as the base to a casserole, as a pilaf to be topped with steamed or curried vegetables or as a hot cereal alone.

Bulgur soy grits take less cooking time (only 15 minutes) than whole soybeans, but for better texture and digestibility they should be simmered or covered with boiling water and allowed to soak for a few minutes before adding to other food.

Try adding bulgur soy grits to spaghetti sauce (a good complement to the protein in the noodles.)

Japanese Rice Pudding

1 cup long grain brown basmati rice

⅔ cup Rice & Shine

Cook the basmati rice and Rice & Shine according to directions, then mix while still warm. In a blender combine:

7 tbsp. soy milk
3 tbsp. sliced almonds
¼ tsp. vanilla extract

⅛ tsp. nutmeg
½ tsp. ground cardamon
¼ cup rice or maple syrup, or honey

Mix the liquid mixture into the rice mixture. Chill and serve. Yield: four ½ cup servings.

Optional: add ¼ cup soaked raisins.

Rice & Shine

Made entirely from brown rice, Rice & Shine provides for a delicious, nutritious hot breakfast dish with only two minutes of cooking. Additional time saving and convenience is provided by the two measured pouches, each containing four servings each. Information is also given for preparing as little as one serving.

The pleasant flavor and satisfying nutrition of whole brown rice make this a product sure to gain a niche among the favorites of hot cereal lovers.

Rice & Shine is more than just a breakfast cereal — the box gives instructions for preparing other dishes as well.

GRAINS

With all the information available these days about the questionable nutritional value of standard manufactured varieties of cereal, it just makes good sense to serve your family whole grain cereals.

All Arrowhead Mills cereals are made from the finest whole grains grown with natural farming methods. We take nothing out and put in no preservatives of any kind.

There are several Arrowhead Mills whole grain hot cereals to choose from, including our hearty Seven Grain Cereal, Cracked Wheat with its slightly crunchy texture and Bear Mush, a smooth and creamy favorite of youngsters.

Our newest hot cereal is 4-Grain + Flax, which blends the good taste, hearty nutrition and creamy texture of wheat and oats with flavorful rye and chewy barley. A true body-building and energy-giving breakfast food with flax to aid digestion.

Rice, barley and millet make delicious porridges and oat flakes cook up into a hot cereal that really sticks to your ribs.

Cold cereals can also be every bit as hearty and satisfying as hot cereal. Arrowhead Mills granolas are favorites for breakfast as well as for snacks.

Triticale

Triticale is the world's first human-made grain.

It was developed by cross-breeding several different species of wheat (botanical name Triticum) and rye (Secale), and has characteristics similar to both its parents. When ripe, triticale is similar to wheat except the grain head is about twice as large.

Triticale is higher in protein than either rye or wheat, and includes a greater percentage of some of the amino acids as well. B-vitamins and minerals are also present in notable quantities.

Tritical has a slightly nutty flavor, resembling whole wheat bread with pecans added.

Research on triticale was published as early as 1876, but only in the last 25 years has much attention been given to it. The grain was developed in Sweden, but serious research began in Canada at the University of Manitoba in the 1960's.

Today considerable quantities of the grain are grown in the "grain belt" states of North and South Dakota, Nebraska and Minnesota, but most of the triticale in Arrowhead Mills products is "home grown" in the state of Texas. Triticale flakes are whole grains which have been quickly toasted (about 15

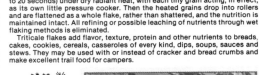

to 20 seconds) under dry radiant heat, with each tiny grain acting, in effect, as its own little pressure cooker. Then the heated grains drop into rollers and are flattened as a whole flake, rather than shattered, and the nutrition is maintained intact. All refining or possible leaching of nutrients through wet flaking methods is eliminated.

Triticale flakes add flavor, texture, protein and other nutrients to breads, cakes, cookies, cereals, casseroles of every kind, dips, soups, sauces and stews. They may be used with or instead of cracker and bread crumbs and make excellent trail food for campers.

Triticale Cookies

1½ cups Arrowhead Mills Whole Wheat Flour	1¾ cup Arrowhead Mills triticale flakes
1½ teaspoons baking powder	1 egg, beaten
½ teaspoon salt, optional	¼ cup milk
1 teaspoon cinnamon	⅓ cup Arrowhead Mills Safflower oil
1/8 teaspoon ground clove	½ cup honey
1 cup chopped dates	

Sift together the flour, salt and spices. Stir one large spoonful of this mixture into the chopped dates. Stir the triticale and floured dates into the dry ingredients. Mix the egg, milk, oil and honey and pour them into the dry ingredients. Mix together thoroughly and drop dough by spoonful onto a greased cookie sheet. Bake 15 to 20 minutes at 325° F. or until the cookies begin to brown around the edges and are cooked through. Do not overbake as the cookies will burn rather easily.

Grains, the Biblical "staff of life," have been basic to the diet of mankind throughout recorded history.

As a nutrition source grains are excellent suppliers of essential protein, bran, complex carbohydrates, B vitamins and trace minerals. They also make delicious additions to hot cereals, soups, stews, casseroles, meatloaves and many other dishes.

To preserve the wholesome taste and freshness of its grains, Arrowhead Mills uses a special three-stage cleaning process. After which the grains are stored in over 100 clean dry bins and fan-blown with cold winter air -- without fumigation.

After screen-cleaning the grain Arrowhead Mills goes another step and runs each grain over a gravity table and stoner to remove all foreign materials. So you know the grain you buy from Arrowhead Mills is a superior product.

In addition to the universal grain staples -- wheat, rice and corn -- Arrowhead Mills markets barley, buckwheat groats, millet, oats, rye and triticale.

Italian Casserole

3 cups water	1 cup long grain brown rice
½ cup soft wheat berries	
Parboil for 20 minutes.	
1 zucchini, quartered and sliced	2 tsp. basil
1 onion, chopped	1 bay leaf
1 8 oz. package mushrooms, chopped	1 cup Tamari Soy Sauce
1 tbsp. garlic powder	3 tbsp. oil
1 tsp. oregano	

Saute herbs and vegetables in oil; when tender, add grain (drained). Then add:

1 28 oz. can whole peeled tomatoes, chopped with juice

Add the Tamari, stir, then transfer everything over to a rectangular casserole dish and bake at 350°F. for 45-60 minutes until juices are absorbed.

Swiss Brown Rice

2 T unrefined sesame oil	1 clove garlic, minced
2 cups onions, sliced	1½ t paprika
3 stalks celery, sliced	1 t sea salt, optional
½ pound mushrooms, sliced	½ t black pepper, optional
½ cup watercress or parsley, chopped	¼ t ground ginger
3 cups cooked brown rice	1 pound swiss cheese, coarsely grated
Garnish: chopped parsley or chopped watercress	

Heat a large skillet. Add oil and saute the onions, celery, mushrooms and watercress or parsley. Add garlic, paprika, salt, pepper and a little ginger to taste. Layer the brown rice, vegetables and grated swiss cheese in a shallow casserole. Repeat layers. If it seems dry, sprinkle with ¼ cup water before adding last layer of cheese. Bake for 20 to 25 minutes at 350° F. Serves 8.

Long Grain Brown Rice

While it is complicated to grow, rice is the prinicpal food crop for about half the world's population.

In the United States, it is grown commercially in parts of eight states, including Texas. Rice requires wet soil and a long growing season of four to six months with a mean temperature of at least 70° F.

Polished or white rice is a nutritionally inferior product, having lost about 10 percent of its protein, 85 percent of its fat, 70 percent of its minerals and most of the B vitamins.

Brown rice has a light, creamy color when cooked, a pleasant but mild flavor and cooks up to be just slightly chewy -- not tough and not mushy. It is nutritionally superior to all forms of processed white rice.

Of the three lengths, short-grain rice tends to be softer and more moist. It is sweeter and the grains stick together somewhat. Long-grain rice cooks up into a drier product, with the grains tending to remain separate.

Medium-grain rice tends to have the flavor of the short-grained rice and the texture of the long-grained variety.

SUGAR

Sugar is not a food, rather it is a drug. It should be included in its own chapter called *Poison*. For an experiment, take a spoonful of sugar and hold it over a flame. What's left? Is it black? If that's not proof of the real nature of this wicked substance, then read on.

In addition, carbonated sodas amount for much of the American average of a one-half pound daily sugar intake.

In almost all of the recipes offered in the food section of your paper, you'll see numerous sugar ingredients. In addition, all types of sugar, whether it be light, dark, powdered, etc., are often on special—save on this destroyer of teeth and bodies.

Not only is sugar terrible for you, the wholesale price of it is now around six cents per pound. An expensive price to pay for something that could plague you with diabetes.

"Educate the masses and tyranny will vanish."
— **Thomas Jefferson**

CHAPTER FOUR
SHELTER

WHY WE NEED ALTERNATIVE SHELTER

Here are photos of two typical homes in central California. While this is admittedly an expensive area to live, the costs are representative of what we seniors are confronted with nationwide.

OLDER HOME
in established section of Redwood City. 3 bedrooms, 1 bath, separate dining room, fireplace in living room, 3 or 4 car garage, some remodeling, new carpet in living room. Fenced & landscaped yard, with fruit trees, 2 wooden decks off kitchen, workshop area. Seller will provide home warranty program. $229,000. Call owner at 366-7686 leave message.

The payments on this modest 70 or 80-year old home would be about 1,700 dollars per month in interest alone.

COZY COURTYARD ENTRY   **$429,000**
Immaculate home with special custom touches thru-out. 3BRs/2½BA's, inviting Mstr BR w/remodeled BA, update kitchen, walk to downtown Menlo Park.

The payments on this home would be about 1,000 dollars per week!

It is obvious from these examples that home ownership is out of the question for virtually all seniors, and for that matter, for every American with an average income.

That's why we are presenting a long list of practical alternatives, truly affordable shelter that has proven itself by actual experience.

PROLOGUE

Let's take a unique view of shelter by observing roofs. In my own perspective, a roof can mean a cozy shelter if you exercise a little creativity. So let's see how many roofs we can imagine:

ROOFS

- on conventional houses
- on barns and sheds
- on all kinds of vehicles
- on underground spaces, caves, mines
- on unused schools and churches
- on shelter that time has passed by (these would include such structures as gas stations, motels, stores, factories, storage tanks, ghost towns)

- on abandoned warehouses and factories
- on various vessels from small boats to liners

This unique concept of shelter was the main objective of an issue of the *San Francisco Minicron*, which I publish when I have some spare change. To make it easy for you to understand where I am coming from, here are selections from an issue I devoted to the homeless problem. It is directly applicable to virtually every senior who has a problem finding affordable shelter.

SPECIAL SHELTER ISSUE

The NEW San Francisco MINI Chron "Truth, tho the heavens crack!"

SHORTER THAN THE BIG PAPER BUT MORE RELEVANT

1st YEAR, No. 2   PAGE 1   25 CENTS

Photo by Kurt Ellison.

Chuck Ellery, left, and Bill Kaysing outside their first Minigranny.

A roof over your head for $1,200

Home sweet home, but only 8 by 12 feet

By PAUL BEILEY

A group of men based in Moss Landing have an idea for putting a roof over the head of everyone now without shelter. Not a very big roof, but a roof.

They've come up with the "Minigranny," a house the size of a garden shed that they say could be home for elderly relatives on the property of a larger home; or, for others, a complete, self-contained unit.

Bill Kaysing, a free-lance

But Kaysing and his partner Chuck Ellery see a much wider use for the Minigranny. The two are "co-pastors" of an organization called the Holy Terra Church, whose purpose, Kaysing said, is to "put everybody under a roof."

That thousands are homeless in this country, Ellery said, is "a national disgrace and a national tragedy. Here we've got an answer.

Ellery has taken a year off from his work as a production-

MICROHOUSES

Imagine a complete house that measures only 8 x 12 feet! Is it really possible? Indeed it is, and here's my proof. Firstly, ships have long since manifested the strategic and efficient use of a small space.

I was once aboard a reproduction of Sir Francis Drake's *GOLDEN HIND* and found that his cabin in the stern was only large enough for a table and his bed. Shifting rapidly through the years we find luxurious cabins aboard nuclear submarines that, while small, make use of every cubic inch. Switching to a more prosaic and less expensive example, we can see that modern recreational vehicles (RV's) are masterpieces of the efficient use of space. Here are some samples:

Now that we have proof that you don't need a lot of space to be comfortable, let's examine the microhouse:

BACKGROUND

About two years ago I was engaged in a study of the Granny House in California. Senator Henry Mello had worked for seven years to gain approval of his Granny House Act. This act allowed a home owner to build a house not larger than 650 square feet on the back of his or her lot as long as the plan was to rent it to a senior citizen. What a wonderful concept; one, however that did not work out in practice. Obstacles exist with any building projects, but it was apparent that the obstacles doubled and tripled where Granny Houses were concerned.

It will suffice to say that very few Granny Houses have been built in California despite the existence of the law permitting them.

I began exploring the possibilities of a minigranny, a house so small that it would not require a permit. It turns out that if you build a structure smaller than 120 square feet, you don't need a permit. The building is classified as a shed or portable building and can be built by anyone without bureaucratic interference.

That was all the encouragement I needed. I immediately began to build the Minigranny or Microhouse as I now call them, shown here.

Microhouse (early model)

Someone bought it before it was finished so I started on a second unit. I built it at cost for a minister for his pastoral living quarters. There was a kitchen and bath in the church, so all he really needed was a bedroom and sanctuary. It wasn't long before we got calls to build other units and then the miracle occured that we had anticipated—people saw the Microhouses and began building them by and for themselves! Hallelujah! You, too can do it with plans and a material list. Here are some of the basic specs and photos. If you need more help, write in care of the publisher, as he will have plans for a modest fee.

Anatomy Of The Basic Minigranny

½" CDX plywood

1x8 Ridge board

15 lb. felt paper

Shingles

2x6 Rafters

Metal drip edge

2x4 Gable studs

1x8 Fascia

2x4 Double top plate

4x6 Header

2x4 Rough sill

⅜" Plywood siding

Door track

2x8 End joist

2x4 Trimmer studs

2x4 Bottom plate

2x4 Studs

Blocking

2x4s

3-stud corner detail

⅝" T&G CDX plywood subfloor

2x8 Rim joist

Entry ramp

6x8 Pressure-treated skid

Pressure-treated lumber

Any carpenter can build this in your backyard in a day or less. Figure about 400-500 dollars in materials; less if used material is used.

As this book goes to press, we are working on a super Microhouse, one that can be built much more inexpensively because it will be constructed of Kaysited cardboard (fireproof and termite-proof) and features Japanese style windows of a new type of rice paper coated with a waterproof material. All in all, it will be cheap, portable, warm, and comfortable—the ideal backyard or remote home for seniors and others.

SOME USES OF THE MICROHOUSE:

- Spare Bedroom
- Business Office
- Guest House
- Sharpening Shop
- Photo Darkroom
- Design Room
- Artist and/or Writer Studio
- TV and VCR room
- Chemistry Lab/Research Facility
- Hot House
- Library
- Growing Room
- Library
- Small Church
- Small Schoolroom
- Mail Order Workroom
- Sanctuary/Meditation Room

- Gun Room
- Hideout
- Trophy Showroom
- Typing Room/Business Office
- Repair/Machine Shop
- Model Shop
- Bakery, Cookhouse, Catering Facility
- Print/Silkscreen Shop
- Fishing Tackle Storeroom
- Smokehouse
- Game Room
- Exercise Room
- Sauna/Hot Tub Enclosure
- Table Tennis Room
- County Fair Stand
- Music Room

As you can see, the possibilities are endless.

While the Minigranny is a good idea, it needs additional items to make it more usable for seniors. Here are a few items that will create a degree of self-reliance for Minigranny residents. Fortunately, our era of high technology has yielded many advancements in power generation, water purification and so forth. Within the next year, there will be an opportunity to plant a Minigranny in almost any location. We'll keep you posted in an update of this book.

THE BOWLI-N.E. (non electric)

The **BOWLI-N.E.** is THE unit for the remote cottager with no source of electric power. This matchless toilet requires NO WATER, NO CHEMICALS, NO SEPTIC SYSTEM and most important NO ELECTRICITY. The **BOWLI-N.E.** handles a family of 4 – 6 for cottage use, with ample capacity for guests. Airflow through the unit is created naturally through a large 4 inch vent pipe. Excess fluid that is not evaporated through the vent, is drained out at the back (The excess tube can be installed either to the right or left). This ensures the **BOWLI-N.E.** to have a very high capacity. The only help the **BOWLI-N.E.** needs is the rotating of the **BIO-DRUM** every 3rd day, if in constant use. Freezing temperatures will NOT damage the toilet or the compost. **BOWLI-N.E.** is a unique product, so well engineered and designed that it will last a life time, always ready to be of service. It now comes with a full *5 year* factory warranty.

TECHNICAL DATA:

Measurements: Width 57 cm (22½"), height 73 cm (29"), length 80 cm (32"), **Weight:** 26 kilos(57 lbs.), **Drain:** 19 mm (¾"), **Ventilation:** Natural, through 10 cm (4") plastic tube, **Enclosure:** extremely durable fire retardant fibreglass **Capacity:** serves a family of 5 – 6 in cottage use.

This unique toilet could eliminate the sewage problem for a Minigranny.

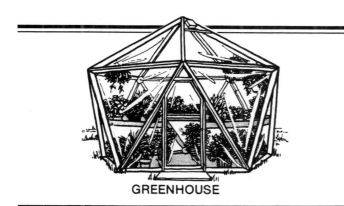

GREENHOUSE

Greenhouse attaches to Minigranny making resident almost self-sufficient in food.

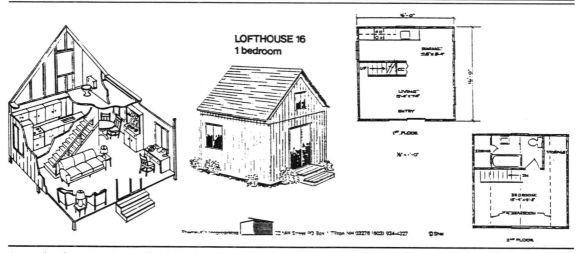

LOFTHOUSE 16
1 bedroom

A complete house just 16 x 16 feet? Yes, it's true and here are the plans courtesy of the *Shelter Kit Company in Tilton, NH.*

THE EASY 2 HOUR FRAME UP!

FROM 3' TO 14' DIAMETER

BUILD YOUR OWN . . .

Greenhouse
Storage Building
Gazebo
Sandbox
Woodshed
Playhouse
Screenhouse
Corn Crib
Machinery Shed
Cabana
Carport
Hutch
Ice Fishing Hut
Display Stand
Grape Arbor
Sauna
Cold Frame
Climbing Toy
Pigeon House

- Cut 25 equal length 2x4's or 2x3's or 2x2's
- Bolt together framework with galvanized steel Starplate connectors
- Free construction plans with connectors show how to add roof, walls, door, overhanging eaves, etc. to finish your project.
- Build big, build small - one set for all sizes!

EACH STARPLATE SET INCLUDES

40⁰⁰

- 11 Starplate connectors
- Construction plans

(Framing lumber, 5/16" bolts, nuts and washers not included)

This bolt together house uses a patented steel bracket called a starplate. With it you can build a sturdy little backyard cabin in a short time. Using the principle of the triangle and its superstrength, the starplate construction method lends itself to a variety of quick and easy structures.

This drawing shows how the starplate structure is assembled. It's obvious that even a person without previous building experience could fabricate one of these

continued on next page

structures. The exterior could be anything—plywood, shingles over particle board, stucco over plaster wire or just plain board and batt. You could even spray it with a Kaysite coating which would hide any mistakes. Also with a Kaysite surface, you could use any type of scrap wood since it wouldn't show. Check with your local hardware or building supply store for starplates and, of course, the lumber to build it.

In addition to the ideas presented here, I visualize a number of these small huts connected to form a communal dwelling facility—bedrooms, dining hall, kitchen, bath, etc., could all be built in the same manner. Floors could be ply on a pier block base with 2 x 6 joists. Put some wall-to-wall carpeting over that and you're home at last!

Simple and inexpensive.

STORAGE BUILDING

SCREENHOUSE

CARPORT

SQUARE-FRONT

LIVE-IN JOBS
SHELTER FOR SENIORS

One reason I joined the Navy rather than the Army during World War II was because of the brutal conditions in the trenches of World War I. I often read about how soldiers lived, fought and slept in deep mud, suffered freezing temperatures, and went without hot food for days on end. On the other hand, I observed that no one had to suffer any of the above conditions on naval vessels in San Pedro, even during combat. The same, of course, held true for the U.S. Air Force.

My point is this; if service in the armed forces may be considered a sort of far-out job, then it is also a live-in job where the choice of service determines what you will have for a roof. In the three years, five months that I spent in the U.S. Navy, I never had to sleep outdoors. If I had to made the choice over again, I would most assuredly choose the Navy over the Army. I realize that many infantrymen would say that at least their foxhole couldn't sink and there are no sharks around their position, but regardless of this ever-present hazard, I would still prefer the steel roof despite a lot of water in the basement. All of this is preliminary to a seldom-considered way of having your own roof—by taking some kind of employment that includes a room and often the board, too. Let's take a look at some examples:

CARING FOR THE DISABLED OR ILL

A couple of years ago I took a job as a companion for a young man who had been seriously brain-damaged in a motorcycle accident. He was articulate, although a little slow of speech. He could walk, but only at a very slow pace. My job was to see that he had his meals, attended college and got some recreation. I did not live-in, although I am sure it could have easily been arranged. The job taught me many important lessons, including being appreciative of good health. I also learned that there are thousands of positions of this kind all over the country.

No home, no money? Then send for a copy of this unique publication that lists opportunities for live-in people all over the nation.

The Caretaker Gazette
P. O. Box 342
Carpenterville, IL 60110

Enclose a dollar or so to cover their postage and tell them that Wild Bill sent you.

COMMUNAL LIVING FOR SENIORS

In the mid-70's, I was living aboard my converted Coast Guard cutter tied up to an island in the California Delta. As part of the agreement I was given the use of 15 acres of fine, rich land with plenty of water available from the nearby canal. It struck me that this would be an ideal situation for an experiment in communal living. So I recruited some homeless young people from the streets of Santa Cruz and we formed an *ad hoc* commune aboard the Flying Goose.

I learned more from that year than I did from seven years at my old aerospace job. Among the aspects of communal living that became clear are the following:

1. There is one basic rule for communal living that makes it all work. You must, absolutely must have privacy. You must have a place that you can call your own completely. In this way, you can feel autonomous, independent, free. I cannot think of a more basic and essential element of communal living.

   The place of privacy need not be large. In fact, almost any nook or cranny on a boat or in a house suffices, even a screen, drapes or a partitions would be fine as long as it afforded a single, secure place for you to establish and maintain territorial imperative.

   Thus, all of us on the Flying Goose had our own quarters and we could retire there any time of the day or night and be absolutely sure that we would not be disturbed by anyone.

   Thinking back to WWII, I recall that the many fights that broke out on our destroyer were caused by people living too close to people without a break. In our engineering crew compartment, we had about 12 men bunking in a space that was about the size of pantry. It's no wonder that someone snoring or playing cards late would generate some violent hostility. So again, at the risk of overkill, let me say that if you want to have a successful senior commune, give each and every member a place which he or she can call his or her own. So be it!

2. Another aspect which can be properly handled in advance is the understanding of the use of personal and communal property. Everyone has little idiosyncrasies about things. So right from the start, a successful commune must determine who is going to use what.

   This includes furniture as well as food, TV as well as the communal car. Once the use of things is reconciled, you can get on with the business of the commune with relaxed demeanors.

   I recall that aboard the floating commune we agreed that as long as we all kept our fingers off the surface of LP records, we could play anyone's. Also, we agreed that the noise level of the music had to be within bounds. After all, no one should have to listen to hard rock when they really like Ravel and Faure. And vice versa!

3. Money can be a touchy subject, especially when you are short of it. No one likes to be the patsy and pay for another person's wherewithal if that person can pay for his or her own. So it is mandatory that some agreements be made on how to handle both personal and communal funds.

   I have seen more fights break out over a bottle of milk in a communal refrigerator than have occured at Madison Square Gardens!

4. One of the best ways to assure that a communal senior facility will be successful is to pattern it after historically successful communes. Take, for example, the Eskimos. They live communally in an environment where few mistakes are tolerated by an unforgiving Mother Nature. Thus they avoid the petty arguments that could destroy their solidarity and bind themselves together with pledges of a united front. When the wind howls, they pitch in and build their igloos

in joyous brotherhood. When starvation looms, they work like a well-drilled team to find food. In short, the Eskimos have had a successful communal lifestyle for many millenia because they know that in unity there is great strength. And that, dear seniors, is the true essence of communal life that works.

ADVANTAGES OF COMMUNAL LIFE

If you travel with a companion, he or she will help you up if you fall, and you the same if they fall. This is the basic truth of life. You are not alone when things go awry. And they inevitably do. Here are some tips, not listed in any particular order of importance, merely what comes to mind from my own experiences.

1. If you own one lawn mower for a household of ten seniors, then there's just one lawn mower to fix. That's a lot easier than having ten seniors worrying about ten mowers. The point is this—shared equipment makes for both economy and efficiency. My friend Barry Reid has coined the phrase, "cooperative efficiency" and the use of property is certainly a valid example of this principle. Just imagine the savings when a group of seniors share the expenses of a van that can hold everyone in the commune. Or the savings when the group buys 500 pounds of winter wheat at a big discount. It's obvious that great savings can be made and a better life created when people share.

2. Elimination of lonliness. That says it all.

3. Possibilities of new relationships, inter and intra and every way but loose. Just because you gets old doesn't mean that you lose the joy of touch. Communal life has infinite potential for learning how to relate, give and share knowledge with fellow human beings.

4. It follows from the above advantage that you can expect that life will be a continual and enriching learning experience. Everyone a teacher and everyone a student!

5. Picture a chilly evening with the communal group of seniors gathered about the fireplace popping corn and reminiscing about the good times past as well as discussing plans for good times to be. How much more rewarding than sitting in a lonely room in some downtown hotel.
   Try it, as you can always go back to being a solitary soul.

SHELTER FOR WOMEN

As mentioned in another part of this book, 75 percent of all poor seniors are women. To help alleviate and diminish this astonishing number of poor women, here are some some non-linear alternatives, a few of which may be a bit way-out.

LIVE-IN JOBS

My ex-wife Carol lives in a lovely home in the foothills of Montecito where she cares for two elderly people. The seniors are in good health, but simply need someone around just in case. Carol draws a good salary, can eat anything she wants and has days off. The house is surrounded by some great hiking terrain and a spectacular view of the Pacific.

This is hardly an isolated case; there are many areas in the country where there are large enclaves of wealthy retired people who need help with their daily activities. Off hand, I can think of several besides Montecito—Scarsdale, New York, Scottsdale, Lake Washington and Bellevue, the suburbs of Washington D.C., parts of San Diego, and Santa Fe.

To get a job like this requires ads, direct inquiry and distribution of your capabilities and references. Nursing organizations will often help you get a caring position. Personally, I prefer the direct approach. I would go to the area that interests me and just go to one or two houses on each block and leave my card and the request that if anyone on the block needs aid, to call. It could be that simple.

There are many varieties of jobs in the live-in category; here is a sampling:

- Care for paraplegics or quadraplegics
- Be a full-time baby sitter
- Be a house sitter while people are on vacation
- Care for a yacht in some quiet harbor
- Care for retarded or otherwise impaired person
- Help an alcoholic or smoker kick the habit
- Care for convalescents and terminal cases
- Look after a family having multiple pets or horses
- Be an assistant gardener to a hobbyist

And on and on. Actually, there are many variations on this theme and hundreds of possibilities!

CARETAKING

There are all kinds of properties that require someone to be a passive guard. No need for a gun; just a phone or an alarm system. These would include such places as equipment storage facilities, lumber yards, boat yards, airports and so forth. A small trailer could be provided by management to keep you cozy. That coupled with a salary for your food and you're set. Again, just make direct inquiries where you want to be.

STORAGE COMPLEXES

One of the fastest growing businesses around is the storage facility with many small rooms and lockers for the storage of personal items. These places all need someone to tend to them. The duties would include signing up the tenants, collecting the money and guarding the premises. Living quarters are almost always provided along with a salary. Just look in the phone book for storage places in the area of your choice.

OLD-FASHIONED SHOPS

Many cities still have the old-fashioned shopping areas with a store downstairs and living quarters upstairs. These have been beautifully illustrated in the paintings of Edward Hopper, and if you're over 60 you may remember shopping in them as a child. Now times have changed and many of these old shopping streets have been partially or completely abandoned. This is your opportunity to either work in a shop in exchange for the rooms upstairs or to open a shop of your own! Many of these places have been lying vacant for years and the landlord would, I believe, be willing to rent it out in exchange for a percentage of the take, or just for keeping the shop from being vandalized.

If you do obtain a shop and the upstairs living quarters, you don't need any capital to open a business. Just take second-hand goods on consignment or allow others to use the floor space for little businesses of their own—a mini-mall! Another good business for a low rent neighborhood is old magazines and books. You can offer these on a cash or exchange basis. Many book stores will GIVE you books just to get rid of them. Also, you can put an ad in the paper offering to take books off people's hands who are moving. Another good possibility is to offer to clean someone's garage or shed in exchange for the books and magazines. There is a shop of this kind in Santa Cruz and they have done nothing but make money and grow. The shop is called *Logos Books* in the Santa Cruz Mall.

RANCHES AND FARMS

Many ranch and farm owners are delighted to have an older person come and live just to dispel their own isolation and lonliness. You can be cook or take care of the garden or the farm animals. I remember a woman who was delighted to be the only female on an all-male ranch in central Nevada. And speaking of Nevada, I was once offered a lifetime of ease on a large ranch about 200 miles north of Las Vegas. No duties whatsoever other than keeping the property intact. No salary, but they provided chickens and feed and plenty of space and water for a large garden. An older woman (or several) could enjoy their own *ad hoc* commune in such a setting!

VESSELS

I have covered boats in depth in another chapter, but it is important to mention that there are many jobs aboard boats for older women. These jobs include light kitchen duties, waitressing, full charge of a small yacht's galley, caring for the children of boat people, charter work and so forth. With the boat population growing daily, this area has much potential.

TRAILER PARKS, MOTELS AND HOTELS

Anywhere that there are transients you need someone to count noses and take money. That's why it should be a great opportunity for older women to be desk clerks in places that offer space or shelter. I recall a woman in her late 70's who was completely in charge of a mobile home park south of where I live. She was a real character who endeared herself to the population of the park and enjoyed every minute of her day.

And don't forget dude ranches, resorts, hot springs and other outlying facilities. There are directories of each of these, often in libraries or travel bureaus. For hot springs, there is *Great Hot Springs of the West*, available by writing the publisher of this book. The book, discussed elsewhere, lists more than 1,700 hot springs in the 11 Western states.

REVIEW

It's obvious that there are virtually unlimited opportunities for older women with limited funds to find that "warm room somewhere" and have enough to eat and some salary besides.

Here's an easy way to get a commune going. Write an ad like this:

> "SENIOR MALE (or female) WISHES TO FORM A COMMUNE TO SHARE HOUSING AND LIVING COSTS. CALL BILL at 408/462 4176."

If you keep the ad simple, you'll get lots of inquiries. Don't limit yourself on the first go-around.

COMMUNAL LIVING

There is a publication called *Communities*, which is produced by the Stelle Group four times a year. If you would like to subscribe or receive a sample copy, write *Community Publications Cooperative, 126 Sun St, Stelle, IL 60919*.

It is best described by reproducing some sample offerings by existing communes.

COMMUNITIES journal of cooperation

no. 66 $5.00

◼DIRECTORY◼

in the following: afforestation; town planning; house construction; health centers; workshops for mechanical design and maintenance; handicraft units; publications; horticulture; arts and music; physical education/ sports; schools and research centers; food production and distribution; Matrimandir construction. Mother and Sri Aurobindo are the inspiration behind the development of Auroville whose stated aims are to realize an effective human unity and peace upon earth.

Auroville International USA

(a) Specific and Primary Purpose:
Supporting projects in the Auroville project in India as the first attempt anywhere to create a universal town where men and women of all countries can live together in peace and progressive harmony, above all creeds, all politics, and all nationalities.

(b) General Purposes:
To promote wherever, whenever possible, understanding and peace between nations and individuals, a living embodiment of an actual human unity, and an environment for unending education, constant progress for mankind.

B

Bryn Gweled Homesteads
1150 Woods Rd.
Southampton, Pennsylvania 18966
(215) 357-3977   John Ewbank

Bryn Gweled is a green oasis in suburbia a mile north of Philadelphia. About 75 homes, each on a lot of about 2 acres, provide a neighborhood in which culture diversity, family autonomy, neighborliness, and honesty can prevail.

Visiting all 75 families and obtaining at least 80% vote are among the pre-requisites for becoming an Approved Applicant entitled to negotiate for the purchase of a house from a retiring member or his estate. House

purchase is synonymous with membership.

Young families with children, childless couples, and retirees, are among recent new members. Members have been active in all minor and major political parties and many Bucks County projects.   By living among non-conformists, there is freedom to spend salary as desired instead of being pressured into manicuring lawns.

Bryn Gweled has hosted Fellowship of Intentional Communitarians, (CESCI), etc.

The Builders
P.O. Box 2278
Salt Lake City, Utah 84110
(801) 364-7396

The Builders' communities are dedicated to the spiritual illumination of humankind, through Christ or cosmic consciousness, a conscious force for good now hovering over humanity. Our founder, Norman Paulsen, is a direct disciple of Paramhansa Yogananda, whose great dream was World Brotherhood Colonies. In this spirit 200 members live, meditate, and work together on a 500,000 acre ranch in northeastern Nevada. We are building commercial greenhouses heated by hot springs, and have a pottery studio, woodshop, and crafts businesses. We farm, have many kinds of animals, and are projecting a full-spectrum healing center into the future. We have our own state-approved schools, kindergarten—12. In Salt Lake City, Utah, we operate natural food stores, and a demolition company. We meditate together regularly and often for this is the key to achieving our goals. If interested in visiting, please write or call.

Breitenbush Community
Breitenbush Hot Springs
P.O. Box 578
Detroit, Oregon 97342
(503) 854-3501

We are a family of 30 adults and 11 children who have restored an

abandoned hot spring resort and have for the last 5 years operated it as a Healing Retreat Conference Center. We eat together as vegetarians, operate our own school for our children, practice a wide variety of spiritual disciplines, have a common treasury, and have a participatory democracy as our form of governance. All visits should be previously arranged by telephone or mail.

C

**Camphill Special Schools —
Beaver Run**
R.D. 1
Glenmoore, Pennsylvania 19345

Camphill Special Schools — Beaver Run is an intentional community for the nurturing of mentally retarded children. Through a 10-month integrated program of schooling, home-life, and therapeutic activities, the handicapped children are allowed to realize their potentials in an enriching and supportive environment. The co-workers strive to being to expression the impulses of social renewal indicated through Rudolf Steiner as Anthroposophy and cultivated by the worldwide Camphill Movement founded by Karl Koenig.

Beaver Run is located in the rolling hills of rural Chester County on some 57 acres of open spaces and woodland. It has been in development since 1963 and consists of 10 extended-family homes, a school house, a craft center, a community hall, and several smaller buildings.

The population of adult co-workers is about 55, half of whom are permanent members committed to the ideals of Camphill, and half are newcomers enrolled in the Seminar in Curative Education. The Seminar is a couse of hands-on experience and formal studies, which allows newcomers to acquaint themselves with the community and its work.

Governing is by inter-related groups with differentiated responsibilities. Decisions are made through

My view of living communally is that it represents one of the best ways for any senior with limited income to not only have a home, but to have friends! What could be nicer than to move into a cozy farmhouse, have a private room and then enjoy all the vigorous outdoor work that a farm enterprise comprises. And beyond that, envision all the wonderful fresh farm produce that you will have three times a day. As I see, it, any senior who is in ill health could be rejuvenated by a sojourn at a rural commune.

And beyond all these benefits, think of the new friends one could make, the social gatherings that would be so rewarding, the formation of a new family network and so forth.

To find live-in employment, you just turn to the yellow pages of your phone book and look for ads under the headings of:

- Nursing
- Home Care
- Health Agencies
- Live-Ins

- Companions
- Homemakers
- Temporaries
- Health Care

Here's a typical ad:

The next step is to register with the agencies. Sooner or later you'll have a job. You can pick and choose in many areas since there is such a great demand for people who will cabably provide this service. You can live in or out, but since we're talking about getting shelter, it is my intent to familiarize you with such live-in opportunities. Many live-in jobs are simply wonderful—you become a member of the disabled or ill person's family, you share their joys, their sorrows. It's impossible not to become involved in their lives. I know I felt a great sympathy for my young ward and his predicament of being partially crippled. I was delighted whenever he showed signs of improvement. And I am sure that this will be the case when you have this type of position.

FACILITY LIVE-INS

Many institutions invite their employees to share their roofs. These include hospitals, nursing homes, agricultural enterprises (large ranches have traditionally had bunk houses for their "hands"), ships, outlying installations, and such unique facilities as lighthouses, guard stations and offshore oil drilling towers. I recall renting a room at a lumber camp for eight dollars a month—a token sum that hardly covered the magnificence of the view.

Take a walk along skid row sometime and see how the employment agencies recruit for remote jobs; it's always listed as room and board and a salary. This is quite a temptation for even the most inveterate wino. I'm not implying that seniors have to become gandy dancers or lumberjacks, it's just that there are a lot of jobs that exist that few people know about. Most people think in terms of urban offices and factories when there are actually millions of people living the clean-air life in faraway places.

For more information on this type of employment, check out the yellow pages for listings such as:

- General Employment Agencies
- Employment Agencies that Specialize in Country-Area Jobs
- Ranches (in areas of ranches)
- Farms
- Institutions (homes, prisons, hospitals, convalescent centers)
- Organizations (churches often have someone live on remote retreat properties)
- Railways
- Lumber Companies
- Oil Drilling Firms

Leave your resume off and then sit back and be choosy if you have the time. Sooner or later, the job of your choice is bound to appear.

SHIPS AND YACHTS

This is a special category, one that is so full of dynamic, romantic and dramatic possibilities that it deserves its own section. When I was about 14, I would hitch-hike down to the local yacht harbor and wait around until I saw someone begin to get their sailboat ready for sea. Then I would politely ask if I could help sail their boat to Catalina, as Catalina was the usual destination.

And I was never refused! The yachtsmen must've taken pity on the sea-loving youth that I was, one who so obviously wanted to see waves close-up. Once on the island, it was even less of a problem getting back since the boat owners knew that I would otherwise be marooned. This experience has generated a lot of interest in exploring the many jobs that may be obtained on various vessels from yachts a few meters long to large "love boats" that travel worldwide. Getting such employment is really quite simple; read yachting publications or those catering to people with large incomes, such as *Town and Country*. Often, you'll find ads offering berths aboard a yacht for a coming world cruise. Many specify "experience necessary," but many also just want someone to help around the boat. Here is a typical ad from a magazine called *Latitude 38*, published in the San Francisco, CA area:

> YACHT CREW REQUIRED—
> Engineer: diesel/electric, exp
> required. CREW: Maint, exp
> req'd, salary based on ex-
> perience, poss live aboard. 95'
> Charter Yacht, Sausalito-
> based. Send complete resume
> and salary req to: PO Box
> 1735, Sausalito, CA 94966. (98)

REACTIVATING A GHOST TOWN

Imagine our surprise. We had been pounding the desolate pavements of northern Oregon for several hours. The terrain was lunar; there was not a tree in sight in the flat high desert that stretched for miles in every direction.

Suddenly, we sighted the town from a rise just a few hundred yards away—it was Hardman, Oregon. We stopped in the center of town and stepped out of our pick-up camper. Total silence, except for the faint strains of metal contracting in our engine.

We began to explore the town. It measured only two blocks in all directions. On the main street, where the highway bisected it, there were several handsome buildings with false fronts and fairly fancy architecture. Paint had long since weathered from the grey lumber, and hardware had that outdoor patina of rust. It was the set of every Western ever filmed in real life! We loved it instantly.

We began a slow walk, almost on tiptoe, through the deserted streets of Hardman. Every house was empty, except for one having the appearance of being lived in. However, no one emerged during our all-too-brief stay.

As it turned out, Hardman was once a prosperous town garnering income from freight haulers and local farmers. But the railroads ended wagon trains and farming went elsewhere. Thus, the town was left to die a natural death, and all alone. Hardman is typical of hundreds, perhaps thousands of towns that have been left behind in the march of civilization throughout the West. And there are, of course, towns throughout the world that have outlived their inhabited lifespan. What they are today are opportunity spots in where to have shelter for almost nothing. Many seniors have taken advantage of this by inhabiting such remote ghost towns as Jerome in Arizona, Silver City in Idaho, and the famous Virginia City, Nevada. I understand that even isolated Bodie (Bad Bodie) in California near the Nevada border is picking up a few residents each year. There are no hard and fast rules for living in a ghost town. After all, they are all so different. But here are some guidelines that I would use myself if I planned to try it for a spell:

1. Get yourself something rugged—a 4-wheel drive vehicle would be ideal though a small car pulling a trailer with an off-the-road motorcycle would do. The point is to have something that will get in and out of remote places. Most ghost towns have become remote because of the circumstances which caused their demise. On the other hand, there are some ghost towns right on major highways such as Rhyolite in Nevada or the aforementioned Hardman.

2. Pick one that has a climate you can handle. Alternatively, pick two, one for summer and one for winter! And there's really no reason you can't have homes in several ghost towns!

3. Be sure that there is a source of good water in or near the town since this is a basic essential to healthy living as well as providing the irrigation for your kitchen garden.

4. Check out the town for existing residents since some ghost towns have people living in them who don't really want any more neighbors. That's why they are there—for peace and privacy. Furthermore, there would be no point in residing in a town with some grouchy misanthropes when there are so many ghost towns from which to choose.

5. Check out the houses to make sure they won't fall on you during the first big windstorm. Oddly, many ghost towns, Like Eureka in central Nevada boast strong stone structures. The strength of those would be my choice, although I can also see fixing up a charming old Victorian in some scenic locale.

6. Supplies should be available either by a reasonable trek to town or by mail via a post office that is hopefully nearby. Of course, with a garden and the dollar a day philosophy, you can become virtually self-sufficient, like many ghost town dwellers.

7. There should be something interesting to do in the town—a little gold panning, a bit of tunneling or perhaps a project of restoring the old "opry house."

There are, of course, many other considerations, but these are some of the more basic. Keep in mind as you entertain this concept that increasing numbers of people are doing—taking over old abandoned towns and making them into very desirable places to live. What follows is a pictorial review of some examples:

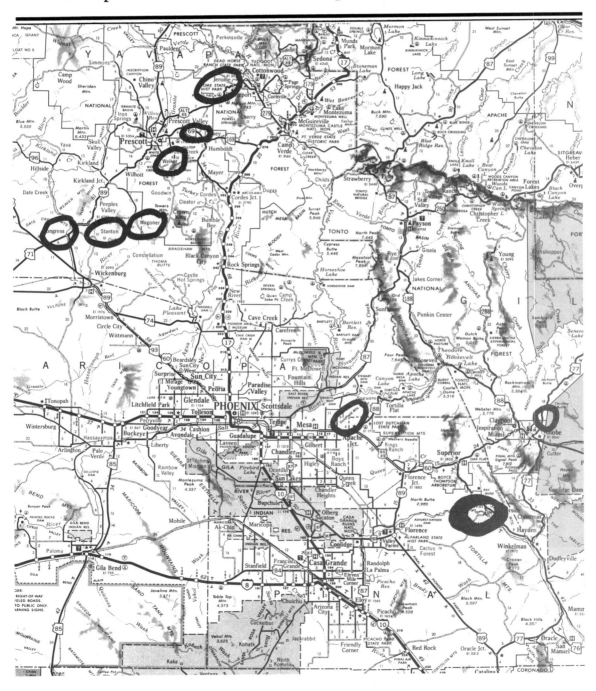

In the early-70's, I was living on a small ranch in the High Sierras. To help out some homeless friends, I rented an entire lumber camp from the lumber mill in Jackson for 75 dollars. This included several dormitories, a mess hall/kitchen combination, a large workshop and about five acres of land which boasted a wonderful clear water spring spouting a beverage better than Perrier or Calistoga. My friends moved up to the camp and were enjoying the challenge of restoring it when a little trouble was generated; it seemed that because my friends had a rather dark skin coloring, the locals objected to their living in the old abandoned lumber camp minding their own business. One thing led to another and my friends had to vacate.

My point in bringing this up is that you would not only have to check out the residents of a given ghost town, but the nearby residents as well. You see, prejudices against color, attire or lifestyle still exist in these United States and we must all learn to either live with this situation or be prepared to change it. And, as I'm sure you're well aware, the change can start with you. As I.F. Stone once said,

"The way we live our lives determines the future."

Arizona's More Interesting Ghost Towns And Mining Camps

GOLDFIELD: Pinal Co. 5m from Apache Jct. on State 88. Mining town in the middle 90s. Four of the original mine shafts, stopes and timbers can be seen.

GOLDROAD: Mohave Co. 23m SW of Kingman. Gold first discovered by John Moss and party around 1864. A new strike was made by Joe Jerez in 1902. In 1949, most of the remaining mining operations and buildings were razed to escape taxes. Now mostly diggings, minor ruins.

HARRISBURG: Yuma Co. Approx. 8m S of Wenden. First town in this part of the desert. Gold was discovered near the town site by Bill Bear around 1886. The town was started by Capt. Chas. Harris on the site of the old centennial state station.

HARSHAW: Santa Cruz Co. 10m SE of Patagonia. Settled about 1875, this place soon boasted a newspaper, "The Bullion," saloons, numerous stores, with 100 working mines nearby. Stone, adobe ruins, cemetery.

HILLTOP: Cochise Co. 36m SE from Willcox on Rt. 186. Mine established by Frank and John Hands. The town of Hilltop was first started on the west side of the mountain, then a tunnel was put through to the east side where an even larger town was established. Today, it is a ghost town.

JEROME: Yavapai Co. on U.S. 89A, 33m NE of Prescott. Estab. 1876, this famous copper camp hit a peak population of 15,000 about 1929 and its main mine produced some $500,000,000 in ore before closing in 1952. Many picturesque buildings and ruins, museum, other points of interest. As the population has grown to about 400, Jerome is now referred to as a restored mining town.

KOFA: Yuma Co. 24m Rt. 95 from point 28m S of Quartzsite on U.S. 60-70. Site of the rich King of Arizona gold mine discovered 1896 by Charles Eichelberger. During its 13 years of prime activity, ending in 1910, official records credit the King with a production of around $14,000,000. Mostly ruins.

LA PAZ: Yuma Co. 8m N of Ehrenberg. Flourished for 7 years as a gold center and river port. Between 1862-1873 the town had over 5,000 residents. The central portion of the town is being reconstructed. Public may view the excavations.

MC CABE: Yavapai Co. 2-1/2m W of Rt. 69 at Humboldt, via yard of Iron King Mine. Mining and milling town dating from late 19th century. Remains of old cabins, cemetery, ruins of large mill, mine dumps, rubble.

MC MILLEN: Gila Co. near U.S. 60, about 10m NE of Globe. Supported by celebrated Stonewall Jackson Mine discovered in 1876. Mine is believed to have produced close to $3,000,000. Ruins.

MOWRY: Santa Cruz Co. 15m SE of Patagonia. Small town grown up around an old silver, lead, zinc mine purchased in late 1850s by Sylvester Mowry, U. S. Army. Lt. Mowry's operations were cut short in 1862 when Mowry was charged with supplying lead for Confederate bullets, jailed at Fort Yuma, his mine confiscated by Uncle Sam. Extensive ruins.

OATMAN: Mohave Co. 32m SW of Kingman. Gold mining town active 1900-1942. Many empty buildings and picturesque ruins. Some small places of business operated by a hardy group of "never say die" citizens.

ORO BLANCO: Santa Cruz Co. 15-20m W. of Nogales. Between 1873 and 1932, $1,130,000 in gold was taken from this locality. Adobe ruins.

PARADISE: Cochise Co. 6m NW of Portal. Briefly active mining town dating from early 1900s. Paradise is still "home" to a few oldtimers who are glad to point out the old town jail and ruins of various businesses. Part of the town privately owned.

PEARCE: Cochise Co. 1m off U. S. 666 from a point 29m S of Willcox. This old gold camp once had a population of 2,000 - all of them well supported by the wealth of the Commonwealth mine. It was discovered by Johnny Pearce in 1894 and in its heyday, the old Commonwealth was the richest gold digging in southern Arizona. Operating store and post office. with many vacant adobes, mine and mill ruins.

SIGNAL: Mohave Co. on Big Sandy R., 60 m NW of Wickenburg. 8 m S of Wikieup on US 93, take dirt road W 12 m. Estab. late in 1870's as milling town for ore from McCrackin and Signal mines. In its heyday, had stores, shops, hotels, saloons and a brewery to supply beer for the thirsty miners. Freight was shipped from San Francisco to Yuma thence to Aubrey Landing, from there it was hauled by mule 35m upgrade to Signal. Prosperous for many years. Mill ruins, one old saloon, foundations, rubble and cemetery.

STANTON: Yavapai Co. 6m E Arrowhead Sta. on U.S. 89, 42m SW of Prescott. Named for Chas. B. Stanton who kept a store and stage station and was also postmaster in 1875, later an active mining camp. Remaining buildings in fair-to-good condition all privately owned.

TOMBSTONE: Cochise Co. 69m SE of Tucson. "The town too tough to die." One of the old west's most famous towns where silver was king. Most of its notorious landmarks remain; OK Corral, Boot Hill, Tombstone Epitaph, museum, shops.

WALKER: Yavapai Co. 6m S State Rt. 69 from a point 4m E of Prescott. Joseph Walker in 1863 led a gold prospecting expedition into Yavapai Co. As a result of his success, Walker came into being. Mill and mine ruins. Walker has a few winter residents and many summer residents.

WASHINGTON CAMP: Santa Cruz Co. 20m S of Patagonia. It once was the major service community for Duquesne, Mowry and Harshaw. At its peak in 1905 it had a population of 5,200 miners and their families. Ruins. Check road conditions.

WEAVER OR WEAVERVILLE: Yavapai Co. 2m beyond Stanton on same side of road. A very picturesque town named after Pauline Weaver, guide, whose party accidentally discovered a rich gold find. When this rich placer was exhausted, the town was a hangout for thieves and murderers. After 30 years of lawlessness, the gangs were chased out and Weaver became a ghost town. Little remains except mine trails.

WHITE HILLS: Mohave Co. 50m N of Kingman off Rt. 93. In the 1890s it was the rowdiest silver camp between Globe and Virginia City. In a brief six years, the 15 now forgotten mines which surrounded it, gave up $12,000,000 in silver bullion. Mostly old diggings.

In order to preserve these remnants of Arizona's colorful past for future ghost town visitors, please observe and respect all posted signs, leave all gates as you find them and do not remove anything from the premises.

Desert regions are subject to flash floods and resultant washouts; wherever possible, make inquiries locally.

Here's verification that ghost towns DO experience revivals and that the trend is likely to increase along with senior population.

CHAPTER FIVE
TIRE TRAMPS

"The worst day on the road is better than the best day at home."

—*old gypsy song*

OVERVIEW

It is estimated that more than 3,000,000 Americans are living on wheels. Many of them are seniors, some of whom are on wheels part-time, but many of whom are retired, home free and void of excess baggage.

They are in motorhomes, campers, trailers and an assortment of miscellaneous rigs such as motorcycles with trailers, pick-ups with camper backs and tug boats.

While it is true that many people are homebodies, there is enough gypsy and nomad blood circulating in the veins of Americans to steadily increase the number of people who opt for wheel estate rather than a fixed address.

Including the many factors leading to this are:

- Increased cost of land and housing

- More seniors opting for a free life

- Growing numbers of campgrounds that cater to the full-time gypsy

- Improved recreational vehicles which are self-contained

- Social changes which make people want to travel and learn rather than merely possess things

- Desire to have a good climate and environment year round

These are but a few of the many reasons why people become tire tramps, as I call them. In a subtler, more esoteric vein consider this:

- Camping on a pristine beach in southern Baja, swimming nude in the clear, cool, emerald-jade water, sunning to a bronze shade which shaves years off of your age, barbecuing fresh fish you've caught over a driftwood fire, reflecting the serenity of a virtually uninhabited world all your own.

- Dawdling along the remote byways of a central Nevada valley in the fall, spotting hidden ranches clustered beneath giant cottonwoods with clear springs gushing forth from nearby red sandstone bluffs, watching wild horses calmly graze in a lush and lonely meadow.

- Exploring 19th-century towns in remote reaches of incredibly beautiful British Columbia, a land where time stopped about 1850 and where you can relive the Wild West at will, panning gold from a roaring stream, staring bemused into a bonfire of willow and poplar in a campground where you are the only visitor.

- Shopping in a border town in Mexico just across from Texas and finding coffee in the bean for about a dollar and a half a kilo, a lunch place with the best-tasting enchiladas ever made, and buying a handwoven, museum quality jacket for so little you can tip the clerk the same amount.

- Parking your rig near the bridge at Concord and sensing the great history of the place, standing on the bridge itself and practically hearing the shouts of the rebels and the clipped orders of the ramrod-straight Redcoats.

Travel, it turns out, is a form of magic wherein you are the magician; you can fly through time and space and mood at a flick of your ignition key, a turn of your steering wheel.

PERSONAL BACKGROUND

Ever since I learned to walk, I have been an inveterate explorer. I recall packing a light lunch at the start of a summer's day in South Pasadena, California of the mid-20's and then taking off, totally free, to see what fascinating things lay beyond the town's perimeter. Sometimes I arrived home after dark and when I was older, not arriving home until the next day or even the next week. To me, there was always something more exciting just over that next rise or hill. And to this day, there still is!

A bicycle made traveling much faster and more energy-conserving. With it, I could go for miles and miles without having to measure my trips in blocks. Later, when I was able to trade in my bike for a motorcycle, my range expanded exponentially; it became possible to visit remote beaches, vast deserts and eventually, other states. Traveling by motorcycle is so dynamic and dramatic—such a tremendous high—I dare not expand on it here for fear of using up the rest of the book just telling you the innermost secrets of two-wheel, high-speed travel. Suffice to say, once you have felt the wind buffet your body and the road sweep you into banking like a gliding gull, you are hooked for life.

Eventually, I graduated to my own convertible. With this promotion, my horizons became essentially unlimited. And when a trailer was added to a pick-up truck, no place on earth was too far.

Today I can look back on some fabulous tire tramping—all over the United States, Mexico and Canada—and sans trailer, all over Europe. What a pure delight and education this life on wheels has been! No wonder I feel motivated to spread the word to those who may not have had this wonderful opportunity.

My major objective regarding tire tramping is to prove that it need not be expensive or arduous. In fact, what you are about to read is based on the premise that almost anyone, regardless of income level, can become a full-time tire tramp if they so desire.

JIMMY ONE

In 1972 I bought a 1966 GMC pick-up truck equipped with a low camper back containing a stove, refrigerator, two bunks and a space for clothes and supplies. Today, almost a decade and a half later, the Jimmy is still running well—it could take off for the east coast with only a little preparation.

The major motivation for buying the rig was because of our experiences with one too many noisy nights in motels and hotels. We were determined to become autonomous. So with the twist of the starter key, we would find ourselves far from radios, arguing couples and switchyard trains.

Often I have been low on funds, as the financial life of a writer is very much a roller coaster. I have had to be prepared to work in other areas at a moments notice. Thus, with the Jimmy on hand, I can toss in some clean clothes, a bag of beans and rice and take off. I have departed for a point 500 miles away with only enough money to get there. However, knowing I can live in the camper and add some wild greens to my beans and rice, what's to worry? The answer comes in one word,

NOTHING!

You see, a small, simple rig like the Jimmy can provide one or two people with everything they need to comfortably survive. To me, anything beyond this just becomes frosting on the cake.

You say, what about sanitation in a small space? Try a portapotty for your toilet and the nearest small waterfall for your shower. If it happens to come from a hot spring, so much the better. You only need one copy of *Great Hot Springs of the West* to locate more than 1,7009 thermal springs in the ll western states.

And if you can't locate a handy source of water, a bucket of water warmed by your engine manifold (via a copper coil) or a campfire with a hose siphon suspended from a tree and presto! You have a shower—au natural!

Improvisation is the key to low-cost comfort on wheels. And it's fun—not a chore. I recall, for example, being out of flour and yet desirous of making some creamed tuna. I found a couple rocks in the desert, ground up some barley Indian-style and made the best tuna dish I've ever tasted. It must have been that fresh ground grain. Another time I was almost out of food and found a once-harvested corn field still bearing many uncollected ears. Again, an improvised stone grinder provided the corn meal for some great corncakes, a la the Wild West.

Without infringing on another part of the book, let me add that while traveling, you often find large quantities of food growing in a free-for-taking mode. Ruth and I once harvested a year's supply of walnuts from an abandoned grove in a remote reach of the isolated San Benito Valley in central California. Often farms begin operation and when water supplies diminish or prices fall, they go out of business leaving orchards and fields still producing crops without attention. On another occasion, we put up dozens of jars of tomatoes from a field that had been harvested by a machine leaving tons of fruit untouched.

My point is this; food is really not a great problem when you are traveling. Food of all kinds, wild and domestic abounds in these productive United States. And since you can select your own routes, just include some places that provide food. Oregon and Washington are typical of states with extensive agricultural development as well as such states as New Jersy and New Hampshire. And don't forget the resources of fish in almost every state.

The other needs, such as propane for your stove and gas for your car do require either money or a method of barter. If you are short, you can stop and work someplace for a while or work in exchange for the energy supplies you need. I have almost never been refused employment where it was logical to apply. I've picked cherries, helped harvest corn, written freelance articles, been a caretaker of a defunct brothel and run a small train at a tourist attraction. As Zorba the Greek says,

"I got hands and feet, what does it matter what I do?"

Tires, car parts and licensing. Yes, all of them require funding too, from time to time, but they need not be too costly. You can buy good used tires, go to salvage yards for parts and pick a state with low license fees for your RV. After all, as a tire tramp you have the perfect opportunity to pick your "home" state.

Doing laundry can be as simple as using a bucket of water from a handy hot spring and hanging the clothes on a line stretched between two trees. They'll never smell fresher! And, as we point out in the *Clothing* chapter, with so many thrift stores around, you won't have to spend much. Besides, as a traveler, you can wear what you please wherever you go. My own costume was always a pair of Levis, a western shirt and boots. I doubt whether I have ever spent more than 25 dollars for clothes in any given year! And to think I was once a minor executive in an aerospace firm and had to put on a shirt, tie and coat every single day, or risk demerits from the boss! How I laugh now!

What more do you need to be an independent tire tramp? Well, how about baking soda for your teeth and some of that wild chaparral shrub for tea. Now if you use those items you can wear your tire tramp badge proudly!

Now that we've covered most of the basics, what about life on the road? What is it really like, where do you stay for free and what do you do all day? Here are some real life anecdotes:

THE SOUTH FORK OF THE COSUMNES RIVER

One sunny afternoon while I was making my getaway from the rat race, I encountered a cohort who was engaged in the same clandestine activity. He was an electronics technician who had slipped away from the smog-festooned town of Pasadena. Here on the sandy banks of the Cosumnes River near Fiddletown in the California Mother Lode, we met and exchanged notes.

It seems that my tech friend had enjoyed diving for gold nuggets as a hobby. It suddenly dawned on him one day that he was not only making as much money from his hobby as his job, he was having a lot more fun and breathing a lot purer air.

His rig consisted of a small pump and SCUBA gear. He was actually vacuuming gold from the nooks and crannies of the river bottom. Every winter, new gold is washed down from the hillsides in the Mother Lode and it eventually ends up at the lowest point of a stream or river since it is so heavy; heavier, in fact, than any other mineral.

He showed me about 25 dollars in what is called specimen gold that he had found in a matter of a few hours. The year was 1963, the sum was substantial. He said that 25 dollars was his quote per day and when he found it, he quit. It was more than enough to pay all his expenses, food and such with some left over for possible lean days.

It was then about noon. The rest of his day was spent soaking up the warm sun, playing water games with my two daughters and finally, cooking a Western barbecue on the sandy beach over a driftwood campfire.

As the glittering stars emerged over the canyon, we talked at length. We agreed that the only problem was; why didn't we discover the life of free-wheeling tire tramp sooner?

Later I learned that he lived either in the back of his station wagon or just camped out in his small tent. He planned to acquire a larger vehicle when his nugget bag was a little fatter. In the meantime, he had no time clocks to punch, no bosses to harangue him, no freeway gridlocks, no bad air to gasp in and only selected friends and new acquaintances to rap with. All in all, his lifestyle was most desirable and one that I was to remember whenever the occasion arose to cite a successful tire tramp.

Many years later when I had become a successful tire tramp myself, I met another rat race escapee at a Nevada hot spring. Also an electronics tech, he had worked out a simple system to meet his money needs. He would work at his trade for a couple of months and live in his camper to save money. Since he worked for high pay, the savings were substantial. With the cash stashed in his money belt, he would travel the entire U.S. smelling the roses and bathing in creeks.

Thinking back, I have had the pleasure of meeting and conversing with many authentic tire tramps. I have never met one that did not radiate great enthusiasm for his or her freedom.

Now that we have answered the question about what you can do if you have some skills, let's consider that you have no marketable talents and that diving for gold is not your bag.

Well, I have found work of all kinds in every part of the country, from apple-picking in New Hampshire in October to packing fish at Moss Landing in California. Farms, ranches, canneries, lumber camps, dude ranches and dozens of other countryside enterprises are always in need of help. After all, most of the help is, by nature, transient. Many tire tramps follow big harvests like wheat in Montana or grapes in California.

Then too, in small towns, there are often little jobs like retouching signs or doing consulting work. Often you can arrange barter if you don't need cash, for example, your work for food or auto parts or even gas. Then there are those ubiquitous flea markets where you can unload all the flotsam and jetsam you may have picked up along the roadside. Speaking of that, I walked with a group of peace marchers last year and found that they were making 40 or 50 dollars a day just retrieving and flattening aluminum cans. I tried it myself and was amazed at how many cans I found in just one 300-yard stretch of road.

Then there was the time that I bought an entire truckload of apricots that a cannery had rejected for a cosmetic problem called *bluestone*. I purchased them for five cents a pound and sold them in a flea market for 25 cents. It was fun and profitable and I had all of the dried apricots I needed for the year, along with lots of apricot syrup and preserves.

In our chapter on *Senior Income* many of the proposed enterprises can be adapted to the tire tramp lifestyle.

Tire tramping—ah yes, even Mr. Toad has something to say about it in the classic children's book, *The Wind in the Willows:*

> "He led the way to the stable yard and there they saw the gypsy wagon, shining with newness, painted canary yellow picked out with green and with red wheels.
>
> 'There you are,' cried Toad. 'There's real life for you embodied in that little cart. The open road, the dusty highway, the heath, the common, the hedgerows, the rolling downs! Camps, villages, towns, cities! Here today

and off to somewhere else tomorrow! Travel, change, interest, excitement! The whole world before you and a horizon that's always changing! And mind, this is the finest cart that was ever built. Come inside and look.

It was indeed, very compact and comfortable. Little sleeping bunks, a little table folded up against the wall, a cooking stove, lockers, bookshelves, a bird cage with a bird in it, pots, pans, jugs and kettles of every size and variety.

'All complete,' said the Toad triumphantly, pulling open a locker. 'You see, biscuits, potted lobster, sardines, everything you could possibly want. Soda water here, letter paper, bacon, jam, cards and dominoes you'll find,' he continued. 'You'll find that nothing whatever has been forgotten when we make our start this afternoon.'"

THE TT RIG

You may not be satisfied with Toad's horse-drawn cart, but there are modest RV's that can be purchased for very little. My own suggestion for you or a couple just starting out as tire tramps would be a small pick-up camper, as small as you can comfortably use. After more than 40 years of the gypsy life, I have learned that you should buy only what you intend to use. I know it is a temptation to acquire a giant motorhome that will impress the neighbors and roadside gawkers but restrain yourself; remember you have to pay for every pound you move around and some of those big rigs get only a few miles to the gallon. Also, the bigger they are, the more susceptible to being tipped in a windstorm. The smaller, lower, lighter the better is my recommendation and this trend is now reflected in many of the latest RV's. I know that for myself, a low rig with just sitting headroom is just dandy. The layout looks like this:

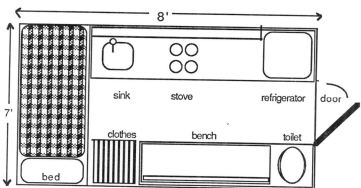

storage above and below

By placing a foam mattress on the floor, it can sleep two, or if you have a short visitor, the front seat of a big pick-up can be used. The important thing about tire tramping is that you will be spending most of your time outdoors enjoying Mother Nature, with only minimal time inside. So there's no need for an elaborate interior when you can sit around a blazing campfire and enjoy all outdoors as your living room. I know that I find myself spending only the time it takes to prepare a meal, rest during the day or sleep at night inside my rig. Of course, if you like to stay indoors a lot, a larger camper, motorhome or trailer would be called for. But on the other hand, if you are really a homebody, you probably should stay at home and just take occasional trips.

After you have spent some time getting accustomed to the nomadic lifestyle, you might want to graduate to a travel trailer in the 20-foot range. Most tire tramps are couples, and from my observations over the last 40 years, a 20-footer has all the amenities that anyone could want to make them comfortable and happy. There's plenty of sleeping space, usually bunks or beds for four or six, a kitchen, dinette, shower, toilet and plenty of storage cabinets, lockers and clothes closets. In the deluxe models you may find stereos, generators and other luxuries that could be added to a standard model when you wish. The above items all fit into an 8 x 20 foot space.

Now, when you get a longer trailer, there is usually all of the above, in addition to a lot more storage space and more leg room and possibly a moveable chair or two instead of one fixed sofa or lounge. With a longer trailer, you don't gain any more of the basics for the simple reason that there are no more to gain! Once you can cook, bathe, have a toilet available, and sleep, there is precious little else that makes much difference. What you must determine is the difference between real needs and totally optional wants. All we need to live is some air, water, food and a bit of shelter. As Marcus Aurelius said, "How little is needed to make a happy life."

Let's take a look at some trailer layouts and see if this isn't true:

My favorite layout!

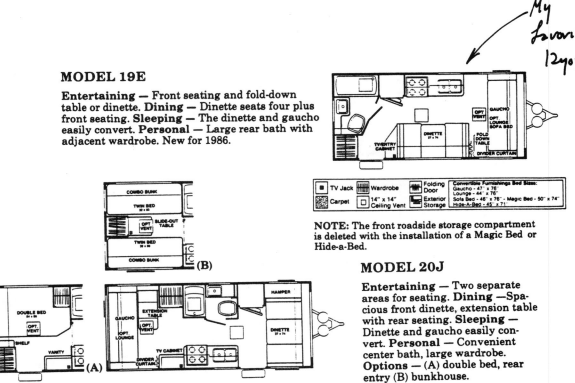

MODEL 19E

Entertaining — Front seating and fold-down table or dinette. **Dining** — Dinette seats four plus front seating. **Sleeping** — The dinette and gaucho easily convert. **Personal** — Large rear bath with adjacent wardrobe. New for 1986.

NOTE: The front roadside storage compartment is deleted with the installation of a Magic Bed or Hide-a-Bed.

MODEL 20J

Entertaining — Two separate areas for seating. **Dining** —Spacious front dinette, extension table with rear seating. **Sleeping** — Dinette and gaucho easily convert. **Personal** — Convenient center bath, large wardrobe. **Options** — (A) double bed, rear entry (B) bunkhouse.

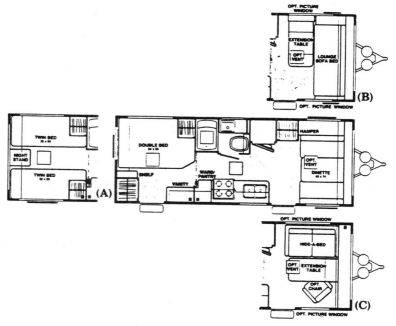

MODEL 23S

Entertaining — Front dinette seats four. **Dining** — Front dinette; extension table convenience with lounge, sofa bed or Hide-a-Bed. **Sleeping** — Double bed, convertible dinette. **Personal** — Generous wardrobe storage throughout. **Options** — (A) twin beds; bunkhouse shown with 20J also available. (B) front lounge or sofa bed (C) side Hide-a-Bed, chair.

MODEL 23M

Entertaining — Front seating and dinette suited for both. **Dining** — Dinette seats four, front seating for guests. **Sleeping** — Rear double bed plus convertible dinette and lounge. **Personal** — Rear bedroom/bathroom privacy. **Options** — (A) side Hide-a-Bed.

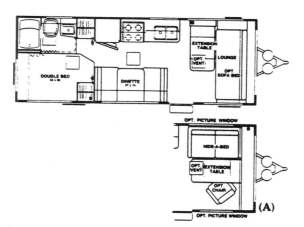

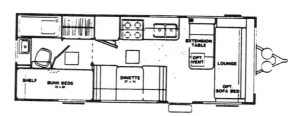

MODEL 23P

Entertaining — Front lounge with extension table plus dinette. **Dining** — Dinette seats four. **Sleeping** — Bunkbeds, convertible dinette and lounge provide choice. **Personal** — Private rear bath, generous personal wardrobe.

WHERE TO GO AND WHERE TO PARK

Once you buy an RV and fill it with your treasured belongings, you'll be free to roam. No place with a road becomes too remote for a well-built, self-contained RV. Today, many tire tramps think nothing of probing the upper latitudes of Canada and then dropping down towards the equator for a nice warm and sunny winter. Others, more affluent, ship their RV's overseas and continue their travels to places where signs say *nicht rauchen*. The entire world becomes your personal playground and that's what makes tire tramping such a continuous delight.

Even after many decades of continuous travel, I still get excited when I am preparing for a departure. It doesn't matter where we go because we have fun everywhere—mountains, oceanside, desert, famous or obscure places. There is that never-ending fascination with what new adventures and sights lie just over the next hill. Try it and you'll see what I mean.

Here are some shots taken on some recent TT trailer trips:

Several times in the past, I have gone to trailer shows and looked at units larger than my present rig. However, I have never found an interior design that satisfied me as much as my present love—a 20-year-old Kenskill.

I have gone both solo and with Ruth, and not once have we ever missed anything important. In fact, just the idea of having a hot shower after a hike up and down the Grand Canyon is fantastic. And imagine the joy of a cold drink on a hot day in the desert. You don't need a complex unit for that—just an old-fashioned icebox is perfect. And napping, or using the bathroom—these are the real needs for anyone who is on the road. These items make the big difference in comfort and cleanliness, not a lot of electronic gadgets or ten feet of added floorspace.

My point is this; when you have all the necessary comforts of a home on wheels, you really begin to appreciate all the things we take for granted at home. Everything on wheels has a new dimension of importance just because it IS on wheels. I recall visiting Thoreau's pond at Walden and thinking of how wonderful it was to park something the size of my hero's cabin so close to his spiritual home.

Even the simple act of preparing and enjoying a meal becomes an event—always a picnic on wheels. Often we savor some regional treat, perhaps a cut of fresh salmon that another tire tramper caught. Broiled salmon, a baked potato and a salad leisurely eaten while admiring a view of a magnificent river in Idaho or Washington has to be what life is truly about.

Therefore, if you only haul around what you really intend to use, you'll save a lot of gas, help reduce pollution and have the convenience of an RV that is easy to maneuver and park and still provides all of the creature comforts we seniors seem to need.

Motorhomes can be fun, but personally, I have learned to live without them. They seem so clumsy and unwieldy with such poor visibilty. Some are even equipped with TV cameras on the back so they can see what they are crunching today. Except when they're out on a flat, open highway, they appear as clumsy as the Mayflower on roller skates. There are some good things to say for them; for example, no trailer to unhitch (which can be an advantage) and you don't have to get out of your RV to eat or sleep, as you're already there.

I personally have always felt more comfortable with the truck and trailer rig. But don't let me dissuade you from what has become a very popular mode of life on wheels. Give them a try, rent a motorhome and see how you relate to it both in the city and the country. Then decide. Make the same test with a trailer and its tow vehicle.

So, that's a review of what's currently available for tire tramps in the realm of RV's. There are new combinations and layouts every year, but basically, the interiors and exteriors don't really change that much from an accepted norm. After all, form follows function and the technology of RV's has been fairly well stabilized for years.

Also, something to be considered is the possibility of buying one type of rig one year and then trading it for another the next until you, like me, find one that is just perfect.

PARKING

Years ago I gave up parking my rig in campgrounds. Too much noise and expense. Ruth and I start looking for a place to spend the night long before sunset. If we are way out in the boondocks, we never worry. There is always a side road, a wide pull-out, an abandoned farm, an old airport, a marina, or a quiet street in a ghost town. I'm sure you get the picture.

If we are in a small town, we drive to the outskirts and find a street with empty lots. Few people are concerned with the parking of a neatly kept trailer nearby—sometimes they object to parking right in front.

My theory, which has been borne out by experience, is that if you don't make any disturbance, no one will have any hostility. After all, many people have taken trips and they know what it is like to have to park in a strange area.

In larger towns we park in shopping centers and with one exception, have never been bothered. Other good places to stop are church parking lots, tourist attractions adjacent to city and county parks, behind gas stations, rest stops, truck stops and so forth.

In time, one becomes expert in judging which place will be free of middle-of-the-night disturbances or police questions. Of course, you are bound to make some mistakes. I once parked off the main road in New Mexico and was awakened about 2 a.m. by police who said that the Indians on the reservation did not like white tourists and they might shoot holes through our rather thin-walled rig. I left promptly. I had not checked to see whether we were parked on Indian property.

Just for fun, here is a brief inventory of places I have found that were just perfect:

- a plateau near Snowflake, AZ during a raging snowstorm.

- a shelf overlooking the surf just south of Half Moon Bay, CA.

- a thick forest near Campbell River on Vancouver Island in Canada.

- an old dry riverbed near Las Mission in Baja, Mexico.

- a ghost town near Darwin Falls not far from Stovepipe Wells, Death Valley, CA.

- behind a gas station in Concord, MA, thanks to the courtesy of the owner.

- an 8,000-acre ranch in central Nevada near Diana's Punch Bowl, a geothermal attraction. Again, thanks to the owner.

- a park full of redwoods in North Vancouver, Canada.

I could go on for a long time. After all, in four decades of travel you get an eye full, and some of it repeatedly!

Lately, I have been reading about people who just drive out into the desert in the Southwest and park for months or even years. These camps have been nicknamed Coyote Camps and if you want information about them, write: *PO 837P, Salome, AZ 85348.* There is not a lot to say about a coyote-type camp. Seniors just drive their RV's down some sandy desert road until they find a place that suits them. Most likely there is no water but the air is clean and the price is right and you have no nosy, noisy neighors. Periodically, they go into the nearest town and fill their water tanks, dump sewage and buy supplies. They spend their time rockhounding, looking for gold and other minerals, reading, or just plain old-fashioned loafing. After all, seniors deserve some time off.

I have done this many times myself and can vouch for the spiritual tranquility that comes from a desert experience. Life becomes simple and easy. Being close to nature eliminates those urban headaches. And with lots of free time, you can actually try to get in touch with who you really are!

I guess if I were to make a broad generalization about tire tramping and snowbirding, I would say this: find a remote area that appeals to you and and then find a specific hideaway spot, preferably near water. Then just squat. If you stay there long enough, you can even file a claim to the land—squatters rights are still a point of law.

America is still a largely unpopulated country. I have often driven for a hundred miles and not seen a single house or human being. That's why I claim that tire tramping has such great potential—you kick those high rent payments, live amidst fine scenery, breathe pure air, drink clear water and do exactly what you please. What could be better?

SECURITY FOR TIRE TRAMPS

A word or two about the possible dangers of staying in remote places far from so-called civilization. In all the years I have trailered and campered, I have never been approached by anyone with harmful intent. Yes, police have checked me out a few times, but that's understandable.

I know there are stories about tourists being attacked by marauders. I think that the chances of being attacked by marauders, however, is much less than if you live in a densely populated urban area.

Sometimes I carry a rifle or pistol with me, but it's mainly to do a little target shooting. My philosophy is live and let live.

COSTS

If I were a single person receiving a small Social Security check, I would certainly opt for the life on wheels. I cannot think of a lifestyle that returns so much for such a small investment. Here's a real life example:

I am driving along in one of the 11 Western states with a full tank of gas, plenty of staples like corn and beans in the galley, and a monthly income of about 300 dollars. If I drive at a reasonable speed and stop often for a few days at some fine riverside camp, there is no question that I can continue indefinitely. I do my own maintenance and repair work on the car, as I keep a complete set of tools with me. I eat simply and frugally, usually on much less than a dollar a day. My life is easy-going since there is no stress caused by money problems.

I keep a lookout for wild foods, which there are many of in all states. And oftentimes, someone gives me a fish or two.

It would be possible to hunt small game, though I no longer have the hunting instinct. I prefer something like a potassium-filled banana.

If I did run up a big bill for RV repairs, I could stop and work somewhere for a while or write an article.

Yes, from my own experience, poverty in old age need not be a reality if you keep your health and can scare up the price of an old camper or other RV. Or, as some people have done, build your own on a good strong chassis you buy from a wrecking yard. Many a good homemade RV has been built on a quality car frame after stripping off the bent metal.

If you need some special advice, just drop me a postcard in care of the publisher.

SOME ANECDOTES (OF TIRE TRAMP ADVENTURES)

Tire tramping is a great way to put some real LIVING into your life. For example, we were once traveling an isolated road in southern Oregon when I decided to stop and check the oil. I had just raised the hood when a light plane flew overhead at low altitude. I waved to the pilot as a casual gesture of friendship and was both amazed and shocked with the pilot banked steeply and made a 360 degree turn and landed on the road just behind our truck/trailer rig. Ruth and I greeted him with apologies—we thought and correctly so, that he had landed to help us; he interpreted my friendly wave as a call for assistance.

I explained and he explained. It seems that in this uninhabited part of America, people are strongly motivated to help one another. Had he crashed off in the distance, I am sure that I would have gone to HIS aid. And so it goes, a chance meeting and little adventures when you least expect them. Incidentally, we learned a lot from this pilot who steered us to the mysterious Steens Mountains just south of where we were. We were told to look for wild horses. That became our next adventure.

As we resumed our trip, we kept a sharp eye out for wildlife. A little further down the road, we saw some water cascading from a steep hillside. Desiring to see the source of the spring and knowing that wild things gather around water, we stopped and I walked towards the spring.

Suddenly I was confronted by a large herd of wild horses that seemed to appear from nowhere. Well, in the front was a huge wild stallion pawing the ground furiously and snorting to announce his possession of the herd. Not wanting to appear fearful in front of Ruth, I held my ground and the horse and I had a staring contest. Apparently, I won because the stallion and his mares and colts sauntered off into the brush. Again, an adventure that was as fascinating as any that one could have in Africa or South America.

Having researched hot springs for many years, it is fitting that Ruth and I have had many delightful and often humorous adventures with them. I recall having 6,000 gallons a minute of 72 degree water pound on my head at Ana Springs near Paisley, Oregon. If you like lots of water, try it—it's free.

Then there's another gusher near Alamo, NV called Crystal Springs. An equal amount pours forth from a rocky fissure.

Once in Oregon, I rushed to jump in a hot pool and tossed my underwear in first. Ruth advised caution, noting the steam rising from the huge pool. And indeed, upon checking the water with a quickly-scalded finger, I found it close to the boiling point. Had I leaped in as I intended, I would have become a good imitation of a boiled lobster. Thanks again Ruth.

In Mississippi, we watched sugar cane being crushed in donkey-powered mill. The freshly made syrup was delicious on our pancakes. In South Carolina, we played a little tag with a giant alligator while in New Hampshire we ate fresh, crisp apples right from the tree. In Vancouver, we visited the EXPO 86 free because we used our press passes. In Lillooet, a hundred miles north, we feasted on freshly baked bread from a commune of young people who live on the banks of the mighty Fraser River. In Mexico, we encountered nopales (cactus) gatherers in a remote canyon and learned how these natives survive on foods they find. In Europe, we dined like royalty at Ruth's cousin's castle in Stainach, Austria. In Yugoslavia we explored the 2,000-year-old walled city of Dubrovnik. And so it goes in pictures, writing and memories.

Yes, travel is wonderful and tire tramping is its best manifestation. You can expect the unexpected every moment. Seldom is there disappointment. To paraphrase the song, *don't sit at home in your room, come to see the wonderful sights of the world as a tire tramper and live!*

CHAPTER SIX
PRIVACY

"I shall be as secret as the grave."
— *William Shakespeare*

OVERVIEW

My personal concept of privacy is COMPLETE privacy. That means no intrusion on your vision, hearing, body, personal possessions, domicile, car, boat, airplane and bank account. Let me give you an example of invasion of privacy and what can be done about it:

A few months ago I was busy writing an article for a boating magazine. The writing, which required a great deal of concentration, was suddenly interrupted by the irritating sounds of a motorcycle. It seems that two boys were riding racing motorcycles on a hillside behind the mobile home park where I was working. The land was owned by a family that lived in the park, so I went over to talk with them. To no avail; they said that the kids weren't really hurting anyone and that they would go right on racing.

Over my dead body.

I canvassed the park and found that many people were as annoyed as I. So I called the sheriff to report a public nuisance. He interviewed the head of the family and issued a citation to appear in court. To date, there has been no more of that kind of noise.

I used the power of the law and support from my neighbors to prevent a totally unwanted invasion of our ears. Had the law not supported us, I would have filed a civil suit claiming damages—loss of income, health hazards due to unreasonable noise and so forth. I would have never given up, as the noise was intolerable.

There is no reason to give up if you are dedicated to the elimination of the problem.

Sometimes it may not be easy to confront the noise issue. Many people, especially those who are quite old, are often fearful of reprisal and will back off and just tolerate the annoyance. If you are one of this group, please write me in care of the publisher of this book, as I have some unique and creative ways to silence noisy people.

Privacy, to the degree you wish, is possible. Here are some practical ways of achieving it:

VISUAL PRIVACY

There are a few good things on television, very few, and a lot of unpleasant spots, like commercials for deodorant. Here's a way of eliminating the sound without leaving your chair. As far as the picture is concerned, just close your eyes. For the sound part, just install a simple switch that will cancel the sound from the speaker.

I have a friend who lives full-time in a travel trailer. To prevent anyone from spying on him, he simply put aluminum foil on his windows. The windows can be opened and he can look out, but when he wants visual privacy, he shuts them and opens a roof vent for air.

Ruth, too, likes her privacy, so we recently planted a fast-growing hedge to shield the mobile home from the neighbors. Also, she painted the front sliding glass doors with an opaque paint. Result? No more dirty looks from the grump across the way.

Visual privacy extends to such media as newspapers and magazines. Don't be leary of cancelling any subscriptions you're not happy with. And do subscribe to some truthful newsletters.

SOUND PRIVACY

As we grow older, we seem to lose our tolerance for unwanted, unpleasant sounds. Rock music sounds great to a person of 16, but when you're 66 it may sound satanic. The international organization that monitors sound says that sound will double in level and scope by the year 2000. So it does not look good for those who hate unwelcome noise.

In the overview, I discussed a problem that I had in my own neighborhood and the solution to it. Admittedly, this was a simple case easily solved with the intervention of the law. But what can one do about noise that persists, such as traffic noise outside your window? As I see it, you have several options:

1. You can move somewhere else, to the country perhaps, but remember, there are lots of small children, motorcycles and chainsaws in the country. You could be going from the proverbial frying pan right into the flames.

2. You can soundproof your rooms, or the one room that you most often use. This can be done by using some of the new kinds of sound absorbent materials. Heavy drapes and rugs will also dampen incoming sounds.

3. You can mask the noise with television or radio, or other sources of more pleasant noise. You can use earphones.

There is a unit that creates "white noise"—pleasant sounds like the surf or wind. Also, there are audio cassette tapes which are actual recordings of real wind and water in motion. Then beyond these are tapes of the New Age music which is made by synthesizers and is often ethereally beautiful.

4. You can soundproof yourself by using some of the new plastic earstops that give almost complete protection. Incidentally, I have often wondered why we don't have the equivalent of eyelids for our ears! It must be so that we can hear sounds of danger, even when we're asleep.

5. All of the above.

Noise can eventually cause your nervous system to deteriorate and rebel. Noise is often the cause of serious illness. If you have been jumpy lately and out of sorts, check the noise level of your environment; if high, do something about it before you suffer physical and psychic damage.

What if the sound sources are from the next apartment or the people who live above you? What then? The first thing to do is obvious; ask them politely to turn down their radio or TV or play their tuba more quietly. If they comply, good. If not, see that the landlord intercedes in your behalf. Often a landlord will defend a good tenant against the noisy ones, especially knowing how hard it is to find quiet tenants. If the noise still persists, ask the police to help you. They are often sympathetic to older folks and may be just the right intimidation that you need to defend you against nervous breakdown caused by noise.

Now if that doesn't work, you might try a little counterattack, like pounding on your ceiling or wall with a big chunk of 4 x 4. Or, rent a bass drum and strike it every time their radio or TV is too loud. If that doesn't do the trick, then buy a large, used speaker and attach it to the surface that divides your place from theirs. I did this in Manhattan Beach, CA when the tenant upstairs refused to turn down his ball game. I pumped Bach, Brahms and especially Mahler and Stravinsky up and into his floor for hours. He got the message and the ball games ceased.

There are audio signal generators that you can buy from electronic stores. These develop sound frequencies ranging from very low to very high. You can hook them to your speakers, turn up the volume and give your noisy neighbors a shot of 16,000 hz while you go shopping. When you come back, I think you'll find your place quiet. After all, the continuous shriek of high frequency sound is more than almost anyone can handle. You can also set the signal generator to low levels; this has the effect of grating on people's nerves without their even knowing it—tit for tat.

There are still other ways of silencing noisy neighbors that I will be happy to supply to the noise-tortured. You see, I have often suffered from severe invasion of my privacy where noise is concerned and sympathize greatly with those who suffer likewise.

PERSONAL PRIVACY

This has been a problem for many seniors living in urban areas and sometimes in rural regions. Mugging and assault is common in large cities such as New York and Los Angeles. My own solution has been simple and direct; I carry a loaded, cocked automatic pistol in my coat pocket and have my hand on the grip and trigger when I am in a dangerous area. I don't have to take it out of my pocket to shoot. I think that muggers must sense this is the case, as I have never been assaulted. My reason for this is that if my wife were attacked due to my fear of carrying a gun, I would never forgive myself. She is such a lovely lady that the thought of someone harming her is beyond my comprehension. Thus, the finger-on-the-trigger solution.

While this may not be your way of handling urban violence, it is mine and I intend to continue with this precaution. You see, even the police themselves will tell you that they cannot prevent crime—they can only take over after it has been committed. I have had policemen tell me that it is intelligent to be your own policeman in this era of violence and rampant crime.

If a gun bothers you, there are other defensive weapons including stun guns and sprays. The new electronic stunning weapons will not kill, but they will lay out an attacker as flat as a pancake in milliseconds. They're not lethal and not expensive. You just touch an attacker with the tip and he is suddenly out of your picture completely. The reason for this is that the voltage is high enough to momentarily paralyze the nervous system. He falls to the ground in a daze while you make a safe getaway. After 15 minutes or so, he is okay again, but so are you! Ask any policeman to tell you about stun guns. They know all about them. If you can't get the information, write to me in care of the publisher and I will be happy to send you the sources of these defensive tools. You can often buy plans to make your own from ads in magazines like *Popular Science*.

Less aggressive are the sprays like mace and cayenne pepper. Personally, I would rather put my trust in something a little more authoritative.

When you're at home, you need not open the door to anyone, even the police, unless they have a search warrant. Also, you can install a stout dead bolt that will keep a battering ram busy while you make your getaway or get your shotgun. So there's no reason to be assaulted or have your home invaded. Just ask through the door who it is or install one of those fish-eye peepholes in the door at eye level. I have friends who have a good system of maintaining privacy at night. They just don't answer the telephone or the door for anyone, even so-called authorities or utility personnel. No one can legally come into your home unless they are police with a signed search warrant. And even then, you can ask for your attorney to be present while a search is made.

If you are law-abiding, it is extremely unlikely that a search warrant will ever be issued for you. In all other cases, DON'T OPEN THE DOOR!

PERSONAL POSSESSIONS

It is getting harder all the time to keep your goods from being stolen and used to buy drugs. Everything and everybody is vulnerable. Of course, you can put alarms on your car, boats and airplane, but don't expect them to be 100 percent effective in protecting against theft. A thief can buy or make a device that will open a car door in seconds. Then he can hot wire your ignition and be off in few more seconds.

Of course, you can have your car or other important items insured. Other than elaborating on fancier alarm systems which can even be deactivated by a clever and experienced thief, it is caution and astuteness that protect your treasures.

I do have a creative solution to the theft problem which I call "grungification." This means that you make whatever you own so ugly or undesirable that no thief will take it. I learned this method after I had lost three motorcycles to thieves. Now I leave my totally ugly 90 cc motorcycle anywhere with impunity because it is so UGLY that no one will even come near it, much less steal it.

Now you may not want to make your possessions this ugly, but you can let it go unwashed, leave the dings unrepaired and generally let it go grungy so that a thief will select a more presentable unit for his target.

MONETARY PRIVACY

This subject has been well documented by many other writers.

If you don't find them in your local library, write to me in care of the publisher and I will help you locate them.

About 12 years ago, I wrote a book called *Privacy*; it is still on sale. If you would like a copy, write me in care of the publisher and I will send information on how to obtain it.

IN CONCLUSION

The desire for privacy is as avid as the efforts made by some unpleasant people to eliminate it through new methods of electronic spying. Personally, I believe that you can have as much privacy as you want. That's because I have met and made friends with a number of people who enjoy complete privacy in their daily lives and are never hassled by anyone.

As I often quote, "take from life what you wish, but be willing to pay for it."

If you want complete privacy, you can have it if you are willing to make the effort.

CHAPTER SEVEN
SENIOR FUN

WILD IDEAS

*"You think too much. You need a little madness.
What you have to do is cut the rope to be free."*

— *Nikos Kazantzakis, Zorba the Greek*

Most of us have been conditioned to live conventional, prosaic, regimented lives within the boundaries of establishment propriety. But notice the people who are having the most fun out of life...they are the ones who have discarded linear thinking. I know that George Burns never has a middle-class thought nor does Steve Martin disbelieve that his cat robs his mailbox and cashes his checks to buy expensive cat toys.

During WWII, a friend of mine spent the winter in the Hurtgen forest where Germans skulked around at night stabbing the GI's in their sleeping bags. To preserve his sanity, my friend decided that although the Germans could kill them, they couldn't, under the Geneva convention, eat them.

"Kill us but you can't legally eat us," was the war cry of the beleagured infantry; this absurd proposition allowed many of our soldiers to have a much-needed chuckle.

In the Pacific, the sailor's war cry was,

"Golden Gate in '48", implying that at least the war would be over at some determinate time rather than drag on, like Vietnam did, for many years.

My own war cry is:

DON'T GET OLD, GET BOLD!

Why not, for example, take up car racing (Paul Newman did) or an acting career, or produce TV sitcoms which deal with real people rather than cardboard characters? Indeed, why not?

Even if you don't have the money, you can always find someone with the funding. All you need is the enthusiasm. After all, I have been able to find backers for some 20 books. If I can do it, you can do it.

Here, then, are some ideas, wild and otherwise, which can lead to putting some fun back into your life.

SENIOR ESCAPE (INTRODUCTION)

Many of us are seemingly trapped in impossible situations. For example, we are committed to a nursing or convalescent home or otherwise robbed of our independence and privacy. I recall how several old men trekked from Los Angeles to a desert region around Lone Pine, CA and established a community in a complex of old Indian caves. They may have been living a primitive life, but at least they were their own bosses. At one point, a nurse from Lone Pine, who had been caring for them, was accused of playing doctor. The old men rallied to her defense in a rousing display of old Western self-reliance and protectionism. The nurse continued to practice.

What follows is what I call SENIOR SCENARIOS, or fantasies based on true adventures, showing how we can escape from captivity and be our own men and women.

BREAKOUT! TEN AGAINST SHADY ACRES NURSING HOME

David Clark, 74, decides that he has had enough of plastic bread and rubber chickens and the stultifying routine of a nursing home. He decides that the best place to escape to is a hot spring where he can have fun in the warm water with his swinging friends. He checks out a book from the local library, *Great Hot Springs of the West*, and makes a survey of possibilities. It seems that there is an abandoned hot spring in a remote area of southeast Oregon. By using a PO box, he is able to correspond with people living near the springs and learns that it is available for restoration through the *Bureau of Land Management*.

Having once been a prisoner of war in a German "stalag" after parachuting from a stricken B-17, he knows the importance of secrecy in any escape plot. So, using the same techniques that he learned in WWII, he carefully selects his co-conspirators; Bill, Amy and Ruth. Two couples seem to be the ideal mix for an escape plot.

Over a period of several months, the foursome become pack rats, saving food and clothing in hidden corners of the nursing home. They also save up their pitiful allowances until they have enough money to buy an old station wagon with a mattress in the back.

The director of Shady Acres, Tom O'Money, suspects a plot to escape, but he is so busy adding up the profits derived from serving junk food that he has no time to make a facility shakedown or question the residents.

The plotters pick a day in early fall when the weather is cool and moon is crescent. Dave secretly fills the gas tank and checks the oil, and around midnight, the group sneaks out of their rooms. Just as they are about to leave, a night nurse spots them them shouts:

"Halt, or you get it with the hypo needle."

In a thrilling chase, the foursome beat the nurse to the wagon and off they go into the night.

The rest of the story is almost routine. The group builds up the ruins of the old broken down hot springs health resort and begins to rent out rooms to travelers. Soon the hot springs is alive with activity; growing vegetables in a geothermal greenhouse, giving massages in the various warm pools, making whole grain breads in the restored hotel kitchen, and selling them to an ever-growing number of delighted tourists who learn of the place by word of mouth.

Since the whole venture is a joint effort of Dave's group and BLM on a long-term, dollar-a-year lease arrangement, there are no payments. The group uses its income to continuously improve the place and to help other senior groups find hot springs of their own.

Fanciful? Far out? Not really. This type of operation has been done by seniors in many areas. For example, I just visited a senior co-op on the river in Santa Rosa, CA. Here, two resolute seniors raised some seed money, bought land and built a wonderful senior housing co-op which is always full. And if you want to see a restored hot springs, take a look at Harbin or Wilbur, both are in the Clear Lake region of north central California.

Just answer these questions:

1. Can you find a copy of *Great Hot Springs of the West?* If not, write me in care of the publisher.

2. Can you get three friends together and buy and old station wagon?

3. Can you negotiate the lease-option of a restorable hot springs?

4. Can you pound nails?

If you can answer yes to those questions, then there is no question that you can do the same as Dave's group. If you need any help finding a hot springs, write me and I will be delighted to help you. It just so happens that I know where there are a few available!

THE KAYSITE KAPER

Cecile and Polly are ex-waves of WWII in their mid-60's. They share a rather dingy room in an old hotel in the San Francisco Mission district. Life on two small Social Security checks is rather grim—the same plain food, the tattered clothes, the view of an air shaft out the one window, and the dangers of muggers jostling each other for space on the litter-strewn streets below.

"Hey," said Cecile, "life wasn't supposed to turn out this way, was it?"

"No way," replied Pol, "but what can we do about it?"

Cece holds up an article:

"What's so hard about finding an old boat and putting on this Kaysite stuff. Then we could live on it like we did when we were in the Navy," Cece said.

CHAPTER SEVEN

"Hey, I'm still game for anything," replied Pol with some of her old 1944 enthusiasm. " Any place would be better than spending another night in this noisy dump."

So the two women took a bus to San Pablo and hitched the last few miles to a familiar marina. They located an old WWII landing craft that they first spotted on a picnic outing.

They asked around the marina and learned that no one wanted the landing craft so it became theirs by default.

Cece and Polly studied the Kaysite process, looked at some boats that had been treated, and then, just for fun, got in touch with the inventor. He volunteered to help them.

With the help of other friends, they straightened up the old landing craft, cleaned it inside and out, and then nailed on the wire. For Kaysite Day they enlisted the help of some seniors who lived on boats at the marina and of course, the inventor himself.

It was like an old-fashioned barn-raising. With lots of sandwiches and drinks, the special Kaysite plaster just flew on the old hull. To the delight of all who worked on it, the job was finished on that one day. Several old men who had watched with skepticism declared that they were going to do the same thing to some other old boats that were just lying around.

"Derelicts for the derelicts" is the way they phrased it.

With the help of the marina tractor and some log roller, the ex-Waves launched their newly-Kaysited boat. As it hit the salt water again, they christened it "Renaissance" with a bottle of Vichy water.

They moved onto the boat with all of their pitiful possessions and soon the boat became the center of activity at the San Pablo marina where they berthed it (for far less than the rent they were paying on the dingy room).

Before long, several other seniors had Kaysited old boats and soon there were enough to create a new floating village in the Delta region near a lush, almost tropical island. A total of seven boats formed the waterborne commune. They shared their income, had wonderful parties, fished all day and slept in the serene silence of the night.

As Cece once said to Polly after they had enjoyed their new floating lifestyle, "This is the only way to float!"

My friend, Vernon Johnson, once said that we have to give ourselves permission to do anything. So give yourself permission to think in unconventional, non-linear terms and generate a life that makes you happy. As Vernon Howard, another astute philosopher commented, "Anytime you want, you can stop living the life that makes you miserable and start living the life that makes you happy."

To help you along, drop me a line and I'll send you a list of places where you can find derelict boats. Also, check out the *Freedom Afloat* chapter for more information on living on the water.

SENIOR EXCITEMENT

It's a few seconds before the 8 p.m. *Fantasy on Ice* show at the Hacienda Hotel and Casino in Las Vegas, Nevada. I am backstage with the entire cast as they are about to go on for the 1,892 time. Their faces, for the most part, are blank, though a few smile rather wanly at each other. As the music rises and the curtain parts, their expressions change to artificial smiles; before a packed house, they all skate out on the relatively small patch of ice. The opening number goes well, as it should when you consider that most of these performers have been doing this and similar acts since they were small children.

To me it is tremendously exciting—seeing a backstage view of professional skater/dancers—the best Vegas can buy. But to the cast, it is just Performance Number One Thousand Eight Hundred and Ninety-Two.

I think my point is clear; what may be exciting to one person may be total blah to to another. When you fly to London or Paris, the pilots are wondering how to fill all those long hours in the air while your little heart is beating with a combination of high altitude willies and the anticipation of a tour of Picadilly and the Champs d'Elysee. The key element is, of course, newness.

Excitement, travel, people, shows, new scenes, new clothes, new everything are what can be the best medicine for many of us older people. Let me give you an example:

About four years ago, I received a call from NBC's *People are Talking* show in Baltimore, Maryland. They wanted me to fly back to talk to their audience of 18,000,000 people about one of my books. That meant that my wife and I would take off from San Jose one morning, appear in Boston the next, Baltimore the next and Detroit the next—three shows in three days in three different cities! Thousands of miles at 550 miles per hour, split second timing to make connections, and then the ultimate—appearing LIVE, no taping, before an audience larger than Mark Twain or Jack London ever appeared before. What an opportunity! What excitement!

I can tell you that my nerve endings were tingling as though 4,000 volts at ten amps were coursing through them. As the day of our departure approached, the butterflies flew higher and faster. Then, almost before I knew it, I was on in Boston. The show went fine, and I was relieved when it was over. One down and two to go.

We flew on to Baltimore over the top of a giant thunderstorm and landed safely. We had a few hours of calm time in our luxurious suite, paid for, of course, by NBC. Then it was up against the wall and my excitement grew as I walked from the green room (a preparation room that is aptly named) to the seat of honor next to the two hosts. The studio held about 100 people in the live audience; there were five giant TV cameras pointed at me and the floor was full of directors, cue people and stage crew. The red light went on and I was asked how I came to write the book.

Well, dear readers, at first the overwhelming aspects of that appearance almost froze my vocal apparatus. But I just started talking anyway and as I did, my courage and self-confidence grew. You have to remember that this was the same man who couldn't bring himself to speak in class, and when called upon for a speech in college, he became a total zombie! But somehow, there was enough energy flowing that day in addition to my dedication to my work—all of this gave me what I needed to make what Ruth calls to this day, "my best presentation."

NOTE: The year that all this happened is a blank except for those three days in the east doing the TV shows. Now those days stand out like lightning flashes in a dark sky.

While not everyone has the opportunity to appear on TV and get a resultant charge, we can all search for excitement in other ways. Here are some suggestions for anyone who has been saying that life is a bore, a drag, a meaningless charade that begins and ends with pain:

1. Go to the nearest hospital with an armful of books and read to the patients, especially the dying children. They are smarter than you think, know they are going and you can help make the transition a little easier. Exciting? Rewarding? Try it for a new view of your own life and times.

2. Ask permission of the warden to visit prisoners in either county or state prison. There are organizations like *Friends Outside* which make this possible. Take books and magazines or something good to eat. You can get hooked on the excitement of helping the less fortunate.

3. Collect castoffs and have a charity bazaar in your neighborhood. Then use the money to help the homeless in America or single mothers or the mentally disturbed who live on the streets—the list is endless in this, the richest of all countries. You'll find a lot of excitement when you help house a homeless person or give some comfort to a single mother and her children. And the excitement will be of a new and different variety, one that will stimulate your best intentions into further action.

4. Go into a retirement home and sit with the 90- and 100-year-olds—the really old people. Help comfort their last days, months or years. I recall taking my two daughters into General Hospital in Santa Barbara, CA and playing music for the oldest people there. What broke me up was that they wouldn't let go of my daughters' hands.

5. Gather up broken toys and repair them for poor kids at Christmas. Fix bikes for kids who have none. Repair clothing for the needy.

I am sure you get the idea—there is great excitement and much reward in helping others. Just read Matthew 10:8 for instructions.

NOTE: I have learned a lot about life by observing it in Las Vegas casinos. I could see that people really wanted to LOSE their money, perhaps a form of expiating old guilts. No sooner would someone become a big winner than they would double and triple their bets and lose it all back. It is no wonder that there are lines of the destitute waiting for a free meal on N. Las Vegas Boulevard each noontime.

I learned also that the so-called glamour of Vegas is on just one side of the curtain. Thanks to my late friend, Fred Blue, at the Hacienda, I was able to watch more than 40 performances of *Fantasy on Ice* and become an honorary member of the cast. The experience taught me that to be a successful performer requires a lot more than just motor skills; it requires an ability to do the same thing over and over until you don't think you can do it again—then you do it anyway!

I recall that Susan Lease, a featured skater, once told me that a few minutes before curtain time she told her partner that she just couldn't go on. She had HAD IT! There was no way that she could do that complex and dangerous performance of spins and twirls one more time.

However, her partner gave her a pep talk that not only changed her mind that time, but for all time.

The point is clear: what often appears to be a romantic, glamorous lifestyle is really taxing and deadening and repetitive. Imagine having to present the same comic spiel at eight and 11 p.m. every night but Monday for years on end!

SUMMARY

Much of life is often routine and boring, but it really doesn't have to be. I know that in my own experience, when life gets a little dull, I go pull the tail of the tiger or take a trip or make some new friends, visit a jail or hospital, listen to music or write a book.

From a hillside in Austria, Bill Kaysing waves encouragement to extend your experience

CHAPTER EIGHT
SENIOR PHILOSOPHY

PROLOGUE

The Seneca Indians have a four-question test to see if one is in harmony with the earth.

1. Are you happy doing what you are doing?

2. Is what you are doing adding to the confusion?

3. What are you doing to further peace and contentment?

4. How will you be remembered after you are gone—in absence or in death?

These questions, the Seneca say, can help anyone evaluate their actions in a way that can bring them into greater harmony with the Earth Mother. They are an effective tool to teach anyone to take responsibility for their own actions and happiness.

The Seneca go on to say that:

- Self-knowledge is the need.

- Self-understanding was the desire.

- Self-discipline was the way.

- Self-realization was the goal.

It is apparent that we have much to learn from people who live close to nature.

THE WAY

"We have it in our power to begin the world again."
— *Thomas Paine, Common Sense, 1776*

The Chinese, with more than 80 centuries of history, have evolved a system for viewing the world that transcends most Western thinking. For example, Lao T'su, who lived before Christ, gently discussed the Tao (pronounced dow). The Tao may be roughly translated as "the way" or a method of living one's life that makes peace, tranquility and understanding an integral part of the daily experience.

What is so interesting is how this philosophy relates to many other modes of living, such as Zen Buddhism or segments of the Hindu religion. Or, drawing from people living in our own country, we might say the Amish and Mennonites have found "the way."

A few years ago, Ruth and I made a cross-country trip, spending some time in Pennsylvania. Here we enjoyed a dinner at an Amish farm restaurant. The people we saw seemed to be so "together," as the present use of the term denotes, that I began a study of this religious sect that pays no social security, fights in no wars and generally has divorced itself from the air-conditioned nightmare so prevalent in our 20th-century American culture.

If the Amish can do it—live self-sufficiently, quietly and productively—then anyone can, especially seniors who have developed an appreciation for the serene lifestyle.

Any or all of these elements can be adapted to life in the U.S., in any area, by any seniors, or, for that matter, Americans of any age. You can give up processed foods for food you grow yourself (see the chapter on *Gardening*). This is possible, even if you have a small space, by using containers. You can eliminate automobiles, since bikes and walking are a more healthful way of getting about. You can enjoy the simple pleasures of life—reading, walking, conversing, enjoying the little events of the day. You can live quietly and with minimal stress as the Amish do. And, you can choose this way of life anytime you wish. Again, if they can do it here in the U.S., you, too, can do it.

INDIAN PHILOSOPHY

For many years I have observed how Indians live. True, many have taken to the ways of white men and drink firewater to their detriment. However, there are countless Indians— Navaho, Hopi, Apache, Paiute, Nez Perce and others who live by the rules of the "old ones." You won't find these enlightened people racing back and forth on a crowded freeway. Instead, they follow the slow, steady rhythms of the seasons. They grow their blue corn, squash and tomatoes, dote on fry bread and gather at the reservation store to converse in quiet tones. What I have always admired about rural Indians is their closeness to nature. Although they might own a pick-up, they still live in such structures as round hogans or picturesque and practical pueblos.

Once, my otherwise faithful old GMC burned out a rear axle bearing south of Isleta in New Mexico. We were compelled to stay there for three days until a new bearing could be found and installed. I was able to make friends with an Isleta Indian family and found them to be calm, peaceful, friendly and helpful. They permitted us to park on their land while the truck was fixed. They invited us to enter their inner village which tourists normally do not visit. Here we saw their clay ovens and smelled the aroma of freshly-baked bread. As we observed them, it became clear that here was a sub-culture close to the electronic research labs of Albuquerque, but eons away from them in the way of life.

I plan to return to Isleta and learn more about how Indians really live. They can teach both seniors and young Americans much about the real values of life.

ARTISTS AND WRITERS

In Emeryville, a suburb of bustling, industrial Oakland, there is a growing colony of creative people who live in restored factories and warehouses. Here they pursue their artistic goals largely free of the frenetic pace of competitive society. Here again is a sub-culture of America that anyone can emulate almost at will. As seniors, a percentage of us have incomes which permit a certain degree of freedom. We can, if we wish, join a colony of avant-garde men and women and learn from them, even becoming artists and writers ourselves! Certainly, a goal of self-fulfillment is one of the worthiest, as the Seneca Indians pointed out. And best of all, it is a proven fact that it is never too late. There are many examples, including the most famous—Grandma Moses taking up painting at 70 and becoming world famous from then on.

MUSICIANS

Ruth's father was conductor of the L.A. Civic Light Opera for many years. He pursued a musical career almost into his 90's. Arthur Kay, like many musically-inclined people, is typical of a man who was transformed by his profession. Notice how long symphony conductors live. It's no accident that they, as a professional class, enjoy not only a long life but a happy one at that! Every day is a delight when you are involved in music and other creative activities. Music, especially, as a way of life, can fulfill many of the longings of the human soul whether it be pursued full or part-time. If there are some big holes in your life, latch on to a musical instrument and have at it. It's never too late and you don't have to attempt something difficult. That's why I play the harmonica. Fits neatly into the back pocket of my Levi's.

HORSE PEOPLE

I have noticed that people who live around animals retain their health and *joie de vivre* much longer than their contemporaries. I have a friend in Santa Barbara, a Lebanese gentleman, Skip Shaloob, who retains the elasticity and musculature of a man in his thirties. Pushing 70, Skip works with horses every day of his life and seemingly gains their strength and serenity by this close association. Another friend, Linda Tellington-Jones, heals the psychic ills of horses through a system of Feldenkries massage adapted to the needs of horses. She, too, has an agelessness about her and serenity plus.

BOAT, AIRPLANE and CAR PEOPLE

Have you noticed that people who enjoy living on boats, flying in planes or driving high tech cars seem to retain their youthful enthusiasms. One of my friends, Bill Shaw, is 57 and still dotes on tooling his fast racer around the big car tracks. This relates back to our original premise—the Tao or Way in which what we do is what we are, or to put it in the formal Zen,

To be is to do and to do is to be.

This then is the key to a productive and rewarding senior lifestyle. I know that it is true in my own life. Writing about things that will be helpful to others is a most fulfilling and rewarding occupation, far beyond the considerations of monetary compensation. I am doing what I apparently was born to do; the result is a rare inner joy that approaches pure bliss on more than one occasion. Writing this ending is one of them.

Peace.

CHAPTER NINE
GARDENING

GROW YOUR OWN (PROLOGUE)

When I first wrote this chapter, I planned to present some standard data from the *National Garden Bureau*.

Then it occurred to me that this kind of information was available in abundance in any library. Also, most seniors have had some experience with growing their own foods, especially those who were poor during the Great Depression. So what I have decided to do is to tell you about all of the unique and unusual methods of gardening that I have either tried myself or encountered in my travels. The emphasis is on gardening for survival—growing good food for your kitchen with the least amount of labor—just the way nature does.

For years, I would ride my motorcycle in the back country of Santa Barbara and in the spring, the wild oats would tower over my head. No one planted them, no one weeded or cultivated or watered them, yet these wild oats were giants. Why?

Well, it appeared that nature had provided everything the plants needed to be vigorous and healthy; a good soil with lots of rotting mulch, plenty of water in the winter and spring rains, lots of sunshine and freedom from harmful pests. Result?

Monster plants that, incidentally, were the staple food of the Chumash Indians who once populated this fair land.

Here's how to pull off the wild oats caper in several combinations.

CUSTOM SOIL

There are some books available on custom soil, but here's a brief outline—sufficient information to get you started.

Most soil lacks one or more of the essentials for a successful garden. It's either too hard and clay-like or it is so sandy it cannot hold water. Further, it could lack the essential nutrients for sturdy plant growth.

So, the answer is, make your own, custom soil. You can start with anything you have—clay, loam, sand or just plain old back yard dirt. Dig some up and put it into a pile. Now add whatever seems to be missing. If it is too hard to work, add some sand—the kind builders use is fine as long as it is clean. You can often get it at a building site where it may be left over from a construction project. Or, you can find sand along river banks.

If the soil is too sandy and porous, add some clay-type soil to give it more water-holding power.

Next, add compost which is nothing more than garden trimmings—grass, leaves and kitchen waste that has been allowed to rot in a heap or container.

I am a strong believer in natural rather than manufactured fertilizers, and since there is so much organic waste around to be had for free, I personally see no reason why anyone would have to go to the garden store and pay money for chemical additives.

Now that you have all the ingredients for a custom soil, mix them well and shovel the result into a raised bed. This can be a rectangle of cement blocks or old boards. It can even be a bed with walls made of regular dirt. Whatever you use, be sure to get the custom soil up and away from existing soil so that you won't have to contend with all the negative elements than can be inhabiting the area you're working. If you lay down a layer of chicken wire of about ½ inch mesh underneath your custom soil, you won't have any gopher problems.

Now that you have a fine, loose bed of healthy soil, you merely drop in the desired seeds and water. Presto, Mother Nature takes over and you should soon be eating crisp lettuce, firm, flavorful tomatoes and some fine dark green chard. Personally, I grow the easy vegetables like those just mentioned. If you have more time for gardening than I do, then you can grow a great variety and provide just about everything you need for your table.

It's a known fact that only a small space is needed to grow all that one person needs—even a half dozen 10 x 2 foot raised beds can produce a monumental amount of food. Try succession gardening wherein you plant a seed for every plant you harvest. Also, practice intensive gardening with plants cheek to jowl on every square inch. And don't forget the benefits of drip irrigation—the Israelis upped their tomato production by a substantial percentage with this method. All you need is a soaker hose. You can make one out of an old hose by just punching or drilling holes in it and plugging the open end.

Gardening is really a subjective art—the more you practice it, the better you will be.

ODDS AND ENDS

Here are some ideas that I have gleaned from a lifetime of being an avid spectator of successful gardens.

One dentist I knew in Santa Barbara grew fabulous vegetables and small fruits by mulching his raised beds with seaweed. As it slowly rotted, it provided all the trace minerals that his giant strawberries and squash needed. Never saw such huge plants.

Another friend in Santa Barbara, Vernon Johnson, told me about a system he has used. Fill a five-gallon container with leaves, grass or and organic material. Press it down so it is really full. Now add water to nearly overflowing. Then sprinkle on a layer or dirt—almost any kind will do since the plants will only use it for support. Add seeds, water and jump back. Periodically, add a five percent solution of fermented urine (your own is fine) and plain water to the water in the container.

What happens is this: the plants germinate and send their roots down into the water where the leaves are slowly rotting. All the nutrients that a plant needs are in the solution, thus making it easy for the plant to obtain what it needs to create a flourishing growth. The fermented urine is a bonus since it contains free nitrogen.

From what I have seen of Vernon's results, this system is the best invention since popcorn. Try it soon and you'll be able to grow everything you need in a battery of discarded containers scattered about your premises.

Incidentally, container-growing is what many pot farmers have turned to in the woods of northern California. They plant seeds in a five gallon bucket; as the Indian Hemp grows they move it around to get the best sun and avoid detection.

"I have often thought that if heaven had given me a choice of my position and calling it would have been a rich spot of earth, well-watered, and near a good market for the productions of a garden. No occupation is so delightful to me as the culture of the earth."

— *Thomas Jefferson*

Jefferson was right, as usual, so let's pursue this thought with a little preliminary story. Along old Highway 99 in Albany, Oregon is the Nichols Nursery founded many years ago by the venerable agronomist whose name it bears. From a small start, he and his family built a very prosperous business growing plants and selling seeds and bulbs. The enterprise is still there and you are urged to go see it whenever you are in a traveling mood.

It seems that he did what any of us can do—he grew a variety of vegetables and small fruits along with flowers and herbs and some unusual and exotic foreign plants. He then printed up a catalogue of his offerings and advertised in various appropriate magazines. His catalogue was simple; a mimeographed production that was as homely as it was honest. His customers loved his practical advice and the business grew. Today, Nichols Nursery, deservedly, is one of the major enterprises in Albany. And although Mr. Nichols has gone to his reward, the tradition of honesty and integrity goes on.

I suggest you write for the *Nichols Nursery Catalogue* and see what marvelous ideas they offer for making an income from plants you grow in your own garden. The address is *Nichols Nursery, 1190 Old Salem Rd NE, Albany, Oregon.*

Here's a typical suggestion from the catalogue: you buy some of their giant garlic cloves. Plant and replant, while gradually increasing your operation. When you have a goodly surplus, you can sell to gourmet restaurants in your region or offer them by mail. There is, at present, a much greater demand for giant garlic than a supply and the price is, of this writing, around four dollars a pound.

Another of Nichol's ideas involves the growing of colorful Indian corn—the ears that sport blue, green, red and purple seeds and attract interior decorators like fishing boats attract seagulls. It is as easy to grow as ordinary corn and brings premium prices. Along with it you could grow those fantastic ornamental gourds.

Nichols also suggests a roadside stand if your output warrants one. Or, you can sell you own salad makings along with a good brand of maple syrup, nuts in the shell, hickory chips for barbecuing, handicrafts from friends and neighbors, seasonal horticulture like holly, mistletoe and wreaths, and of course, seeds, booklets and other garden-related items.

Recently, I discovered a most prosperous home business in the Watsonville, CA area. A couple are growing baby vegetables for gourmet restaurants on just a few acres of land. The work is minimal, the rewards are great. I am sure that the Nichols people have something relevant to say about that senior-style enterprise. I know for certain that they can supply the right seeds and directions.

SUMMARY AND CONCLUSIONS

Growing your own food makes good sense and I hope that the above suggestions work for you. If you have any questions or suggestions, write me in care of the publisher. I'll be happy to correspond with readers.

CHAPTER TEN
PLACES

PROLOGUE

I have never found a place where I would like to spend ALL of my time. Sure, there are some great spots on this planet but as far, none of them have had ALL that provides for everything I need. The one failing of every place is that sooner or later I grow tired of it, boredom takes over.

Once in lovely Lake Tahoe a man said, "Just how much of paradise can you stand?"

This was a sage observation and has been confirmed many times in the years following. A woman from Miami who I once hired as a yacht salesperson told me, "How many times can you take a 60-foot Chris Craft to Nassau and then jet back?"

Same situation, proving that every place is subject to burnout. Keats said it best, "Ever let the fancy roam, pleasure never is at home."

It is clear that you and I will probably never find our completely ideal place because it does not exist in terms of human usage.

However, there ARE many places that are delightful and will reward visitors or residents with many wonderful days. I have had the good fortune to have lived in many places that are considered resorts or vacation destinations. These would include Miramar Beach in Montecito, California, Santa Cruz in the Golden State, often my semi-permanent hangout, Bellevue in Washington, Las Vegas and many other places, mostly in the 11 Western states.

I've also lived aboard boats in San Francisco bay and the fascinating Mark Twain country of the California Delta. I've lived, too, along the roads of America in all sorts of recreation vehicles. With the latter, you can change your picture window view daily if you wish! What a delight—I always look upon recreation vehicles as modern magic carpets, right out of the Arabian Nights fantasies.

Here then, for your approval are descriptions of some places that I have enjoyed for a visit or as a residence.

LAS VEGAS

This town is a mecca for seniors for a variety of reasons:

- It's a 24-hour action town with stores and hotel-casinos open around the clock, seven days a week all year long! If you find you cannot sleep, which is a common failing of seniors, you can get up, get dressed and go downtown or the the Strip to bustling, wide-open action and activity. Enjoy a New York delicatessen-type pastrami sandwich on Jewish rye, a cup of herb tea in a natural foods restaurant, play cards with fellow seniors, see a free lounge show for the price of a chilled mineral water, take a walk along the strip to see the colorful signs hundreds of square feet in size, enjoy a low-cost buffet of fresh fruits and crisp vegetables (they are very cheap from midnight on), and have many chances of meeting seniors like yourself from every state in the union!

I've done all this and it can be exciting and rewarding for anyone who likes music, action, meeting new people and having urban adventures.

- It has a great climate for about eight months of the year, but be sure and find another spot on this earth from June through October. The mid-summer heat is sufficient to boil you if you're caught outside. You would be forced to live inside for several months, unless you like to fry eggs on the sidewalk in front of your home or apartment! Of course, if you really enjoy dry heat, be my guest but my own preference is a bit of coolness. I spent too much time in the fireroom of a WWII destroyer in the Pacific to have any love for the blistering heat.

- Vegas is a seething mass of contradictions; you can live in the desert for a reasonable price and yet the town has more churches per capita than any other American city. Also, when there is a need, it is the best town on earth for fund-raising. In short, there is heart among some hard-hearted.

A TRIO OF ATTRACTIONS—*(Left-to-right)* Hoover Dam, a Lake Mead yacht tour and the "wild, wild west" re-enacted daily in "Old Vegas", are three of the most popular tour attractions for visitors to Las Vegas. Hoover Dam, the 726-foot high engineering marvel, was the first dam to harness the mighty Colorado River; the one-hour yacht tour of Lake Mead, created by Hoover Dam; and the gun fights at "Old Las Vegas" are an exciting change-of-pace from the glitter and and glamour of the entertainment and casino action of Las Vegas. *(Photo courtesy of Las Vegas News Bureau.)*

Personally, I like Vegas because it represents the best and worst of American life and culture in microcosm. As a writer, it appeals to my sense of drama and life lived in the fast lane. I can learn more about human nature in 24 hours in Vegas than I can in a year of prowling around San Jose or Wichita. Besides, it's much more interesting to live in Vegas than a conventional American city. Where else can you see someone lose their life savings on the crap table in a matter of minutes? And more importantly, conjecture why. Where else can you sit at the same table as the costumed performers enjoying lunch at nine p.m? Where else in America do prostitutes have their names on the license plates of their brand-new Cadillacs and Lincolns? And where else can you feast on a Lucullan display of salads, fruits, meats and cheeses, breads and drinks for a dollar or so? Tell me and I'll check it out.

If you need more information on Vegas, write to:

Las Vegas News Bureau, Convention Center, Las Vegas, NV 89109.

Here is a the text of a personal letter from Ken Evan of the News Bureau, typical, I think of the friendly welcome you can get in Vegas.

I include it because it has a lot to say about seniors:

Dear Bill:

In response to your letter, here is a standard press package and some photos. You mentioned housing so I am enclosing the classified section from the L.V. Review Journal, the main daily newspaper. Rent in the private sector is fairly low here compared to your part of the world. The prices you see will change little from season to season and have not increased much in five years. As for subsidized housing, I will refer you to Ms. Suzanne Frost. She is head of the local office of the state division of aging services, 1050 E. Flamingo Rd., St. 242, Las Vegas, NV 89109.

While living in Vegas is quite easy for those on moderate to low incomes, it is all but impossible for those who rely on government assistance. The state is very stingy when it comes to social programs.

Entertainment is cheap. There are a dozen movie theaters that offer bargain prices on first-run films and lounge shows are quite inexpensive (free in many cases).

Many retired people make their homes here and find the warm dry climate to their liking. There are many service-oriented and part-time jobs available to those who want to supplement their Social Security checks, though they are generally low paying. Employers are becoming increasingly aware of the value of seniors as employees.

If you have a specific question, please feel free to contact me again.

Regards,
Ken Evan

I will take the liberty to extend that invitation to all readers. What follows is a selection of information from the many pages that Ken sent.

- Las Vegas is a big town, about 18 square miles with about 200,000 people. But despite this, the air quality is quite good, since it's in the open desert and the wind does blow!

- The surrounding county is about the same size as Massachusetts—nearly 8,000 square miles.

- Principal industries are tourism, mining, manufacturing, government, agriculture, warehousing and trucking. Gambling is the largest revenue source and is included under tourism. Since you really cannot win in the long run, I suggest you stick to the penny slots.

- There are 236 churches with 40 denominations refuting the contention of some people that Vegas is a God-forsaken place.

- You can get married and divorced very quickly.

- The sun just loves Vegas; it shines there 320 days a year. As mentioned previously, it does get very hot and sometimes as much as 117° F. It can get very cold in the winter. But you won't get wet, as rainfall is negligible.

- If you arrive in an RV, you can choose from more than 16 RV parks and over 3,000 full-service spaces.

I like the one at the Hacienda Hotel Casino; it has lovely green lawns, huge cottonwood trees, pool, tennis courts and a location at the south end of town with much less traffic and congestion.

- There are 13 golf courses and 200 tennis courts open to the public.

- Vegas is host to 450 conventions per year with an attendance of over a million people. Personally, I love to go to the conventions and see all the high tech goodies on display. You can learn so much from them and the presentations pertaining to the cutting edge of arts and sciences and many professions.

- There are many public events ranging from rodeos to desert races with cars and cycles.

- The University of Nevada at Las Vegas has a stunning campus with one of the finest libraries I've ever seen. It is open to the public and you can get a library card. Many pleasant hours have been spent there studying about desert herbs and Nevada history.

Besides the attractions of nearly 40 hotel casinos, some of which, like the new Tropicana swimming pool, are truly spectacular, there are such appealing places as:

1. Mt. Charleston, a high country playground with snow in winter and wonderful hiking trails all year.

2. Red Rock Canyon with lofty bluffs of bright red sandstone. Nearby is charming old Bonnie Springs Ranch and my favorite Old Nevada ghost town (a recreation that is so authentic you will think you are a time traveler). Close at hand is the Hughes Ranch which is open to the public and full of interesting Hughesiana legends.

3. Water sports abound on nearby Lake Mead which has 500 miles of pristine shoreline, many boats and houseboats for rent and fishing all year for many varieties of fresh-water fish. What I like best is a campfire on an isolated beach and communion with a billion glittering stars.

   Incidentally, there are no camping restrictions around Lake Mead. As far as I know, you could live there on your boat untroubled for as a long as you like.

FUN TIMES IN VEGAS

There are many single seniors in Vegas, so it is easy to make instant friends. You can go to senior centers or clubs, though I prefer to strike up friendships at the casinos. All the old ploys work just like when we were teenagers. I have never had anyone spurn my friendly overtures; in fact, I have found Vegas to be one of the best places in the world to meet a senior friend and lots of younger people, too!

Here's a typical adventure: I had been hired to write some articles for a local magazine which involved a trip to my favorite Hacienda Hotel Casino. The boss gave me *carte blanche* to see the show for free as many times as I wished. I met the cast and actually became an honorary member of the cast of *Fantasy on Ice* for several months. I viewed the show from backstage, the audience, the lightbooth, the orchestra pit and just about every vantage point possible. I became so familiar with the show and cast that I plan to someday write a book about Vegas revealing the astounding lifestyles behind the scenes.

Could anyone become a part of the Vegas scene? Why not? There are, as Ken points out, many part and full-time jobs for seniors. When you have a community that invites 14,000,000 people to come an visit each year, there are plenty of opportunities for everyone.

Of course, there is also opportunity to walk up N. Las Vegas Blvd. and see the homeless "people" lining up a free meal at a charitable facility. Most were gamblers who blew their bankrolls and either can't or won't find work. It is important to tell about the reverse side of the chip. Vegas can be a letdown for those who are into heavy gambling and alcohol. If you don't have will power to avoid these double disasters, then stay in Fallen Leaf, Idaho or Talahassee. Otherwise, enjoy!

If you like entertainment, then you should know that Vegas is the entertainment capital of the world. No need to sit in front of the TV at home when you can "come to the cabaret" anytime you wish. Don't die until you see one of truly spectacular shows like *Lido de Paris* or *Hello Hollywood*. These live shows feature dancers, singers, acrobats, jugglers, animal trainers, magicians and just about everything else that you would expect in a continental revue. Many of these shows have been performed for decades and have been constantly improved with wonderful live music, the latest lighting, including lasers, and beautiful casts. Costs are moderate for what you get—I promise you won't forget what you see.

Then, too, you will have the chance to see world-class performers like Sinatra, Davis, MacLaine and many others. I have had the great good fortune of seeing virtually many of the major performers at least once. I can still remember almost every detail. Sammy Davis is peerless—one-of-a-kind and he did an extra half hour because the audience was so responsive to his sensitive and outstanding presentation. There is magic in being a few yards from people who have become world-famous for their entertaining ability—mystique creates a special aura about them. As a result, you will probably be as excited and rewarded as I always am.

Vegas has more than 300 fine restaurants with an endless array of foods, many drawn from ethnic cuisines of great appeal. I recall bursting my belt with a German dinner that would have filled a regiment of Hussars to capacity. Then, too, a Mexican buffet that challenged my will power to the limit. I recall one memorable feast at the Desert Inn where the guests were hosted by a radio station opening to a complimentary celebration. They had prepared a buffet that would have bankrupted a Roman emperor. There was every conceivable kind of hot and cold dish, meats, cheeses, salads, vegetables, fruits, baked delicacies along with wines and fruit juices. I especially remember the giant, ten-pound loaves of authentic European rye bread with sweet butter. I could have been content on a meal of that alone! The flavor was that of genuine Jewish Russian rye—the most robust in the world.

Shopping in Vegas, whether you buy or not, is a "trip." Dozens of elegant shops from which to choose clothes, gifts, souvenirs and specialty items that you will find only in Vegas. There is a huge complex called the *Fashion Show* on the Strip near the Frontier Hotel Casino. Here are 150 stores ranging from boutiques to large, elegant department stores. Not far away is the giant 80-store center known as the *Boulevard* and still another, the *Meadows* about five miles west of the Strip.

I once met a Canadian who felt that the hotel casinos had a sameness about them once you entered. I had to disagree, since I lived in Vegas long enough to sense the unique character and personality of each opulent facility. For example, you can sense the grandeur of Rome when you visit Caesar's Palace and see, among other wonders, an exact reproduction of Michelangelo's "David." Or wander through the charming, old-time rose garden back of the Flamingo-Hilton and enjoy the perfumed blooms, made more lush, the legend has it, because some of hoods buried there in the era of Bugsy Siegel. And don't miss the wondrous view of the emerald city from the rotating restaurant atop the Landmark Hotel Casino. At night, with millions of colored lights sparkling amidst the deep black velvet of a desert night, you will believe that the tales of Arabian Nights have come true here in this fabulous and improbable city.

If spectacular surroundings (some call them garish) pall, then drive into the surrounding desert, stop your car and listen to the silence of the infinite. Often I took a break from the Strip to enjoy little springs surrounded by lush trees, remote mountain hideaways where desert rats and prospectors still seek that pot of gold, and in many places, genuine ghost towns that evoke a rich and dramatic past. Sandy, only a few miles from Vegas, is such a town, complete with an old mill. Sand dunes, old diggings and fascinating desert flora and fauna are within walking distance of the paved road. Not too far away is Goodsprings, a rock hound's paradise with many semi-precious gemstones available for the taking. It too, yielded much gold in times past.

Then there is Eldorado Canyon, 40 miles southwest of Vegas near the hamlet of Nelson. Narrow, rugged and scenic, it now displays the ruins of a mine that once produced millions in gold bullion before it was shut down at the start of WWII. Personally, I like Searchlight and the mysterious Rhyolite with its grandiose ruins of mighty buildings and a strange, disenfranchised railroad station. Ambling amidst these relics of a recent past, you can almost hear the voices of the departed adventurers. Imagine, from a peak of 10,000 residents, only six people remain today. *Sic transit gloria munda!*

IDAHO

Although I have never lived there for long periods, the state is one that calls me constantly. I love its mountains, rushing rivers, lovely scenery, clear air and especially, its great open spaces. Idaho has one of the largest wilderness areas in the country.

It is a state that appears as though the year were 1887 rather than 1987. For long distances on the fine highways you will see no sign of habitation or development and often, not even another car. Take a tour with me and see why this state has such appeal to a western wanderer.

The southwest portion is so productive, its overwhelming— corn tall and free, crisp, sweet watermelons, peaches by the box for practically nothing and, of course, those tasty Idaho spuds. I could live on them alone.

You will never see such rich land as that which lies on either side of the mighty Snake River. It's certain that anyone with even a moderately green thumb could grow all they could possibly eat on a parcel 20 x 40 feet and have food left over to give away.

As you drive northward, you pass strange areas that look like the surface of the moon and enter old towns like Shoshone. This one is a railroad town with tracks bisecting it on main street. While you might hear a few trains at night, you'll be compensated by the town's other charms. The Little Woods River also bisects the town and provides it with one of the best swimming holes I've ever tried. You can leap off the bridge and then raft yourself down to the rapids; if you like excitement, go on through. And all around are the green lawns and the big shade trees of a small park. Take the time to have a picnic there and let the rest of the world turn on its own axis.

Then, famous Sun Valley, a town created by the railroad near Ketchum. Nearby is a new addition, Elkhorn. All have grown in the last few years, as people discover the delights of living all four seasons in a natural environment. And, as everyone knows, some of the best ski runs in the world are above Sun Valley's charming alpine architecture. Don't forget to pay a visit to Elkhorn, a small village that has no auto traffic. You park your rig outside and then walk or bicycle through its clean streets. In the center of this "town of the future" is an all-year ice skating rink, a crowning touch for a regal city in a royal setting.

To me, Elkhorn is a city/concept that should be replicated many times in many parts of the world.

As you journey further north, you will pass frontier towns like Stanley and Challis. Here residents are heavily into nature with horses, pick-ups, river rafts and the total outdoor lifestyle. River rafting is almost a way of life in central Idaho, where the famous Salmon or River of No Return, slices through some of the most remote and lovely terrain in America. You can leave from the town of Salmon, travel for many days and not see any human habitation of any significance. In fact, as you look at the map of Idaho, you'll note that there aren't even any roads in this area!

The Selway-Bitteroot Wilderness Area is just north of the Salmon River region and provides a gigantic playground for anyone who wants to live like Lewis and Clark's wilderness explorers. And if this weren't enough, the northern-most panhandle part of Idaho is too exquisite to describe. Even these pictures can't create this rare and timeless beauty.

I can't resist telling you about the summer when we drifted south from northern Idaho and bumped into a really unique town—Gayway Junction near Fruitland. Oh yes, we bought a lug box of ripe peaches there and had the ultimate feast—peaches with fresh cream poured over them. I can still taste those sweet, juicy Freestones awash in cream as only Idaho's cows can produce. The cost of the entire lug was less than what one often pays in a big city market for rock-hard imports.

We've only covered a small part of this fabulous, untroubled state that remains, for the most part, pristine. Land is inexpensive outside the cities, wood is plentiful, water, both hot and cold, flows from ten thousands springs and you can grow all the food you need in your back yard. The only adverse aspect that I can think of is that of the harsh winter weather in some parts. But, as I have pointed out, you can always migrate down to Parker, Arizona or Nogales or Yuma and soak up the sun from about November to April.

IDAHO AND SENIORS

Many seniors who are city-bound long for the wilderness—the wide open spaces that sweep from mountain crest to crest all over the country. Here is just one example of what's available in Idaho:

You are viewing a parcel of ten acres located in Kootenai County, Idaho. This property is near Spirit Lake and Lake Pend Orielle, about 23 miles from Coeur D'Alene. I can almost smell the fragrance of those young pines and wildflowers.

What you build or do there is your own business. And best of all, you can own this ten acres for under 3,000 dollars down and less than 200 dollars a month, about 11 percent interest. If you have cash, it's under 20,000 dollars total price. Just 2,000 dollars for an acre of land is a bargain in my book.

My suggestion would be to get ten friends and have them each take one acre on a draw-straws option. That way, the down payment per person would be only about 240 dollars each with payments as ridiculously low as 20 dollars a month.

IDAHO AFTERTHOUGHT

Can you imagine driving down this road with your RV and then turning into your own property? Well, it can be a reality if you want it to be.

It seems that a company called *National Associated Properties Inc, of PO 1122 Coeur D'Alene, Idaho, 83814* has this land for sale. The terms are as follows:

Full price for five acres as shown . . . . $11,850 CASH
Down payment $1,420
Interest. 10¼
Monthly payments (including interest) $150

It is 35 miles to Coeur D'Alene and 40 miles to Spokane, WA.

THE SOUTHERN OREGON COAST

Of the many Oregon coastal villages, Bandon is my favorite. Now let's take a look at the region which surrounds this cozy little town.

Just for fun, I would like to place my own observations of these scenic ports alongside of the text from a tourist brochure. This will hopefully give you a more complete picture of the region. Then you can make a decision as to whether or not you would consider this area as one of your choices for work, play, retirement or all of these options.

Florence: I love this town because it's replete with everything that makes a tourist/traveler happy—lots of stores, many selections of smoked salmon, plenty of spaces to park you rig without any hassles and all manner of exploring to do, both in town and out. There's an interesting fishing boat harbor, a wide river and a fascinating restoration of Florence's Old Town. We've visited here several times and always enjoyed at least one seafood dinner. We've parked our trailer in nearby Honeyman Park and have been surrounded by beautiful blossoms which have the added feature of providing privacy and natural perfume.

Florence is obviously a prosperous town because it has always been busy when we've visited. And recently, I heard that some of their fishing fleet sailed off to provide fish for foreign factory ships; this proves the courage and resourcefulness of these resolute Oregon fisher folk. The Oregon coast offshore can be formidable, but the Arctic Circle is even rougher. More power to people who love a town so much they are willing to take some big chances to live there.

Winchester Bay and Salmon Harbor: Ruth and I have a running joke about the Umpqua River. It's not so translatable to print, as it involves pronouncing the word as the Indians might have. But one thing is communicable—the fact that the Umpqua River Valley wild blackberry is the largest we've encountered in a lifetime of world travel. They look as big as small plums and are so juicy and sweet!

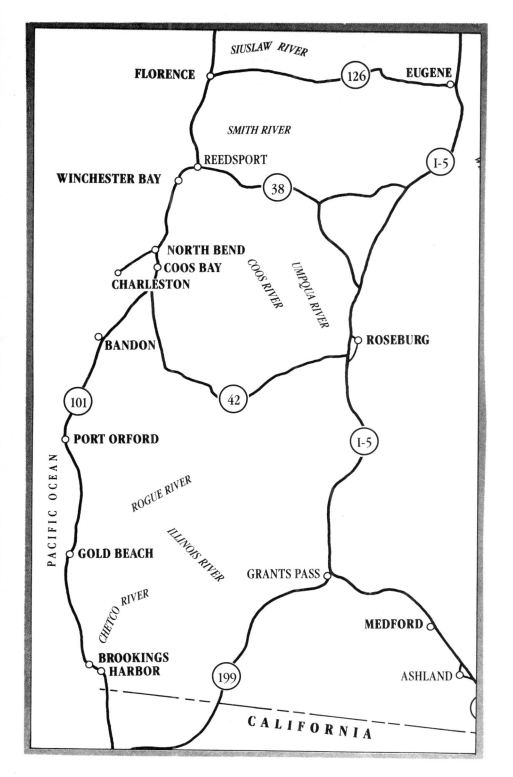

This coastal town is rather loosely connected with itself, thus lending an air of low-density population. Actually, there aren't a lot of people here since the economy base is rather tenuous—a little fishing and some tourists. My own personal love is the tiny but charming houseboat community along an oxbow off the main channel of the Umpqua River. Most are occupied by seniors of advanced age who obviously delight in their waterfront views.

You will never feel rushed or pressured in this coastal community because the natives obviously avoid that condition with great diligence.

COOS BAY, NORTH BEND and CHARLESTON

Now this is a real seaport with giant freighters from all parts of the world steaming up the wide Coos River to a moor at huge docks in the heart of town. While driving through this community, if you feel surrounded by water, it's because you are; the river inlets are as large as bays in other seaports. The town itself would win no beauty prizes since it's a rather garish palimpsest of several historical periods; the old Victorian buildings often have plastic make-up so that you cannot decide which architectural theme is predominant. But there are plenty of stores, a selection of unique restaurants serving fresh seafood and natural dishes and lots of places to park your RV while you tour the attractions. As with all Oregon towns, you get the feeling that you are most welcome.

I found nearby Charleston especially intriguing with its huge marina packed with some 700 plus boats and many charming coves, little bays and inlets. All about are picturesque boats at anchor or beached or tied to old piers. There is a combination of action and retreat in this part of the area—active yachting merging with an apparently declining fishing industry (evidently, many fishing operations are moving overseas where labor is cheaper).

Two things are outstanding—the two lovely state parks with formal gardens south of Charleston and the tranquil South Slough Sanctuary with its sagging barns and abandoned homesteads in a setting of serene backwaters.

The people are as friendly as people can be—I even had the gift of a free boat to restore from the marina owner. So, three cheers for this seaport as a place to visit or live in active retirement. Fishermen will go absolutely bananas here!

PORT ORFORD

We have all heard of the cedar that comes from this famous old port a few miles south of Bandon. Today the cedar is largely gone and the only exports from this sleepy, 19th-century village are memories and a few fish. The town appears to be going through a slow transition from a busy metropolis into a declining seaside township; this is happening to Port Orford as well as other southern Oregon seaports. The sea is often so cruel here that the fisherfolk haul their precious boats out of the water and store them safely on a stout pier nestled behind a strong sea wall.

A few years back a restaurant named "Madelaines" served the best vegetable stew and blackberry pie we've ever tasted. But it, too, has been a victim of harder times. What will become of Port Orford? I conjecture that it will slowly transform into a vacation village retreat for retired Oregonians and Californians. Already there has been an influx of nuclear scientists who have discovered that Port Orford is the safest town in the U.S. as far as nuclear fallout is concerned; it is the western most town on the continent.

It has plenty of places to park your RV and no hassles to date. Try the spot down by the pier—you'll have a marvelous view of Port Orford's bay and the coastline sweeping south.

GOLD BEACH

Here's where the great Rogue River emerges from its mountain fastness and joins the vast Pacific. While the town has little appeal architecturally (a typical hodgepodge of facades), the surroundings are well worth an exploration. You can see the Rogue's riverbanks by a jet boat tour or you can drive inland along a winding road that allows glimpses of its blue waters. There are an abundance of restaurants with seafood specialties and a large marina and small airport. Gold Beach has a bustle about it since it is a tourist attraction of world renown. Personally, I like the scenery but would recommend a little more of Bandon's charm and Port Orford's serenity.

BROOKINGS

Almost a sister city to Gold Beach, this town is the first one north of the California border. It has a much larger marina than Gold Beach and a wonderful 440-acre park right on the beach, offering all of the amenities that a tourist would need. We've haven't spent too much time here because of the draw of the bend in the road ahead. South of Brookings are productive farms growing lilies and my favorite elephant garlic. In all, a prosperous community offering what southern Oregon is famous for.

IN SUMMARY (OF THE OREGON COAST)

We love the Oregon coast and this love grows with each visit. It has the charm that is often lacking in more populated regions where freeways and heavy traffic make life so frenetic. Peace, quiet, friendly people, great fresh food, especially from the sea, and spectacular seaside scenery make this region a delight at any time, but mainly in the summer. We have never braved the rainy season, but plan to try it just for the experience.

Try this area in your RV and you will come away enriched with your close contact to Mother Nature at in her most beautiful and loving persona. You just may want to stay much longer.

SANTA BARBARA BACK COUNTRY

The Los Padres National Forest is one of the largest in the U.S. It extends from the rugged mountains back of Ventura, CA to the beautiful slopes near Monterey. Here you will find everything you have ever dreamed of—clear rivers with few visitors, wonderful hot springs in sylvan settings, jagged mountains studded with tall Ponderosa and Sugar pines, fields of wildflowers in spring, tall wild oats in the fall and sprinkles of light snow in the upper elevation in winter.

It is a pleasant and totally relaxed land, all but unknown to most people. You see, most of us are so busy hurrying up and down Highway 101, that we seldom take the time to enjoy nature at its best, just a few miles inland.

I began my explorations of the back country in the mid-60's and have continued to this day. Take a ride with me and see if you would like it as much as I.

We can start up the mountains in Toro Canyon on the eastern edge of the posh community of Montecito. From a rather arid beginning, the road quickly becomes lined with tall sycamore and oaks with willows hugging the creek. Water begins to flow alongside the road, a clear stream that originates from all-year springs up the mountain. If we are quiet, we can surprise deer on the road and watch them leap swiftly and gracefully into the chaparral. The further we go, the more lush the mountains become, until finally we are in a jungle of vegetation where pools of crystal-clear water gather beneath gentle waterfalls, where giant ferns festoon the glades and tiny sandy beaches invite you to sit and meditate on all this loveliness.

I recall that once when I visited a particularly lovely grotto with a friend, I told him that THIS was my real world—that that paper shuffling I was doing down below was just so much wasted effort.

From the glades, we can travel downhill to the valley floor where the Santa Ynez River flows serenely towards the Pacific Ocean some 60 miles away. If you turn off the main river road up a rocky canyon, you will discover a great hot springs—Agua Caliente, the springs that changed my life. I can thank my two daughters, Wendy and Jill, for introducing me to this springs during a picnic we had one summer in the sixties. While not the most picturesque, it can provide a relaxing warm bath, winter or summer, fall and spring, day and night, seven days a week, at no cost. It's hard to beat something as beneficial as Agua Caliente.

Nearby the cemented pool is a cool stream that provides a startling contrast to the 115° F water of the hot springs. At times, we have rigged an impromptu shower and frolicked about in the steaming water, even when the air temperature was in the low-50's or less.

I recall one night when I was camping near the pool; it had become quite chilly in my sleeping bag, so I rolled out swiftly and into that lovely warmth of Agua Caliente—it was like no other sensation I have ever had, but it did point out that this old earth can treat its guests with great compassion.

From the hot spring, you can hike for miles in all directions, enjoying the completely unspoiled and natural wilderness. Indians (the Chumash tribe) lived in this area for many centuries; if you are sharp-eyed, you may find old arrowheads about, especially at the confluence of two streams where wildlife often gathered.

Only a few miles from Agua Caliente is still another hot spring often called Little Caliente. This one is quite primitive, thus having more natural charm. It has as its source, an outpouring of hot water a few yards above the pool. You can usually reach there all year unless the fire danger is high and the region is closed to travelers. There is no charge, either. My friends and I have enjoyed this geothermal wonder on many occasions and I revisit it every chance I get.

All about are giant trees and nearby is the slow-moving Mono River, a tributary to the Santa Ynez.

Sit with me on an old log and listen. There is a near-silence, but you can hear the buzz of wild bees and the song of a finch or mockingbird. The wind rustles the leaves, the grass bends, all is serene and exactly the way Mother Nature made it. Stay a while, perhaps a week or even a month and renew yourself. There are few restrictions in this vast area and fewer interruptions in this, the land of slow time and spiritual renewal.

NOGALES, ARIZONA

Jumping southeast in a giant leap finds one along the Mexican border. Here are towns of which Nogales is typical. It has two parts, the U.S. side and the Mexican side. I suggest you park your rig on the American side and walk across. The exercise will do you good and you won't have any parking problems. Shop around after you trade your dollars for pesos—about 1,200 at last report. We found strong, rich coffee for 75 cents a pound and lots of tropical fruits for equivalently low prices. The dollar/peso exchange does, of course, favor the Americans and, admittedly, is hard on the poor Mexicans. If you spend some of your dollars down there, tip generously, donate to beggars and children—you will be helping them more than if you just ignored their financial stress.

In any event, shopping in Mexico can help a needy American senior make his or her social security check go further. As you know, many seniors have gone to Mexico to live full-time. I am sure that there are many advantages, but personally, I like it north of the border for a variety of reasons. But visiting a foreign country so close to the U.S. can be enjoyable.

There are many RV camps on the U.S. side of the border, including around Nogales, so my suggestion would be to take your rig down there and try it out for a season or two. A scenario for a couple on social security would be to buy a used park model trailer with pop-outs. Then haul it down to Nogales or another border town, park it and so most of the buying on the Mexican side. An income of just 500 dollars would translate into 600,000 pesos—a not inconsiderable sum and one that represents a lot of buying power, even considering the rampant inflation of Mexican prices.

Besides, haven't you often wanted to brag a bit and say that you had a half a million of currency?

So, hasta la vista.

IN SUMMARY

This chapter on *Places* is, of necessity merely cursory. After all, we could easily write a very large book or series on the virtually limitless places that a senior could visit or live. But what we have presented is a sampling that is, I believe, characteristic of what is available in America.

CHAPTER ELEVEN
FREEDOM AFLOAT

SOME THOUGHTS (ON LIVING ABOARD BOATS)

Living on the water can be most rewarding, fulfilling and interesting—the sights and sounds of the sea coming through the porthole or hatch is dramatic, dynamic, exciting and ever-changing in a way that land never achieves.

Movement of the water itself is fascinating—white waves curl back from the bow while the wake bubbles and froths with spiral whirls and whorls creating patterns, no two alike.

I recall watching the massive propellers of my WWII destroyer create an ever-lengthening helix as the microscopic animals that exude light were activated. *1945, Pacific.*

Then, much later, lying in my spacious bunk aboard my very own converted coast guard cutter observing the flashing light show overhead as the sun reflected its light off the glittering waves. *1975, at anchor.*

Gasping for breath as the anchor pulled me downward in a near-drowning accident when I was 17—an incident so mind-wrenching I cannot completely recall it to this day. Yes, the sea is totally fair, but totally indifferent to your welfare. Make one mistake and it can claim you forever. *1940, Catalina Island, CA.*

It is midnight and I am awakened by the raccoon squabble in the willows and tules behind my boat. It is obvious that one raccoon has come home late and is getting a severe scolding from his raccoon wife. Then, as I peer into the darkness, a long black shape swishes by with minimal noise. No lights, no indication of a person. It is, no doubt, one of the clandestine drug-carrying boats that ply the vast labyrinth of the California Delta. Then suddenly, the boat is gone, the ripples of its wake lap almost noiselessly on the sandy shore, the raccoons kiss and make up and it is silent again on the waterfront. *1976, Bradford Island, CA.*

The stern of the destroyer comes up high and then free falls into the trough. As I make my way across the wet deck wearing my usual two life jackets, a wave picks me as though I were a chance piece of driftwood and carries me aft. Just as I am about to be swept overboard, I grab for the steel life line and hang on for all I am worth as the rest of the wave sweeps by me. Then, frantically I work my way across the deck and into the crews' quarters, dripping gallons of cold sea water. I make it to safety just as the next huge wave crashes over our slender ship. Down below, all is quiet and the red lights warmly glow. The off-watch crew are asleep as I take off my soaking clothes. As I do, I recall the rule that a ship at sea during wartime does not usually stop for anyone overboard. *November, 1944, Pacific.*

The book has been sold and a check for 750 dollars is in my pocket burning away. A party! That's it. A big bash aboard the Flying Goose for all the wharf rats and other friends. We buy beans and rice, tortillas and tamales and make up tostadas and enchiladas. Wine comes on board by the gallon. The colored lights make the long pilot house festive as the guests come on board. Eight hours later the bean pot is empty, guests are draped over the rail and I am playing my harmonica for a girl half my age. What a party—only on board a small ship could you have such joyous times. *1974, Oakland Estuary.*

SOURCES OF FREE BOATS

1. Go to a boat yard and ask if there are any abandoned boats that you can have. Many yard owners are delighted if you take their old boats away. After all, to most people, an old boat with a bad hull is junk. But with what I call the Kaysite process, a bad hull can easily be facelifted. Kaysite is an inexpensive cement-based refurbishing treatment that I developed many years ago with tremendous results. Be careful to determine if there is going to be a significant cost to get the boat moved for any reason. Moving boats can be expensive. Often a free boat can cost more than one already in the water.

2. Often a boat is advertised over and over for a low price. Call the owner and see if they want to give it away. You'll be surprised how many boat owners are just waiting for someone to take it off their hands.

3. Cruise the backwaters of harbors. Here's where you will often find completely abandoned boats. I know that the California Delta region is full of old hulks that people have left to rot. Of course, you must be discerning since many of them would be too expensive to restore even with a low-cost process like Kaysite. Be sure you won't spend more money on restoration than it would cost to buy an equivalent boat ready to live on.

4. Check with government installations near you. Often they will give a boat away rather than try to dispose of it conventionally. The local surplus officer can make this decision. If you are part of a non-profit organization, you have a better chance. I recall a visit to Bremerton, WA recently and the man in charge of surplus boats tried to give me a complete (except for guns) WWII destroyer! While I am a dedicated boat lover, that boat would have been a little large for my slip. But when you think of it, why couldn't a senior group take over a large ship and turn it into living quarters. I have often thought about that as a solution to the waste of large ocean liners.

In summary, there are thousands of old boats around that you can acquire for little or nothing, since most old boats really have little salvage value other than their value if restored. That's where Kaysite comes in. For a detailed explanation of the Kaysite process, please write me in care of the publisher. Now you can have a home on the water for the rest of your life at an affordable price.

This fishing boat was 67 years old when it was hauled for restoration.
The bill for one plank was 1,800 dollars. So owner Mark Russo decided to
Kaysite it instead.

Expanded wire mesh with 3/8'' stand-off is being applied with ring nails.

Kaysite coating being applied by expert Kaysite workman.

After, the vessel ready for sea. On first trip, encountered 50 knot winds with no leaks. Now operating out of Moss Landing and Half Moon Bay, California.

Returned to its berths at Moss Landing, California, the *Manna* looks foward to many years of useful service as a pleasure/fishing boat.

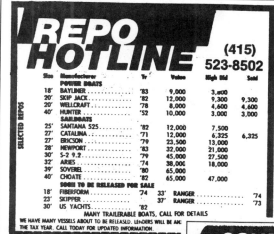

In metropolitan areas, you may find an organization like this that devotes itself to a continuing problem of what to do with boats that people cannot pay for.

They advertise widely and allow bidders to set their own prices. Recently, a friend of mine bought a perfectly good Hunter cabin cruiser, 42 feet long for less than 5,000 dollars. It is now his permanent home after spending a few weekends cleaning and refurbishing.

If you can't find a repo company, then simply go to the banks or other institutions that finance boats and ask them what's available.

In the event that the boat you buy has an unrepairable engine, here's a viable option. A new diesel with transmission and spares.

If 20 HP is not enough, then install two or even four dual engines. At this low price, you just can't go wrong.

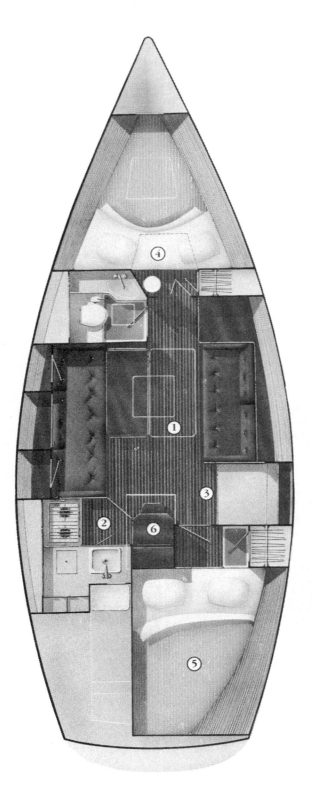

FORWARD CABIN. Berth is 7' at the shoulder, 6'6" in length. Hanging locker is topped with a shelf and protective riser. A drawer and stowage are located below the berth. Ash battens finish the hullsides and the look of a comfortable cabin for two with an opening deck hatch overhead.

There's a molded fiberglass unit that is easy to clean in the head and the bulkhead is mirrored from ceiling to countertop. Both this sink and the galley sink are located near centerline for efficient drainage on either tack. A towel and vanity locker is located above the head. A shower may be fitted as an option.

AFT CABIN. A pleasant surprise in a 30 footer: 6'6" long double berth, 6' wide at the shoulders, lined hanging locker and an opening port into the cockpit. Fine sleeping quarters for guests or kids.

ENGINE COMPARTMENT. There probably isn't a more accessible inboard engine anywhere. This Yanmar 2 GM 20F is mounted right below the companionway, aft of removable steps. Once exposed, note the vibration-absorbing rubber engine mounts and the foil, foam and lead insulation to minimize engine disturbance. A molded-in drip pan prevents any unexpected leakage into the bilge.

The modern 30-foot yacht, *Freedom 30*, sports a spacious layout. Completely state-of-the-art.

BOAT INTERIORS

For a solo senior or couple, the interior of a boat, new or old would be a comfortable and easily-maintained environment. Small, compact, easy and cheap to heat or cool, the galley, bathroom and general living quarters of a 30 to 50-footer would be ideal.

To me, the most advantageous feature is quick heating and cooling. A small wood, coal, oil or butane stove would get a boat's insides toasty warm in minutes. I have often warmed a small boat with just a kerosene lantern!

The views here are from a 1950 *Chris Craft* catalogue showing designs of that era. Naturally, if you were to acquire a boat of that vintage, there would be opportunities to update it with foam, new rugs, thick drapes and creative accessories. Again, because the area is small, the cost of redecorating would also be minimal.

A compact galley makes for easy clean-up.

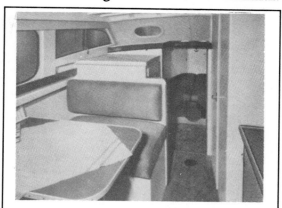

Typical dinette can be the focal point of boat living.

Today, yacht designers are alert to what customers want in the way of interiors and are competing to produce the most luxury and comfort at the lowest cost. The result is home-like surroundings even in relatively small boats.

EPILOGUE

Yes, dear readers, life afloat is like starring in your own waterborne movie. As you can plainly surmise, I love boats—always have, always will. If you would like more information or are interested in the possibility of saving an old boat for yourself, please send for more information on the Kaysite process.

In hopes that this introductory information is helpful and encouraging to you so that someday soon you, too, may enjoy the fabulous world of freedom afloat.

nan CLASSIFIEDS. . . .

AT LEFT, SOME TYPICAL OFFERINGS IN POWER. BELOW, SOME OF MY OWN SELECTIONS..

OPPORTUNITIES

SALESPERSON WANTED. Full-time opportunity to sell boats. Live on the water, enjoy the great outdoors, 200 berth marina. Submit resume or call for interview. (916) 776-1668. P.O. Box 231, Walnut Grove, CA 95690. Att. General Manager.

POWER

PATIO CRUISERS, Inc.
Custom
Pontoon
Houseboats
All Sizes
Factory located at
11088 Midway, Chico, CA 95926
(916) 342-6674

36' CHRIS CRAFT CONNIE, 1961, New paint - FWC Twin 350 Chevs, Asking $26,500 or Best Offer. Call (415) 459-4307. (93)

38' CHRIS CRAFT COHO, 1980, Wet bar & ice maker on flybridge, twin 454 6.5 KW, vacu flush, power windlass, bristol, $103,500. (916) 662-4485. (94)

43' VIKING Dbl. Cabin 1980, bristol, one owner, Twin 671 Detroit diesels (450 hrs.), 7.5 Onan, 250 hrs. Dual stations, glendining sync., 2 VHF, 2 depth finders. Motivated seller, make offer. (916) 776-1166 (97)

40' CHRIS CRAFT TRI-CABIN 1948, Twin V-8. Trade considered. Nice Delta liveaboard berth, Possible owner financing. (209) 333-1836. (97)

28' GLAS-PLY CRUISER, 1981, twin BMW gas. Many extras. For Sale by owner. Asking $30,000. Call after 5pm, (415) 797-7419. (97)

POWER

26' WELLCRAFT AFTCABIN 1984, excellent, 58 hrs., full electronics, trailer, trimtabs, canvas, h/water, stove, refrigerator, shower, sacrifice, $29,500 or trade equity. (415) 937-2739. (100)

18' AMERICAN SKIER PLEASURE CRAFT, 1980, Competition ski boat. Stereo, low hours, excellent condition. 350 Ford Commander engine. Includes Pleasure Craft trailer. $9,800. (415) 686-5715. Weekdays after 5p.m.

You can place your **Classified Ad** by phone, call (415) 865-7504 Monday thru Friday 1-5.

23½ SUNRUNNER 1979, Volvo IO, aftcabin, tandem trailer, 12/110 volt refrigerator, maserater, pressure water, D/F, VHF, full canvas, more. $18,000. (209) 474-8268 (103)

19' SEARAY SRV-190, 1972, V-8 188 M.C., D.S., trailer, ski-ready, extras. Freshwater boat. Closed bow. 400 hours. (916) 726-3856. $7,000. (103)

44 GIBSON HOUSEBOAT, 1984. 14' Wide, 6.5 Onan gen., 125 hrs. on twin Crusader engines. Two A/C double head interior customized. $90,000. (415) 634-5394. (103)

47' SHANE CRUISER 1943, Clasic, twin FWC Chryslers, ideal liveaboard, cruising excellent condition. Asking $35,000. Garrison (415) 589-6995 Eve., (415) 285-9193 Days. (103)

27' BAYLINER VICTORIA, 1978, Sunbridge, aft cabin, twin Volvo 140, head w/ Macerator, VHF, depth finder, full canvas, stove 120/12, refrig, stereo, sleeps 4 — Exceptional condition — $21,000. (415) 538-6974. (103)

POWER

56 HOLIDAY MANSION 1976, Royal houseboat cruiser offered at $75,000. Fast, economical cruising. Many comforts: wood-burning fireplace, heat/air conditioning, electronics. For liveaboard Bay/Delta. Low hours, low maintenance, good condition. Note: Considering time share to houseboaters at excellent rates. Stu, 3952 Nelson Ct., Palo Alto, CA 94306. (415) 424-9089.

28' APOLLO RANGER, 1980, 10' Beam, twin Penta Volvo Diesels, Fiberglass, marine radio, depth finder recorder, tape player radio, CB, galley, head, with treatment system, (209) 683-5251 (103)

36' GIBSON HOUSEBOAT 1978, Merc 228 I/O, VHF, CB, AM, FM radios, sounder, ref-freezer, stove, shower, sleeps 8, under covered berth, $28,000. (707) 576-1300 9-5. (103)

36' TROJAN 1946, tri-cabin, generator-electric stove, refrigerator, shower, fully equipped, flybridge. (415) 228-7249 (103)

43' CHRIS, CONNIE, 65' Fresh water vessel, flush deck, aft cabin, extended hard top, aft deck enclosure, twin G.M. diesels, Onan generator, VHF, autopilot, 2 fathometers, hailer, 2 heads, T.D.X. sanitation system, teak swim platform, air condition, heat, CO'2 & halon, hull refinished '85, custom interior, "MINT CONDITION". (707) 864-1356. After six. (103)

POWER

83' WHEELER YACHT, 1944, GMC 671's, 10K & 25K, radar, VHF, full galley, washer/dryer, 3 staterooms, 4 heads, 2 showers/tub. Fireplace, liveaboard, $75,000. (415) 668-5565. (102)

43' STEPHENS CRUISER, 1931, Allure is professionally maintained in a covered berth. Twin Chrysler V8's, Light plant, charger, shore power, auto fire system, electric winch, depth finder, shower, two heads, sleeps seven, dinghy, VHF/FM & AM/FM. Bristol. (916) 482-5790, Mr. Niello or Mr. Kinney. (97)

65' CRUISING HOUSEBOAT Diesel 671 with 3 to 1 reduction gear, extremely economical, 1000 mile cruising range, heavily constructed, a big boat with a bargain price, $29,000. (916) 422-3040 or 922-5041 (100)

86' CLASSIC WOODEN TUG BOAT, '42, perfect for houseboat conversion; offer above $24,000; good hull condition survey; (415) 664-1006 home, (41? 620-2210 office. (101)

CHAPTER TWELVE
CLOTHING

PROLOGUE

For the past 20 years my good friend, Dan Clark, has kept me supplied with clothes. I have no idea where he gets these fine suits, pants, shirts, coats and unique imports. And I don't ask. He once said that while some men drink, smoke and carouse, his only vice was to acquire fine clothes. And that he does; his own wardrobe would rival that of a billionaire—rack after rack of magnificent garments and elegant accessories. Just the castoffs from this array have enabled me to make a presentable appearance for over 20 years.

I have, among other things, a silk gabardine suit in a distinguishing shade of gray that must have cost 500 dollars new. It is magnificent and I only wear it to state occasions.

Then there is the fine Shetland wood sport coat that would be at least 300 dollars new in a posh men's store. It is still like new! That's the usual state of clothes that Dan gives me—better than what you get off the rack at any store. Like the electronic salesmen in Woody Allen's *Sleeper*, "I got vools, I got vorsted, I got vot ever you vant." I have taken to giving away some of the items that Dan has passed on to me to the homeless in Santa Cruz. You can bet that they appreciate the clothes even more than I do.

So what is my point? Simply this: there are so many fine clothes in America going to waste; if we find a way, as Dan has, to recirculate them, we seniors won't have to spend much money to dress well. Sure, this might be tough on the garment industry, but like other enterprises, it should be based on reality. The garment industry has been guilty of promoting "fashion" purposely and intentionally for profit. I have often noted that wealthy people make their own fashions and will wear clothes they like as long as they like; they care not two cents for what the masses are doing in the way of designer jeans and floppy coats made of rough linen.

SOURCES OF CLOTHES

If I didn't have Dan to supply me, where would I go for clothes? Simple, to the nearest Goodwill, Salvation Army or other charitable/religious thrift shop. And if I couldn't find what I wanted there, I would go to the local flea market (which now operates three days a week in Santa Cruz, CA). There I would find hundreds of lineal feet of racks containing every conceivable type of garment. In addition, there are boots and shoes, accessories, jewelry, hats, raincoats, and a lot of interesting items like leather vests from Mexico and sandals from Guatemala. The prices are low; if you can't pay what they ask, offer what you can afford. That's what flea markets are for. Incidentally, I just acquired a wonderful pair of Dingo boots that probably cost close to a hundred dollars new for just nine dollars. And they are in top condition with new soles and heels. That's typical of what you can save if you just spend some time checking out the bargains.

Do you know where much of the clothing that appears in thrift shops and flea markets come from? From the deceased. After all, people die constantly at all ages and their survivors usually donate their clothing to a charitable organization. Naturally, much of this clothing is in excellent, often new condition. After all, when you and I die, we'll leave behind a lot of great finds, right? I will, since I'll still be wearing Dan's donations, and of course, my almost-new boots.

PRICES

If you have never shopped at a thrift store in your life, you are in for a most pleasant surprise. Shirts that retail for 15 dollars new can be found for from one to three dollars. Pants for men and slacks for women will be under ten dollars and often five dollars in some places. Perfectly good dresses, some of them worn perhaps once to a party, will go for one dollar up. I recall that Ruth and I once went into a thrift shop while visiting Tucos and found that everything in the store was priced at just one dollar. We pigged out, snatching up armloads of great shirts, pants, jackets and many other items. If we couldn't wear them, we could give them to others or the homeless in our base camp in California. I never expect to see bargains like that again but then, who cares, once is enough!

One item that is becoming increasingly costly is shoes. But here you will be amazed at the bargains you'll find. Most of them are in good condition since the thrift stores have learned that people don't usually keep shoes in poor repair—it costs to fix them these days. Look for the brand names; since many shoes and boots today are made of plastic, they have a rather short life span and are not rebuildable.

A SUPER BARGAIN

Ruth and I were in Vegas once when she found a leather coat with fur trim that must have sold new for at least 250 dollars. Guess what? She paid just three dollars for it! We couldn't believe it, but then when you consider Las Vegas and its weird money practices, it becomes understandable. People in that fantasy town will buy new clothes for one evening and then give them away. This evokes a thought—you will probably do real well in such posh communities as Beverly Hills, Scottsdale, Aspen and Scarsdale. Affluent communities naturally cast off expensive clothing on a high frequency schedule.

I want to wind up this totally subjective presentation with a comment from Ruth who is an expert on clothing.

Ruth here: "Although somewhat fussier than Bill about adhering to fashion, I too will check the thrift shops. I have often found nearly new, fashionable clothes there. Since these shops will take your clothes on consignment and sell them for you, I regularly go through my closet and weed out seldom-worn garments to sell. In about two months time, there's usually a check waiting for me and the unsold clothes get donated to the goodwill store.

Another method is to purchase yardage on sale and make your own clothes. This I do on a modest scale with easy to sew items. But when thrift shops and my own skills can't fulfill a special need, I resort to the purchase of new items. In this instance I follow one cardinal rule—purchase at least one piece of merchandise that is on sale.

One last suggestion: If you are the same size as a friend or relative, try swapping clothes occasionally. When my youngest daughter gets bored with her wardrobe, she comes over and picks out something of mine to borrow, thus saving herself the expense of a new purchase while fulfilling her need for variety."

CONCLUSION

In conclusion about clothes; not only are they one of life's necessities, they are vast and varied and can create a desired image, help make you feel a certain way about yourself, or simply do what they were originally set out to do: protect your body.

Notice how these protective coverings come to you in many forms...from new to used, from tailor-made to thrift-store chic, from thin housedresses to ribbed fisherman's sweaters, from currently fasionable to timeless and classic, they are ever-present and easily attainable. So, my one last word of advice: be comfortable in the clothes you wear.

CHAPTER THIRTEEN

INCOME OPPORTUNITIES

OVERVIEW

The average Social Security check issued to seniors is about 285 dollars per month, as of this writing. I am sure you'll agree that that is a laughable amount by standards of the U.S government and linear thinking. The government sets the poverty level for a family of four at about 10,000 dollars per year.

I read some typical classified ads from a California newspaper showing housing suitable for seniors. It is obvious that 285 dollars is not going to even provide shelter under conventional circumstances.

Now while the basic premise of this presentation is to save money rather than earn it, it's logical to assume that some readers will want to have a supplemental income. Thus, here are some of the most creative and innovative ideas that have come our way in recent months. Our belief is that with so many people having so many needs, it should not be too difficult to fill some of those needs and earn some honest returns in the process.

MELODY'S COOKIES

This income plan is one of my all-time favorites since I was able to learn about it first-hand under the most delightful circumstances. We were vacationing in the charming town of Mendocino on the northern California coast; a bit of New England's sea frontier transplanted to the West.

While ambling about the picturesque town, we found a tiny building hardly 8 x 12 feet with a bold sign on top:

MELODY'S COOKIES

Who could resist a fresh, hot cookie on a chilly morning? The interior consisted of no more than a large display case, the cash register and Melody herself. The case was full of giant cookies, 12-inches in diameter—truly the most monstrous cookies I had seen in my entire life! There were chocolate chip, molasses and peanut butter. Prices were reasonable considering how large they were; just one of them would last even an inveterate cookie bandit like myself all day long.

Melody, a charming young woman of perhaps 25 or so, told us that she couldn't find a suitable job in town so she set about to create her own. She had been an experienced baker, and was on her way to becoming a cookie specialist. So it was logical that she bake some of her favorites and then find a place to sell them to the many tourists who come to Mendocino all year long.

An old real estate office with reasonable rent was the perfect choice. A sign, a case and cash register were all she needed to open her doors and when she did—instant success. She usually sold out everything by NOON each day and used her free time to study comparative religions, her main interest. I learned later that she earned enough money from her cookie venture to semi-retire to Lake Tahoe for more education.

Now what is to prevent an enterprising senior from emulating Melody? Nothing really—it's so simple to bake cookies and most seniors, men and women alike, have done it. A small building or space within a larger one are not that hard to come by in most tourist areas. The usual bureaucratic paperwork must be obtained, of course, along with health permits and inspections, but that is not an insurmountable obstacle. Start-up costs can be almost what you want to make them. And if you don't want to run a shop, do what another young woman did in Carmel Valley; she simply put her cookies out for sale in grocery stores. The last time I saw her, business was so good, she had a full-time assistant.

Currently, muffins are the "in" thing and next year it may be something esoteric like apple strudel or French pastry. Perhaps YOU can guess what baked delight will capture the public's fancy next. And then you'll be out in front.

Not only is this a fun business, but the broken pieces and bits you get to eat taste as good as the whole ones!

TAKE MOST OF THE DAY OFF

One of the most relaxed enterprises I know for people of any age is to provide lunches to office and factory workers. This requires that you to make up sandwiches and snacks early in the morning, make your rounds from about 11 a.m. to say, 1 p.m. and then you're free!

When I was helping to produce one of my books at Straight Arrow's book division in San Francisco, I became acquainted with a young woman who had developed a successful sandwich route. She made up the most delicious looking sandwiches in the morning, using lots of sprouts and fresh tomatoes with organic cheeses. She then carried them around in a basket to sell to the *Rolling Stone* (a Straight Arrow publication) employees.

She also took orders from the regulars to prepare special sandwiches and dessert goodies. She told me that she only needed a few places to provide her with an excellent income and best of all, she could spend a lot of her time studying guitar.

Again, this is a simple, low investment business. Anyone can make a sandwich and then bank on the fact that people who work get tired of lunchrooms and bringing their own brown bag. There are many variations on this type of enterprise, including one that I just heard about.

In this food business, you rent a facility that has a kitchen and space for tables and chairs. Every day you cook a hot lunch—popular dishes like chicken and spaghetti. Then you offer the lunch for a fixed price to business people who enjoy a hot meal at noon. Let's say you get 100 takers at a modest three dollars each. Okay, that gives you a budget of 300 dollars to prepare 100 plates. Now everyone knows that most restaurants provide food for about 25 percent of the selling price. Thus, if you use their standard, you can buy the food for 100 meals for about 75 dollars. The rest of the money is overhead and profit. How you balance these out depends on your skill.

I think that this boarding-house approach could be very successful in many areas and could be extended to breakfast and dinner as well.

ELECTRONIC REPAIR

Most American homes have at least one TV set. The new rage is the VCR or video cassette recorder. There is no doubt that barring a major depression, millions of these will be sold over the next ten years and many of them may need to be repaired.

They are expensive items, too costly to toss in the trash like the ubiquitous audio cassette recorder. So here is an opportunity for any senior, woman or man, to learn how to repair them, set up a small shop in their home or apartment, and then either run ads, hang a sign in the window or simply pass out handbills in the immediate neighborhood. If the income from VCR's is insufficient, then offer to fix other electronic items.

You can learn how by studying books in the library or by picking up a copy of *Popular Mechanics*—they always contain ads offering home study courses for electronics and related fields.

To me, this is the perfect opportunity for a retired or semi-retired senior. You can work as much as you wish (there is always the possibility of sub-contract work from an established TV repair shop), take time off when you are restless or sleepy, eat lunch at your workbench when busy, take your pay in cash or barter and pay little if any to the tax man. Also, there is a tremendous feeling of accomplishment to take a defunct, complex item like a VCR and make it hum again. The more machines you fix, the easier the repair becomes.

CONSULTANT

Most seniors have developed one or more skills in their lifetime. Some have been librarians, others airplane mechanics, still others chefs or ship fitters, salespeople or even writers. There are few professions, white or blue collar, that do not lend themselves to a follow-on business of being a consultant.

Take that librarian for example. He or she can offer his or her services to a large company to get their documents in order and keep them that way. Many wealthy people have large personal libraries that could probably use organizing. Then too, a librarian is familiar with what people like to read, so it's possible that consultant work could be obtained to advise publishers and writers as to the market potential.

A retired aircraft mechanic could set up a small office in a nearby airport and offer to advise plane owners as to the safest and least expensive ways to maintain their planes. By keeping up with the current trends in engines, electronics, navigation equipment and so forth, a consultant could easily earn his client much more in savings than the consulting fee would cost. When you consider how expensive plane ownership has become, this makes a lot of sense.

The same consultant opportunities would exist for someone who spent a lifetime around boats. A boat consultant could set up shop at a marina and offer to help boat owners get the most for their dollars. Following up on ancillary enterprises, you could emulate a man I know in the California Delta area who services yachtsmen's boats so that they have freshly-charged batteries, filled water and fuel tanks, and are ready to cast off when the owner arrives.

Let's say that you have been a chef; there are increasing numbers of restaurants in America, as eating out has become a social and cultural in-thing. A simple business card offering food preparation advice to various local restaurants is all that would be required to start this interesting business.

Incidentally, in any type of consultant work, you could ask to be paid in barter. For example, a restaurant consultant could take out his pay in meals while an airplane consultant could be compensated with free air time.

Yes, consultant work is going to be a tremendous opportunity for seniors as the need for relevant information to survive becomes mandatory. And this is a business that can be conducted from your home or even an RV. Just think, you could be a traveling consultant going north in summer and south in winter. What could be more pleasurable?

On a personal note, I found that I had no problems becoming a publications consultant after I left that tech writing job in aerospace. Often I picked up a fee from the client for advice on printing and a commission from the printer for the job.

SPECIAL THOUGHTS (FOR FEMALE CONSULTANTS)

Consultant work is ideal for senior women since it can eliminate the male/female employment bias that exists in so many labor areas. A person who is sufficiently skilled to be a consultant will be hired regardless of sex. After all, companies want RESULTS; very little else matters.

ADVERTISING

This afternoon, a women in her mid-50's came into the office where I am finishing up this book. She had delivered an ad which was to be used by my publisher in mail order sales. It was a handsome preparation and I complimented her on it.

She appreciated the kind words but was quick to comment that jobs were becoming fewer and fewer for her. So I suggested something that I learned when I managed a surgical instrument company. It seems that there are many people who make a living by improving ads. All that is required is that you have the necessary skills in graphic arts—a sense of good design, attractive layouts, knowledge of type and printing and so forth. Then you merely clip out ads that you feel need improvement and mail them to clients with a cover letter. This letter asks if the ad was successful and if not, what the chances are of you preparing a better ad for a reasonable fee.

This type of enterprise can be conducted from any point on the planet and can extend to any area. You can start by helping people with local ads and then graduate to regional, statewide and eventually national advertising. Your sources of clients can be in any print media. And just think, if you have television skills, you can offer to improve commercials which, God knows, need the improvement.

This field is one of those that is open-ended. There is no predictable or foreseeable limit to what could be done. After all, the field of selling through advertising is a multi-billion dollar business and there is always room at the top.

For more information, go to your handy-dandy library and check out books on marketing and advertising, art and graphics. Then study ads so that you have a feel for what is being done and more importantly, what CAN be done. Just remember that from a pragmatic standpoint, the business of America is business and barring some incredible changes, it will be for some time to come. Thus, you have the opportunity to improve such things as truth in advertising or the marketing of really worthwhile products like pure foods. So to merge altruism and honesty with an extra income, I suggest that you eschew what is known as booze, butts and buggies (whiskey, cigarettes and cars) ads and go for the selling of products that benefit mankind.

I once was offered the chance to help sell Cadillacs, but my heart was just not in peddling those giant gas guzzlers. Now if you were to offer me the opportunity to sell Volvos, I might consider it!

KAYSITE

In the *Freedom Afloat* chapter, Kaysite is illustrated in more detail. This method of boat restoration really works as I have proved in many instances.

I will be happy to help any senior who wants to set up a Kaysite facility in his or her community. Just write and tell me what you need to know in addition to what is presented in the chapter. I'll do my best to answer all letters personally.

Kaysite was developed with Third World countries in mind, since boat failure is a matter of life and death to those who depend on fishing or other waterborne activities for their daily bread. When I visited Mexico I learned that many of the Mexican fishing boats are in poor repair and often sink. Sheathing an old hull in a strong and durable coating of special cement is a logical way to maintain hull integrity for a long time. I estimate that this process will provide at least 20 years of leak-free service. I mention this because if a senior wishes to start his or her own *ad hoc* peace corps, he or she could visit or live in one of the poorer countries and teach the citizens there how to restore boats with the Kaysite process.

Then, too, this country has some 18,000,000 boats of good size; the market for restoring them has never been better. An article in a yachting magazine produced more work than I have been able to handle. That's why I would like to recruit some people who would like to have a spare or full-time income from interesting, outdoor work.

Write to me in care of the publisher and tell me how you would like to participate.

SECURITY

In a country where there is a disappearing middle class and a larger population of have-nots, the necessity for protecting life, limb and property becomes increasingly essential. Since it is an ill wind indeed that blows no good, this situation becomes a burgeoning opportunity for any senior who has an interest in this field.

There are many ramifications. One could be a security consultant or install dead bolts. Or anyone who likes to sleep in the daytime could be a night watchman. Then, on a high-tech level, there is the need for people to design and install sophisticated sensing systems.

Generally, this type of security business goes best in a wealthy area or one of concentrated business enterprise. But there are many chances to operate in ordinary neighborhoods as long as one makes systems affordable.

Personally, I can't think of any business that is more in demand than security.

To get started, go to your library and ask at the reference desk to see periodicals and books on the subject. Or call up your local security concerns and tell them you want to get involved.

Incidentally, most security firms want older people for security work since they have proven themselves more reliable.

NOTE: The following income suggestion is especially oriented towards women. Men have long dominated the medical field but now, with rapidly changing public views toward health, women have entered the healing arts in great numbers. Pick up any of the magazines in health food stores on well-being and you'll see ads for many women who are skilled practitioners of the alternative healing modalities.

THE HEALING ARTS

As we have mentioned in the chapter on health, there is a rapid change in what is being offered to the ailing. Ten years ago, hardly anyone had heard of acupuncture. Today it is a licensed specialty in many states. And how about feldenkreis or rolfing—methods of correcting muscular or skeletal imbalance. Or how about the re-emergence of homeopathy, a method of healing popular in the last century.

It is obvious that there are more chances than ever to participate in a full or part-time way as a member of the healing team. No longer do you need to go to medical school and serve a decade-long internship. Today, a course in shiatsu massage might take as little as a month. Or if you want to be a nutritionist, there are courses available by mail. The point is, you can become whatever you would like to be in a reasonable period of time.

From then on, it's up to you as to how much healing you want to administer. There are estimated to be about 100 million Americans who are acutely or chronically ill or both. So your marketplace is very large. I have known people that just distribute their massage service cards in mobile home parks which have a high percentage of seniors and never have to solicit business again. After all, if you are good at what you do, word of mouth will take care of the need for customers.

Personally, I feel good about recommending the healing arts to those who need or want a supplemental income. I can think of no greater reward in life than to have someone say that you relieved them of pain. This happened many times when I was involved in the distribution and use of DMSO and I must admit that many times I acted like a doctor, but without any official sanction.

So, if service to suffering humanity excites your benevolent bones, go for it! Most alternative medicine fields now have their own publications, and a large university is one of the best places to find these periodicals.

COTTAGE INDUSTRY

We once stopped by a house in Mendocino County, CA to ask directions. As often happens, the lady invited us in for a chat. She had been busy winding small transformer coils on a little machine placed on her dining room table. I learned that she was earning about eight dollars an hour for simple, non-taxing although repetitive work.

"It's really nice," she said. "I'm my own boss, set my own hours, and if I want I can lie down or go out and feed the chickens."

She went on to explain that she had worked in an electronics assembly plant for some time and had semi-retired to the picturesque Anderson Valley near Philo.

This incident triggered continuing thoughts on how a senior could supplement a low income by taking on various jobs which could be done in the home. I would canvas local industry to see if there were segments of work that could be done at home with or without equipment. I met one man who had invested in a machine that would deburr small machine parts. This work was transacted by mail and UPS to and from a large city. The final work was done by hand by seniors on a piece-work basis. Another piece work operation was the making of stained glass items in an Oakland, CA warehouse. I noted that these could have been made at home since the only tool was a soldering iron.

There is one mode of work that I do myself—writing. All it takes is a second-hand typewriter and some paper. It requires some ability, but more of just plain gumption and perseverance.

So, if your Social Security check is not covering all the bills, check out your community for homework. Recently, I learned that in the Orient, they drop off a large, hardwood log to a family and come back a year later to buy the hand-carved items that have been made from the log. So, it's just a matter of finding your "log."

MUSIC

Ever since the Beatles came on the scene in the early 60's, there has been a renaissance in the music world. Many years ago, during the era of Beethoven, Bach and Brahms, society was closely linked with both music and its composers and performers. Men like Wagner were social lions and performances by Mozart were attended by large crowds in Vienna and elsewhere.

With the advent of the industrial revolution, music fell into a period of decline. There was a brief period of new interest following WWI, but little of world interest occurred until 1963 when the Beatles burst into an era of anxiety and apathy with their fresh, vital, lively, enthusiastic and iconoclastic words-music. The world was transformed.

The Beatle's music is humanistic and is revealed in such songs as *Yesterday*, *Michelle*, and *Here, There and Everywhere*. Their social commentary appears in *Strawberry Fields Forever* and *All the Lonely People*, in addition to many others.

Their melodies often transcend the impact of their lyrics with many of them arranged for symphonic presentation.

Beatles music appeals to all ages, races and sexes. It is truly universal. Furthermore, John Lennon, the tacit leader of the Beatles, was heavily into the international peace movement and was said to be able to create a million-strong mass of peace-advocates in any city on earth in just 24 hours.

This preamble to the discussion of methods to earn a living from music on a senior level is provided to prove the incredible impact of music on the human soul and resultant changes on a global scope. We are all familiar with the strange and powerful emotional responses we have to some much loved and familiar song.

I know that WWII vets share my feelings about Jo Stafford's haunting ballads and the lift we all got from the clarinet of Artie Shaw or Benny Goodman. And many of us can't hear the strong, complex chords of Rachmaninoff without sensing the unique creative powers of this remarkable Russian composer to call forth feelings uncommunicable in words. And for the American scene in sharps and flats, who can evoke more passionate pictures than our own Aaron Copland?

Yes, I cannot think of any aspect of the arts where a senior could be more rewarded in far more than monetary terms.

Here are a few approaches for seniors with an interest in music.

AD HOC PAY FOR PLAY

Many years ago I met a delightful young woman who dedicated her life to the harp. She started with a small Irish version and later graduated to the symphonic harp. In between, she earned a modest income by playing on street corners in San Francisco and in nightclubs. Today, she is ranked as first harpist in symphony orchestras and is called on for the demanding work of television commercials. She has done what few people do—made a full-time career out of her love for music and her skill in producing it. Congratulations and greetings, Natalie Cox.

Now as I see it, you can do the same if you have the motivation and persistence and at least a modicum of musical talent. And you can achieve any level of accomplishment; it is entirely up to you.

If you are content to play in clubs, fine. If the busy street scene interests you, great. Recently, I heard two black musicians play flute and percussion at Fisherman's Wharf and after they finished one number, many people stepped forward to buy their recorded tapes.

There are opportunities for musical presentations in cities and towns worldwide. I have often thought of taking my harmonica and and old ten-gallon hat and playing Western melodies like *Down in the Valley* and *Clementine* on street corners, just for fun.

TEACHING MUSIC

If you can play well, then teach. Go to a music store and put up a card or poster. Tell the store manager that you would appreciate his or her cooperation in contacting any buyer of the same instrument you play for possible lessons.

Go to local schools and offer to tutor music students. Run small ads in local papers and periodically ask the local music writer to do a feature story on you.

Appear on radio and television as chances occur. Before long, you should have a class of students to teach and as they advance, you advance.

My son-in-law is a guitar virtuoso and not only has private students, but teaches at a state university, and all by virtue of his persistence and much talent. I want to also add that he and my daughter are well on their way to success with their *Miles and Miles* musical group. Again, all due to their refusal to ever even think of giving up the struggle. Incidentally, *M and M* play in clubs, at weddings and other social events and are always prepared for a "gig."

One way they obtained experience was to play for people in hospitals. You can do the same; just call the director of any institution and ask for permission to play in the wards or in prison courtyards. You'll seldom be refused and I guarantee that you will be well-rewarded with riches of the soul.

COMPOSE, ARRANGE, PUBLISH

Just the other day I had the great pleasure of hearing the famous Bob Wills Jr., a world-renowned Western swing singer and bandleader, perform in person. At 60, he had just recovered from two strokes and was getting his health back by practicing at home. He regaled me with fascinating stories about the musical profession and pointed out that there are always opportunities to create your own original music, arrange it, perform it and record or publish it.

It is beyond the scope of this presentation to go into all the details involved in the above, but there are many books in the library on the subject.

Incidentally, one of Ruth's friends composed the famous song *Ruby*, which produced a handsome royalty each month for the composer's entire life. And one of my neighbors in Topanga Canyon (Los Angeles area) wrote *Nature Boy* and could have retired on the proceeds.

You only need one hit song to be financially independent for your entire life and it's never too late to start.

WRITE ABOUT MUSIC

Many publications welcome freelance reviews of new music and local performers. Just phone or write the editors of local papers and offer to be a "stringer" for them. That means that you are considered a reliable and steady source of news or "copy" and will be paid, usually by the line. If you are really capable, you could become a weekly columnist. And don't forget the many music magazines which need articles in every issue.

DEMONSTRATE INSTRUMENTS

At many fairs, conventions and similar events, you will often find an organ or other instrument being demonstrated. If you can handle an instrument with professional skill, offer to supply this service. See your local dealer or write to major musical instrument manufacturers and distributors. Also contact local convention bureaus.

REPAIR INSTRUMENTS

If you play, learn how to repair your instrument. Then offer this service through local music stores.

NOTE: Turn on your radio. Notice how much music is being played right now. It should convince you that music is one of the most active arts abounding in opportunities for seniors. And as we all know, there is always room at the top, which is where I hope you'll be headed!

MUSIC EPILOGUE

Check out the longevity of performers and conductors as well as composers. You will find that musicians like Casals and Rubenstein have lived long, rewarding and fruitful lives with many unique experiences along the way.

Music; it is really the language of the universe; when you learn to speak it, you will gain great understanding.

MINIATURES

In a museum in Santa Fe, New Mexico, I recently saw an exhibit that absolutely stunned me. Imagine an old motel-gas station circa 1928 reduced to about one cubic foot. It included a weathered building, peeling signs, a pop machine with bottles not a half-inch high, old tires out back and even wear patterns on the tired old screen doors, litter in the driveways, struggling plants and every indication that real people, a few inches tall, were inside the rooms reading the paper and looking out at the arid landscape.

I kept coming back to this display and spent part of two days studying this flawless artistry.

We've all see dollhouses, small artifacts, ship models and the like, but until I saw this unique accomplishment, I had never seen a masterwork. I considered this work a museum piece worthy of the Louvre or Metropolitan—priceless, of course. It did have a tag in four figures indicating that it had been sold and reloaned to the Santa Fe museum for a special presentation of New Mexican artists.

What this leads to is this: many seniors love to work with their hands in craft projects. Here is a wide-open field that is perfect for those who have the patience and skill to be masters at miniaturization. I can see where there could be a large following for works of this type. I know I would love to own one.

Materials would be inexpensive—small pieces of wood and metal comprised the bulk of the miniatures that I saw. Paint, glue and some real earth would provide most of the other needs. I imagine that five or ten dollars would provide more than enough materials for a generous project. And if you are a scrounger, you might be able to get most everything from scrap sources.

How to do it would be a matter of learning from books on model building and then taking off by yourself where the book leaves off. I am sure that the young man (he was about 24 I learned) had a background in model building before he attempted his masterpieces. You would be wise to learn something of the basics of modeling before departing on a major project. But all things considered, anyone with the infinite patience of a true artist/craftsman could duplicate this marvelous work. And the rewards would be both artistic and financial.

The field of art is so large that we don't have space to discuss all the other possibilities. But as always, your local library can be a source of books on any aspect of the art world.

"Everyone on earth makes a living by selling either goods or services."
— *Robert Louis Stevenson*

SELLING

When I was about five or six, I began to sell magazines, newspapers and other items on the streets of my hometown. I also went door-to-door. I learned very early in life that selling something can be hard, disappointing work. And yet selling is really the mechanism that makes the world economy function as it does. Without someone to sell and someone to buy, there's no commerce and with no commerce, few people could live above a mere subsistence level.

So what we have developed unwittingly is a tough way to go on this planet. While it is not likely to change overnight, it may be headed, hopefully, in the direction of more cooperation and less competition. Until that happy day, here are some thoughts on what a senior can do in the selling game. My purpose is to take some of the pain and anguish out of the activity that was so destructive to Willy Loman, Arthur Miller's famous salesman in *Death of a Salesman*.

1. As the song says, make it easy on yourself. Get something to sell that has at least a fighting chance in the marketplace. During the depths of the depression, I tried to sell American flags door-to-door. No one wanted to be reminded of how little the government was doing to alleviate the misery of 1932. I don't recall selling a single one in many months of trying with great diligence.
   Take life insurance as an example of a toughy. Out of 100 people who start selling insurance, only one of them is still at it at the end of a year. While I am not advising that you exclude insurance as a means of senior income, it is a hard-sell because of the outrageous competition. I would much prefer to find something like a new VCR or a new type of copy machine if I were to hit the streets again making cold calls.

2. Sell something that will help a person have a more efficient and successful business. My opening line on a prospect was, "Do you want more business?" Well, of course the person did. Not a bad way to start off a sales pitch, don't you agree? I found that if I was selling something like a sales-aids, low-cost printing or advertising, it was not too difficult to make some sales every day.

3. Set a quota for the day and then meet it with due diligence. It's difficult to just go on and on with sales calls and no end in sight. I found that if I programmed myself for a certain number of calls with the toughest ones first, it made the day go by much easier.

4. Have a variety of things to sell if you can. My own philosophy was to carry around a lot of goodies so that if a client didn't buy one, he would buy another. I felt like an old Yankee peddler sometimes, but with two girls and a wife to support in the Santa Barbara of the 60's, I was heavily motivated.

5. I found that selling something that provided a little action each day was heartening. If you are stuck with something gigantic that only sells once a year—a million dollar computer system for example—then you are probably going to be discouraged long before that sale is made. This is what often drives people out of the real estate business —too much time between sales. Incidentally, a friend of mine once discovered that the average real estate salesperson in Santa Barbara was earning about 40 dollars a week in the mid-60's, hardly a living wage. So real estate is often so competitive as to make it impossible for any but a select few to earn a satisfactory income. Of course, as a senior earning income as a part-time, supplemental effort, you can afford to go along with the game.

In summary, while selling is tough, it can be most rewarding to the persistent and persevering. Since it IS tough, there are often lots of openings and lots of things to sell. Load up your Yankee peddler's wagon and go to it. I'll leave you with a bit of homely wisdom from our American past—the dog that trots about eventually finds a bone.

BE A TEACHER

It is predicted that by the end of this century, half of every dollar spent will be on some aspect of information or communication. This would include books, films, television, business and technical data, advertising, education and so forth. Obviously, with this much information flowing around, there must be people to teach it to others. Thus, there are myriad opportunities for seniors to take what they know and transfer the knowledge to others for a fee.

In a recent article in *Town and Country* magazine, called "Schooling the Sportsman," it was pointed out that many people want to know more about a specific sport with sports being defined in the broadest sense of the word. A variety of schools for sportsmen and women were reviewed including those for fly fishing, motor racing, sailing and alpine ski racing. For example, it described the Bob Bondurant School of High Performance Driving, conducted at the Sears Point Raceway in California. Bob teaches anyone who is interested to race cars, drive stunt cars and escape terrorists by car. The Annapolis Sailing School in Maryland offers 26 courses in such categories as live-aboard cruising, basic sailing and advanced boat-handling techniques.

These are typical of many in each category and the thought that it sparks is that almost anyone has developed a skill or skills by the time they are seniors. Thus, why not offer training in your skills to others? After all, the apprentice method of teaching is one of the oldest in the history of mankind and still functions beautifully.

Let's say you are a former photographer. This is a hobby/profession that intrigues millions of Americans. If you have the work to prove your expertise, there is no reason why you can't go into business as a professional photographer/teacher and provide training to eager students nationwide.

There isn't any profession that would not lend itself to this teach-for-pay concept from welding to writing, from railroading to roustabouting. All skills are teachable. What a super-rewarding way to help others as you help yourself.

Just happened to think that one of my desires has been to start a motorcycle safety school, since I have been riding those captivating two-wheelers since 1940. Now just maybe.

THE DREAM OF EVERY AMERICAN FULFILLED

Las Vegas has fascinated me for many years. Vegas IS America condensed; everything good or bad about this country is on view in a form which makes it all too visible. Generosity and greed, lust and love, talent and ignorance are displayed in a fishbowl environment. This makes for greater understanding not only of how the American culture functions, but it also suggests improvements (I recall Hank Greenspun, publisher of the *Las Vegas Sun*, once saying that the town would benefit if gambling were eliminated!).

But while in Sun or Sin City, whichever way you wish to call it, not all my time was involved as a writer/researcher. Instead I found plenty of time to enjoy myself in a variety of ways. One of the ways proved to be a lifelong dream realized and this is how it happened.

Just a few miles south of Vegas is a faithful reproduction of a Western mining town. It's called Old Nevada and the builder used the same type of lumber used in the 19th century. Thus, the authenticity is peerless. In addition to the buildings, he hired young men to stage gunfights and hangings on the streets of the town for the amusement and amazement of visitors. He also installed a half-scale railroad complete with an 1880's passenger train. I will give you just one guess as to who ended up running that train.

Yes, it was your old friend Wild Bill who put on the engineer cap each day, fired up the locomotive and drove excited tourists from the parking lot below town to its entrance. I just can't remember when I had so much fun. The pay was negligible in monetary terms (room and board and tips) but in the "coin" of smiles and laughter from the enthusiastic kids and their parents, I was a millionaire. Actually, I was having so much fun, I would have gladly worked for free or even paid for the privilege!

You just cannot imagine the exhilaration of being a railroad engineer to a train load of wide-eyed children who are also living out a real-life fantasy. And most of the adults had their eyes wide open, too!

I just fell into this job by volunteering to take over when the regular engineer quit. But I can imagine that a senior with an adventurous inclination could find a similar position. After all, there are model railroads all over the country. And if you can't find one, then BUILD YOUR OWN!

Happy train whistles and bells to you!

BIRDS

Many seniors have combined hobby and income with activities relating to birds. My daughter Wendy proved this at a young age by writing articles on birds for avian journals.

To start, just read some of these magazines at your local library or check out books on the subject. You might consider breeding birds for fun and profit. The little parakeets or budgies are easy to handle and can live in moderately-sized cages which you can have in your room or patio.

Remember how the famous *Birdman of Alcatraz* had hundreds of birds in his tiny cell and became an expert on avian diseases?

Then there's a wonderful opportunity to become a bird photographer. Just put a wild bird feeder in your backyard, set up a camera with a telephoto lens and you're in business. Good shots can be sold to fancier bird publications or the general market. Unusual pictures of birds seem to be always in demand. See back issues of *National Geographic* for some great examples of bird photography.

These are only samples of what could be done. Think about helping to prevent the extinction of rare birds, the culture of homing pigeons, the raising of parrots (very popular right now) and so forth. By the way, watch those parrots, they have a habit of snapping their beaks on hapless fingers when you least expect it.

COUNSELLING

We seniors have a great advantage—most of us have experienced some of everything. From war to warthogs, from marriage to madness, from aardvark steaks to zebra rugs. Thus, we are in a great position to counsel those younger who have not had our diverse experiences with life.

Counselling is a vast field with so many ramifications that it would take a book to just list them—drug, career, marriage are just three which require an enormous inventory of people and skills. For example, let's take a brief look at Reginald and Renee, counselors at Paraiso, a lovely hot springs resort near Soledad, CA. They have the free use of a cozy Victorian home and all the springs, and they derive income from their counselling work which helps people obtain and maintain physical, mental and spiritual health. I once took a semi-paralyzed friend to Reginald and after a treatment, my friend said, "I've never felt better."

There are countless opportunities to work at counselling in a setting of your choice. It's a matter of selecting a place and fitting your expertise to the circumstances there. For example, if you are expert at counselling children, there are plenty of schools in outlying regions all over America. Somewhere, as the song says, there's a place for you.

PHILIP MARLOWE ANYONE?

What follows is a brief description of a course in how to be a private detective. Since many seniors suffer from boredom, here's a chance to have excitement and get paid for it.

Richard Alex of *Central Investigation and Security* offers a course of lessons in how to be a private eye by mail. As he points out (and I agree), crime is still rising in the U.S. and the need for skilled investigators is up. He cites pay of 20 to 50 dollars an hour as being possible if you have the training which he offers in a correspondence course taught by a skilled instructor. Employment as full or part-time in private investigation, hotel detective work, insurance investigation, undercover agent, agency management, narcotics investigation, store detective, etc., is cited. If this appeals to you, write to *Richard Alex, CIS, 1031 N. 500 West, Provo, UT 84603*.

Being a private detective seems a very natural arena for seniors—seeking out clues and applying your innate wisdom, let alone putting to use your intuitive abilities and your biggest magnifying glass.

SUMMARY AND CONCLUSIONS

There are obviously many ways that a senior man or woman can make extra income. Ruth still punches away at her typewriter when an attorney friend needs a legal document typed. And I am always on hand to help out when someone needs publicity for an event. Sometimes the pay is not really commensurate with the effort expended, but money is not everything. I have often been paid in spiritual riches and found that to be far more valuable than mere money.

I'll conclude by saying that I can find no reason why a healthy and enterprising senior can't find a source of extra income. Chances for part- or full-time employment or self-employment abound, especially in those areas of increasing demand. And seniors are welcomed in many fields because employers know that you and I are reliable.

CHAPTER FOURTEEN
TIPS AND POINTERS

Here are some ideas which have arisen while writing this book. While they could be placed in some of the other chapters, I feel comfortable having them in a chapter all their own so that you can browse through them periodically. Hopefully, they will help you directly and also trigger some new ideas of your own.

FLEXIBILITY IS THE KEY

One stormy day in the Pacific my destroyer was heaving and tossing. It was so rough, even the captain was seasick.

Standing on the stern gun platform was McGregor, an old sackhound whom we called "Bedsores" because he spent so much time in his bunk. Suddenly, a rogue wave appeared, so huge that it engulfed even our formidable 300-footer. The stern went down into the rogue's trough, the entire gun platform was swept by a mighty rush of water and McGregor was hurled into the sea directly above the razor-sharp propellers spinning at 200 revolutions per minute. A vortex of blood appeared just as McGregor bobbed to the surface. A sailor on deck shouted to him,

"Are you OK?"

"Sure, I'm fine except the propeller cut off my leg."

And indeed, it did. Mac was rescued and despite the loss of most of his blood, lived to see the end of WWII and a return to civilian life with a serviceable wooden leg.

The thought that has remained in my mind all these years was his complete equanimity in the face of a horrendous personal disaster. To be able to say, "I'm fine," under those circumstances must be the penultimate application of flexibility.

The opposite of flexibility is rigidity and it is this state of being that is often the basic cause of disease. As Marilyn Ferguson points out in her great classic work, *The Aquarian Conspiracy*,

> *"If we are flexible, able to adapt to a changing environment,*
> *even a virus or damp air or fatigue or spring pollens,*
> *we can withstand a high level of stress."*

Theoretically, many diseases seem to be metaphors for the activities of the mind. For example, cancerous growths could be manifestations of the need to grow but with the growth frustrated. Arthritis with its crippling of joints seems to be the outward symptom of a mind that has crippled and rigidized itself. Multiple sclerosis with its steady encroachment on the utilization of the body could be a metaphor for a retreat from life due to fear or frustration or a combination of both (how often have authors cited that someone was "paralyzed with fear," a condition that often exists).

The moral is,

WHAT WE THINK, WE BECOME.

FLEXIBILITY, PHYSICAL and MENTAL

Physical flexibility is the easiest. All you need to do is to stay as active as possible within the constraints of aging. It is a truism that the more you exercise, the easier it will be. Give up exercising for a month or so and you'll probably have trouble doing those deep knee bends.

Then there are a great many new techniques of physical flexibility including rolfing, feldenkreis, acupuncture, acupressure and a cornucopia of new massage methods. Each or all can be a part of a daily program of bodily "looseness."

But mental flexibility—it's a bit tougher. How often do older people develop a mindset that is seemingly too rigid to change? If your negative thoughts rule your mental state, the negativism is only supported by dozens of other negative affirmations. In simply perusing the daily paper, there are reasons by the dozen to point out that the negativism is in the air. Your world view can be internalized by the rigid belief that it is too late to change. Many people are convinced that after 60 or so, no old dog can be taught new tricks.

This fallacy has been disproved ten thousand times a day as seniors take up sailboarding, hang gliding, flying or any number of less active and nevertheless exciting activities.

To remain flexible all through your life requires the willingness to at least try a new approach to old problems, habits and routines. For example, the other day I needed to be somewhere 35 miles away and there was no bus service and few cars on an isolated country road. So I climbed on my bike and just rode that distance with no real difficulty. In fact, I think I handled it better at 65 than I would have at half that age. After all, I have a better diet now. The key element here was the willingness to try, to see if I was both physically and mentally flexible enough to handle a long trip.

Is it uncommon to be spry at 65 or 75 or older? Not really. The exploits of men and women in the recent senior Olympics would prove that age has little to do with one's over-all health. And just look at some of these people from the new book, *Growing Old Is Not for Sissies*, a Pomegranate Press publication.

In summary, be like a rubber band; stretch, bend, extend yourself in mind and body and you will hardly feel the encroachment of age at all.

JOHN TURNER
age 67

A psychiatrist, John Turner leads a sedentary professional life ("I sit and listen to people all day"), so he compensates by weight-lifting, jogging and taking long walks. "I think physicians have a responsibility to sell health at least as much as they sell pills," he said. After photographing him, I was sold.

F. EDWARD LITTLE
age 71
and MARIE WILCOX,
age 61

Edward and Marie are competitive
masters swimmers, pictured here at
the national masters in Ft. Lauderdale,
Florida, in 1982. Both still weigh the
same as they did in high school.

FIRST AID

Everyone has been in an emergency situation. Knowing what to do in case you, your friends and family or a stranger need help can ease your mind and make your first aid treatment easier.

In our ever-increasing high stress society, it is not uncommon for a senior to have a physical problem needing immediate attention in a public place. For example, after a long day and an evening meal out in a restaurant, chest pains may occur. This section on first aid addresses some of the more common, yet potentially life-threatening emergencies in seniors and what to do in case of:

Shortness of Breath: May be due to heart or lung disease. Heart failure is the most common cause of shortness of breath.

Symptoms include pain in the chest, upper abdomen, shoulder or jaw, clammy skin and heavy perspiration.

What to do to help in addition to seeking medical help:

1. Determine age and general health of the person.

2. Try to find out if the person takes any heart medication or has a history of heart or lung disease.

3. Help the person to sit up or semi-recline, whatever is more comfortable for him or her. Loosen any constricting clothing. Be reassuring.

Chest Pain or Heart Attack: May be a lung or muscle problem caused by indigestion, strained muscles, or shingles and so forth.

Danger signs and symptoms of the more serious include: pain lasting more than two minutes that is usually described as "tight" or "crushing"; it is usually in the center of the chest and sometimes spreads to the upper abdomen, shoulder (usually the left), neck or jaw pain, gasping or shortness of breath that improves when the person sits but gets worse when he or she lies flat, severe anxiety, a pending doom feeling, weakness, heavy sweating, pale or bluish skin or lips, nausea or vomitting, irregular pulse.

What to do:

1. Get medical help immediately. Call 911 (if available in your community).

2. Help the person to sit up or semi-recline, whatever is more comfortable for him or her. Loosen any constricting clothing. Be reassuring. Keep him or her comfortably warm.

3. If the person loses consciousness, lay him or her flat on back. Check for breathing and pulse (with your middle, index and ring fingers in the neck or wrist). If the person vomits, turn head to the side and clean mouth.

4. If the person is conscious and has medicine for *Angina Pectoris* (temporary shortage of oxygen to the heart), help him or her take it. This medicine will most likely be a nitroglycerine pill under the tongue.

179

5.   If breathing stops, CPR (Cardiopulmonary resuscitation) is required.

Choking: An important tip about choking is that the person's cough is more effective than first aid. If the person is not coughing strongly and cannot speak, first aid is essential.

Symptoms include the inability to speak, difficulty in breathing, suddenly collapsing and the universal choking signal. Without having taken a course in CPR, back blows and the *Heimlich Maneuver* can be useful in some situations.

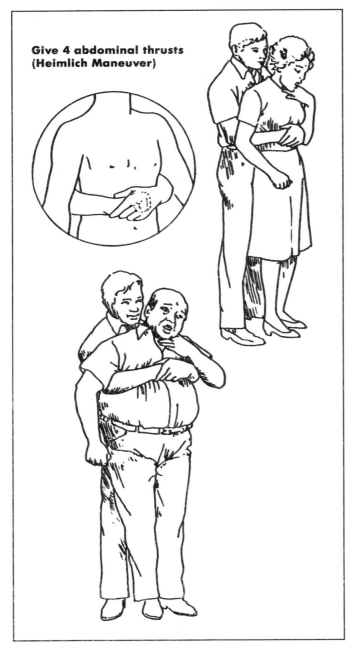

Give 4 abdominal thrusts (Heimlich Maneuver)

WHAT TO DO:

1.   Stand behind the person. Support his or her chest with one hand and bend the head forward (so that head is lower than chest). Give 4 blows to the back, between the shoulder blades. Hit rapidly and hard enough to dislodge the object.

2.   If the person continues to choke, put both arms around him or her and perform the *Heimlich Maneuver*: Press the thumb-side of your fist against his or her abdomen, halfway between the waist and bottom of ribs. Grasp your fist with your other hand and perform 4 quick, hard inward and upward thrusts. Note: If obesity makes this impossible, perform the thrusts against the middle of the person's breastbone.

3.   If the first 2 steps don't work, continue the cycle. Don't give up. Repeat the 4 blows and the 4 thrusts and have someone call for medical assistance.

4.   If the person begins to cough forcefully or loses consciousness, stop first aid. CPR is required.

5.   If you are alone and choking, you can perform the *Heimlich Maneuver* on yourself or you can push against your abdomen by leaning over the back of a chair.

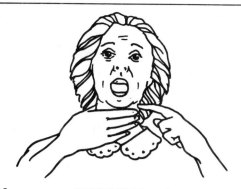

If you are CHOKING, give a signal
Let other people know. Give them an unmistakable signal by clutching your throat with one hand. This is the universally recognized signal of choking.

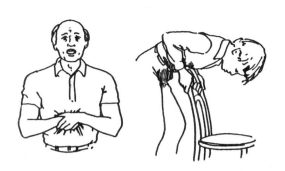

If you are ALONE and CHOKING
You can perform the *Heimlich Maneuver* **or** you can push against your own abdomen by leaning over the back of a chair or other object.

Stomach and Intestinal Problems: A very delicate problem because it can be common indigestion or something quite severe.

Watch for signs of relief and symptoms including doubling over, heavy sweating, nasuea, shortness of breath, rapid pulse, a vacant expression, enlarged pupils, shallow or irregular breathing, diarrhea, constipation. As you can see, the signs are many and there for you to be sensitive to.

The result can be a heart attack if the pain is in the upper abdomen, appendicitis if the pain moves to the lower right with tenderness of that area, loss of appetite, fever, nausea or constipation, a strangulated or trapped hernia if the sharp pain comes and goes (strong and intense cramps) continuously. Food poisoning, too, can result in some of the same symptoms. Save food samples if possible.

For more details on first aid and other life-saving procedures, go to your local library and check out first aid and safety books and sign up for courses such as CPR techniques provided by such organizations as the *American Red Cross*. A good book that we referred to is, *The Johnson & Johnson First Aid Book*.

WILLS

Few people are aware that you don't need a lawyer to create your last will and testament. All you need do is write out your will in longhand and sign it. A witness is optional. And that's all there is to it.

Of course, if you have a lot to give away and the terms are complex, you might seek legal help. But since the average senior dies with a very small estate, you might as well save the money (I learned that by the time the doctors and undertakers get through with the average deceased senior, there is an estate of less than a thousand dollars). So no need to spend a lot of money to give away a mere thousand dollars.

SPECIAL INFORMATION FOR SENIOR WOMEN

About 75 percent of all senior women are poor. Thus, this segment is devoted to ideas that will help this group in the growing part of our population whose fate is seemingly one of poverty and need.

I do not believe that anyone has to accept a standard of living that fails to meet real needs.

For 18 years I have had the pleasurable company of a charming, witty, trim and courageous lady who turned 71 on August 21, 1987. I consider Ruth a wonderful example of a person who has obtained much from life by virtue of adherence to basic fundamentals. I'll let her tell it in her own words:

"My own conviction is that exercise is number one in staying well. But I am also aware that we are not all alike and what one can do may be impossible for another. For example, I have been athletic all my life. I emulated my father's example of daily exercise because we were very close and I admired him tremendously. Now if you haven't had this sort of conditioning and have never been active physically, you aren't likely to jump into strenuous program of aerobic exercise. But you can start walking. No matter what your impairment (short of paralysis), take a step at a time and keep walking. Set a goal each day and try to increase it. You'll be amazed at how good you begin to feel. It will improve your circulation, clear your brain and trim your figure. Get a friend or neighbor to join you. It's a great way to socialize. I love to chat while walking and have sometimes been able to resolve problems in this fashion.

As Bill points out in another chapter, good nutrition is the second most important adjunct to well being. One of the early bibles in this area is Adelle Davis' *Let's Eat Right to Keep Fit*. It's the best introduction to nutrition that I know of because it's not too technical and it makes so much good sense. Although Ms. Davis is no longer with us, her books remain as popular as ever and as relevant today as when they were first published.

Sometimes, due to limited income, we senior women feel frustrated in efforts to satisfy all our needs. One answer for me was barter. Where we live there is a Barter Network which anyone can join for a modest fee. Your work capabilities are then listed in their directory. Perhaps you can bake or sew or type or garden or babysit or do whatever. In exchange for performing any of these services, you earn credits. These you can then apply towards using the services of another Barter Network member. In my case, I do typing. In exchange, I had some carpentry work down on our mobile home and I also enjoyed a number of wonderful massages, a luxury I could never have otherwise afforded.

If such a barter group doesn't exist in your neighborhood, start one yourself. Or simply do it on a one-to-one basis. Bill, for example, has done public relations work in exchange for dental services. I made a fried chicken dinner for a man who painted our porch. The possibilities are unlimited.

It is possible that you may feel hesitant to try some of the suggestions contained in this and other chapters. Perhaps you are the introverted type and feel shy about plunging into some of these new activities. One way to overcome this problem is to take a course or read a book on assertiveness training. My friend Emma was always afraid of hurting people's feelings or being disliked for trying to run things. As a result, she became a doormat, never letting her own wishes override those of others, including her husband. You can suppress your needs for just so long, then—like a steam kettle—they burst forth in some form such as high blood pressure or emotional outbursts. This is what happened to Emma. Then she took a course in assertiveness and as a result, is learning to express her needs without stepping on any toes in the process. It does work and you owe it to yourself to try. Your health may depend on it.

One of the toughest things senior women face may be widowhood. I lost my first husband when I was 50. But unlike some women, I was already out in the world working as a secretary. Bringing home my own paycheck gave me a sense of independence. However, for many women, this is not the case. As homemakers, they may have left all of the handling of finances to their mates along with car, house and garden work. Suddenly faced with all of the responsibilities, a widow feels helpless. The problem is, she has no preparation for coping with these matters.

The obvious solution is to start preparing now by learning as much as possible about what your husband is doing in running his part of the household. If possible, get him to prepare written instructions in case something happens to him. The husband of one of my friends failed to acquaint her with any of their family finances and when he died suddenly of a heart attack, she was left with a nearly hopeless financial mess to sort out.

If you are already widowed, it's not too late to pick up some knowledge. For example, banks are happy to instruct customers about the mysteries of handling money. Senior centers have volunteers to answer questions about Social Security and Medicare as well as the SS offices themselves. You can even take women's courses in auto repair and other previously male-dominated areas.

What is sometimes the most difficult can really prove to be the most important step of all. In two words, it is GETTING INVOLVED. If you are not working as I was, try volunteer work. Hundreds of humanistic organizations are out there crying for your help. Choose one that can use your particular skill or experience and one that you will enjoy helping. It will do wonders for your self-esteem and bring you a whole new circle of friends.

Since my retirement, I have dabbled in 20 different types of volunteer work, a lot of them using my secretarial skills, to be sure. But the one that I liked best was acting as host or a senior radio program in which we interviewed guests and played music or performed short plays. I became acquainted with a bevy of local people from a wide variety of organizations and since the goal was bringing helpful information to a senior audience, I felt good about what I was doing. Whatever you choose, I am sure you'll learn a great deal. And remember, you can switch any time you wish."

JACK LONDON

From a letter to the author from Russ Kingman, one of the world's leading scholars on London, his life and work:

Michael, Brother of Jerry, a book by Jack London was so powerful that it did away with many animal acts in vaudeville. *John Barleycorn* was written to do away with alcohol and it did, at least for a time.

Any person who reads all 59 of Jack's books, and all 192 short stories, numerous essays, poems, plays and letters will be a changed person, rich in spirit.

Here is my favorite selection from London's *The Iron Heel*, a powerful novel of the future that rings with authenticity and prescience:

Author's note: Most of us can cite a single book which has greatly influenced our lives. For me it was *The Iron Heel* which Ruth handed me one night in a northern California library. I read

CHAPTER 7

The Bishop's Vision

'THE BISHOP is out of hand,' Ernest wrote me. 'He is clear up in the air. Tonight he is going to begin putting to rights this very miserable world of ours. He is going to deliver his message. He has told me so, and I cannot dissuade him. Tonight he is chairman of the I.P.H., and he will embody his message in his introductory remarks.

'May I bring you to hear him? Of course, he is fore-doomed to futility. It will break your heart—it will break his; but for you it will be an excellent object-lesson. You know, dear heart, how proud I am because you love me. And because of that I want you to know my fullest value, I want to redeem, in your eyes, some small measure of my un-worthiness. And so it is that my pride desires that you shall know my thinking is correct and right. My views are harsh; the futility of so noble a soul as the Bishop will show you the compulsion for such harshness. So come tonight. Sad though this night's happening will be, I feel that it will but draw you more closely to me.'

The I.P.H.[1] held its convention that night in San Francisco.[2] This convention had been called to consider public immorality and the remedy for it. Bishop Morehouse presided. He was very nervous as he sat on the platform, and I could see the high tension he was under. By his side were Bishop Dickinson; H. H. Jones, the head of the ethical department in the University of California; Mrs W. W. Hurd, the great charity organiser; Philip Ward, the equally great philanthropist; and several lesser luminaries in the field of morality and charity. Bishop Morehouse arose and abruptly began:

'I was in my brougham, driving through the streets. It was night-time. Now and then I looked through the car-

[1] There is no clue to the name of the organisation for which these initials stand.

[2] It took but a few minutes to cross by ferry from Berkeley to San Francisco. These, and the other bay cities, practically composed one community.

it in one sitting and found my life totally transformed. I think that the most influential chapter is the one reproduced by permission here. One should know that this book was written in 1906, just a few years prior to the covert act that allowed the privately-owned Federal Reserve Bank to usurp financial control of the entire United States. Once these unseen powers took over the economic reins of government, the conditions for the events described in this chapter could take place, the suppression of news, for one prime example.

London is able to expose the hypocracies of the church establishment at the same time he presents details of how we could live with compassion for the weak and helpless ones of the world.

Currently, some of the churches in the San Francisco Bay area are being used for housing the homeless, only proving London's message is not entirely lost on those who have followed.

riage windows, and suddenly my eyes seemed to be opened, and I saw things as they really are. At first I covered my eyes with my hands to shut out the awful sight, and then, in the darkness the question came to me: What is to be done? What is to be done? A little later the question came to me in another way: What would the Master do? And with the question a great light seemed to fill the place, and I saw my duty sun-clear, as Saul saw his on the way to Damascus.

'I stopped the carriage, got out, and, after a few minutes' conversation, persuaded two of the public women to get into the brougham with me. If Jesus was right, then these two unfortunates were my sisters, and the only hope of their purification was in my affection and tenderness.

'I live in one of the loveliest localities in San Francisco. The house in which I live cost a hundred thousand dollars, and its furnishings, books, and works of art cost as much more. The house is a mansion. No, it is a palace, wherein there are many servants. I never knew what palaces were good for. I had thought they were made to live in. But now I know. I took the two women of the street to my palace, and they are going to stay with me. I hope to fill every room in my palace with such sisters as they.'

The audience had been growing more and more restless and unsettled, and the faces of those that sat on the platform had been betraying greater and greater dismay and consternation. And at this point Bishop Dickinson arose, and, with an expression of disgust on his face, fled from the platform and the hall. But Bishop Morehouse, oblivious to all, his eyes filled with his vision, continued:

'Oh, sisters and brothers, in this act of mine I find the solution of all my difficulties. I didn't know what broughams were made for, but now I know. They are made to carry the weak, the sick, and the aged; they are made to show honour to those who have lost the sense even of shame.

'I did not know what palaces were made for, but now I have found a use for them. The palaces of the Church should be hospitals and nurseries for those who have fallen by the wayside and are perishing.'

He made a long pause, plainly overcome by the thought that was in him, and nervous how best to express it.

'I am not fit, dear brethren, to tell you anything about morality. I have lived in shame and hypocrisies too long to be able to help others; but my action with those women, sisters

When I first read this poem I believed that Jack had written it and still believe he could have. After all, he was the author of more than books; he wrote plays, essays and poetry and gave many impassioned speeches in many places.

of mine, shows me that the better way is easy to find. To those who believe in Jesus and His Gospel there can be no other relation between man and man than the relation of affection. Love alone is stronger than sin—stronger than death. I therefore say to the rich among you that it is their duty to do what I have done and am doing. Let each one of you who is prosperous take into his house some thief and treat him as his brother, some unfortunate and treat her as his sister, and San Francisco will need no police force and no magistrates; the prisons will be turned into hospitals, and the criminal will disappear with his crime.

'We must give ourselves and not our money alone. We must do as Christ did; that is the message of the Church today. We have wandered far from the Master's teaching. We are consumed in our own flesh-pots. We have put mammon in the place of Christ. I have here a poem that tells the whole story. I should like to read it to you. It was written by an erring soul who yet saw clearly.[3] It must not be mistaken for an attack upon the Catholic Church. It is an attack upon all churches, upon the pomp and splendour of all churches that have wandered from the Master's path and hedged themselves in from His lambs. Here it is:

'The silver trumpets rang across the Dome;
    The people knelt upon the ground with awe;
    And borne upon the necks of men I saw,
Like some great God, the Holy Lord of Rome.

'Priest-like, he wore a robe more white than foam,
    And, king-like, swathed himself in royal red,
    Three crowns of gold rose high upon his head;
In splendour and in light the Pope passed home.

'My heart stole back across wide wastes of years
    To One who wandered by a lonely sea;
And sought in vain for any place of rest:
"Foxes have holes, and every bird its nest,
    I, only I, must wander wearily,
And bruise my feet and drink wine salt with tears."'

The audience was agitated, but unresponsive. Yet Bishop Morehouse was not aware of it. He held steadily on his way.

[3] Oscar Wilde, one of the lords of language of the nineteenth century of the Christian era.

TIPS & POINTERS

'And so I say to the rich among you, and to all the rich, that bitterly you oppress the Master's lambs. You have hardened your hearts. You have closed your ears to the voices that are crying in the land—the voices of pain and sorrow that you will not hear, but that some day will be heard. And so I say—'

But at this point, H. H. Jones and Philip Ward, who had already risen from their chairs, led the Bishop off the platform, while the audience sat breathless and shocked.

Ernest laughed harshly and savagely when he had gained the street. His laughter jarred upon me. My heart seemed ready to burst with suppressed tears.

'He has delivered his message,' Ernest cried. 'The manhood and the deep-hidden, tender nature of their Bishop burst out, and his Christian audience, that loved him, concluded that he was crazy! Did you see them leading him so solicitously from the platform? There must have been laughter in hell at the spectacle.'

'Nevertheless, it will make a great impression, what the Bishop did and said tonight,' I said.

'Think so?' Ernest queried mockingly.

'It will make a sensation,' I asserted. 'Didn't you see the reporters scribbling like mad while he was speaking?'

'Not a line of which will appear in tomorrow's papers.'

'I can't believe it,' I cried.

'Just wait and see,' was the answer. 'Not a line, not a thought that he uttered. The daily press? The daily suppressage!'

'But the reporters,' I objected. 'I saw them.'

'Not a word that he uttered will see print. You have forgotten the editors. They draw their salaries for the policy they maintain. Their policy is to print nothing that is a vital menace to the established. The Bishop's utterance was a violent assault upon the established morality. It was heresy. They led him from the platform to prevent him from uttering more heresy. The newspapers will purge his heresy in the oblivion of silence. The press of the United States? It is a parasitic growth that battens on the capitalist class. Its function is to serve the established by moulding public opinion, and right well it serves it.

'Let me prophesy. Tomorrow's papers will merely mention that the Bishop is in poor health, that he has been working too hard, and that he broke down last night. The next

CHAPTER FOURTEEN

The list of men and women who have defied the establishment and have gone to prison or were dealt with more harshly is long and getting longer daily. *The Iron Heel* exists.

mention, some days hence, will be to the effect that he is suffering from nervous prostration and has been given a vacation by his grateful flock. After that, one of two things will happen: either the Bishop will see the error of his way and return from his vacation a well man in whose eyes there are no more visions, or else he will persist in his madness, and then you may expect to see in the papers, couched pathetically and tenderly, the announcement of his insanity. After that he will be left to gibber his visions to padded walls.'

'Now there you go too far!' I cried out.

'In the eyes of society it will truly be insanity,' he replied. 'What honest man, who is not insane, would take lost women and thieves into his house to dwell with him sisterly and brotherly? True, Christ died between two thieves, but that is another story. Insanity? The mental processes of the man with whom one disagrees are always wrong. Therefore the mind of the man is wrong. Where is the line between wrong mind and insane mind? It is inconceivable that any sane man can radically disagree with one's most sane conclusions.

'There is a good example of it in this evening's paper. Mary M'Kenna lives south of Market Street. She is a poor but honest women. She is also patriotic. But she has erroneous ideas concerning the American flag and the protection it is supposed to symbolise. And here's what happened to her. Her husband had an accident and was laid up in hospital three months. In spite of taking in washing, she got behind in her rent. Yesterday they evicted her. But first, she hoisted an American flag, and from under its folds she announced that by virtue of its protection they could not turn her out on to the cold street. What was done? She was arrested and arraigned for insanity. Today she was examined by the regular insanity experts. She was found insane. She was consigned to the Napa Asylum.'

'But that is far-fetched,' I objected. 'Suppose I should disagree with everybody about the literary style of a book. They wouldn't send me to an asylum for that.'

'Very true,' he replied. 'But such divergence of opinion would constitute no menace to society. Therein lies the difference. The divergence of opinion on the parts of Mary M'Kenna and the Bishop do menace society. What if all the poor people should refuse to pay rent and shelter themselves under the American flag? Landlordism would go crumbling.

There's nothing I can add to this powerful presentation other than to advocate that you read *The Iron Heel*.

It may be at your local library but if not, write to:

Jack London Bookstore
PO 337
Glen Ellen, CA 95442

THE BISHOP'S VISION 77

The Bishop's views are just as perilous to society. Ergo, to the asylum with him.'

But still I refused to believe.

' Wait and see,' Ernest said, and I waited.

Next morning I sent out for all the papers. So far Ernest was right. Not a word that Bishop Morehouse had uttered was in print. Mention was made in one or two of the papers that he had been overcome by his feelings. Yet the platitudes of the speakers that followed him were reported at length.

Several days later the brief announcement was made that he had gone away on a vacation to recover from the effects of overwork. So far so good, but there had been no hint of insanity, nor even of nervous collapse. Little did I dream the terrible road the Bishop was destined to travel—the Gethsemane and crucifixion that Ernest had pondered about.

HELP THEM KICK THE HABIT

A friend of mine in Vegas once sold packs of cigarettes with this label:

People bought them by the carton to give to friends to encourage them to quit. However, when my friend reordered, the factory refused to fill the order. So I suggested that he sell the label by itself. After all, the labels fit neatly inside the cellophane of any regular cigarette package. Then, each time a smoker picks up the pack, he or she is reminded of the risk.

You are encouraged to reproduce the label at your local printers and distribute it freely in your community. After all, Surgeon General Koop says that we can have a cigarette-free U.S. by the year 2000 if we work on it.

As one radio listener put it, "Smoking is respiratory rape."

A FLOAT FOR YOUR FLOATING HOME

An inexpensive float for a houseboat can be made from a large inverted plywood box reinforced with 2 x 6's and floated on lots of empty, sealed plastic bottles—the kind that are used for bleach are perfect. This float will last indefinitely since you can replace any of the bottles that might fill and sink.

AIRPLANES

There are lots of older airplanes around for under 5,000 dollars. I saw a fine Tripacer in Bandon, Oregon for just about that price. If you can afford one, buy it and take out the right hand or co-pilots seat. Install a foam mattress and a Portapotty. Pack a bag with staples like beans and rice, a cooking pot and some matches. Don't forget your sleeping bag and if you can't fly, take some lessons before you leave. Incidentally, it is lots easier to fly than to drive a car. Any pilot will tell you that.

Now you are all set for the most thrilling adventures of your entire life. Take off with a full tank and then fly as free as a bird to whatever place you wish—the Grand Canyon, the open spaces of Montana, the Florida Keys, offshore islands like Catalina or any other place you have been longing to see.

I foresee a sky full of aerial gypsies in their 60's and 70's and beyond. Why not? At our age, we have little to lose, and still have the capacity to enjoy nature from 3,000 feet.

Often an airport will offer a trial lesson for ten dollars. Take it and convince yourself that you CAN learn to fly, no matter what your age. My daughter Jill, 33, on her first flight, took off, flew around and landed without the instructors aid. In my own case, after a couple of hours of dual, the instructor told me that he had nothing more to teach me. He said that all I needed was practice.

Just one flight will convince you that it's a whole new world up there. Just remember, the sky is not the limit, it's the beginning!

"You cannot fly like an eagle with the wings of a wren."
— *William Hudson*

See you on Cloud Nine!

LAST CHANCE RANCH

Currently I am considering a suitable property on which to establish what I call "Last Chance Ranch." It would provide diversified services to those who have been told by their doctors that they have a finite period to live. The concept is simple—if you are going to die anyway, you might as well take a "last chance" no matter how remote the possibilities. Therapy would include:

- Nutrition
- Exercise
- Detoxification
- Yoga
- Prayer
- Visualization
- Feldenkreis
- Lots of sunshine
- Pure Water
- Fasting

The ranch would accept anyone regardless of age, color, sex, or disease. Patients would pay what they could afford or use Medicare or insurance. If they couldn't pay, we would find some foundations to support the LCR.

Staff would include regular M.D.'s as well as chiropractors, faith healers, metabolic nutritionists, fasting experts, masseurs, and our specialists—the M.D.s, or Mirth Doctors. These experts in humor would make people learn to laugh with comic films, jokes, feathers or just plain tickling. We all know how good we feel after we have had a good laugh. Norman Cousins proved to his own satisfaction that laughter can and will help people get well, even recovering from serious, terminal diseases. Laughter stimulates the flow of blood as well as those magic endorphins, the human body's own great booster.

If this plan interests you, write me in care of the publisher.

THE SENIOR DATA BASE

A data base is defined as a source of specialized information available by computer links. For example, if you follow the stock market there are a number of data bases which provide all you need to know on this subject. If science is your forte, then there are many computerized sources of this type of information. To contact a data base, you can subscribe or go through a broker. Either way you will make contact through your modem or computer telephone link. Within a short time, the data you seek is on your monitor screen. Just call a local computer store for more information.

Now what I propose is a *Senior Data Base* which will have relevant information for seniors of which this book is typical. If you have interest in this service, write to me in care of the publishers and we'll try to put it together.

YOU AS ONE LINK IN A CHAIN

We have mentioned that 75 percent of all senior women are poor. Not too many of them will own this book. What I would like to do is to provide free copies to as many impoverished seniors as I can. So send me their names and I will do my best to get them copies somehow.

As part of this effort, we can expand what already exists—a senior network. The plan is to have seniors connect with other seniors with the intent of each one helping the other in any way possible. The Senior Data Base mentioned previously could be a "central" for the senior network. For example, let's say that you have a property that needs a caretaker. Okay, you let the network people know that it's available. Someone is sure to need a place to live and the connection is thus made.

I am sure you get the picture...networks can be local, regional or national and eventually all would be connected.

Let's do it!

FOUR ACRES FOR FREE

A friend of mine has a well-furnished travel trailer. After many years of living on the streets and getting hassled by the police, he has found a home. It happened that he saw a parcel of four acres that was a resting place for abandoned cars. He wrote to the owner of the lot and offered to be a no-cost caretaker and thus eliminate the junk problem. He was accepted and ended up with a two-year contract to guard the property. He plans to grow a garden on part of it since there is a water supply.

So, if you are a trailerite, consider this method to end up with some land for free.

Another method is to file a mining claim on 20 acres. Write to the *Superintendent of Documents, Government Printing Office, Washington, D.C.* and ask for their brochure on mining claims—it gives all the information you need to take advantage of this on-going opportunity.

INSURANCE

Having once been in the insurance business, I know what a racket so much of it really is. So it does my heart good to see some seniors defying the rip-off premiums. More power to them and to you if you can do the same!

Senior citizens group defies insurance hike

By JANE SARBER

Members of the Santa Margarita Senior Citizens Club voted Tuesday in regard to exorbitant insurance rates. The result: Cancel.

Speaking on behalf of the club's board of directors, President Vi Wiita explained to members that the rate of $1,600 for insurance to cover the club building in 1987 is "simply too much."

She said that in case of a claim against the club, "a claimant must prove negligence."

"We keep everything in good repair; there are no stairs or ramps, and we have the floors professionally cleaned so that they are not slippery," she said. "Why should we keep paying the insurance company year after year when we have not had claims?"

Explaining to club members that if the building is not rented to other organizations for use, and if all members continue to share the responsibility of keeping the facility free of hazards, there should be no problem. The vote to cancel insurance was unanimous.

Speaker of the afternoon Thanksgiving luncheon was Neal Royer, advocate on senior affairs who declares that since he is 70, middle age is about 85, halfway between his age and 100 years of age. The busy speaker who is on the staff of Senior Magazine and a representative from this area to the Senior Legislature in Sacramento applauded the action taken by the host club on the insurance vote.

He outlined the top ten state priorities recommended by the California Senior Legislature, including AP-61 on liability insurance. This measure would create an insurance fund for insuring against legal liability of non-profit entities which operate programs funded by the government financed by premiums paid by non-profit entities.

Another train of thought was brought up by the plucky friend of

TWO LEADERS in affairs concerning senior citizens stood together Tuesday during a luncheon meeting at Santa Margarita Seniors Center. Club President Vi Wiita was supported by the seniors board of directors and members in cancelling insurance on the building because of exorbitant rates. Neal Royer, representative to the Senior Legislature from this district, declared that his group intends to alleviate the current insurance rate problem for seniors with a new bill to be introduced when the state Legislature returns to work in January.
—Photo by Jane Sarber

senior citizens. Royer told the nearly 100-member audience that there are currently 17 organizations in this county handling various problems of retirees in the matters of Social Security, help with filling out health insurance claims, providing meals to shut-ins, consumer fraud involving the elderly, tax filing and others.

Royer's new goal is to establish a 'one-stop' senior problem center to handle all such matters now controleld by federal, state, tri-county and city levels. He admitted that upsetting 17 bureaucracies will not be easy, but he hopes, with the support of rational citizens of this county, he can accomplish that goal within two years.

DATES

These little sweeties are a natural candy bar in case you get a craving for sweets as many senior do. About 20 calories each, they have no chemicals unlike so much current candy. They keep well at ordinary temperatures, so make a fine food to take on a tire tramp or hike. Nutritionally they are great—lots of minerals and vitamins and food energy with little fat. They do have a lot of natural sugar so go fairly easy if you have a predeliction for diabetes.

If you live in a temperate climate, grow a grove of date palms and astound your neighbors. Plant a date about two inches deep and keep it moist but well-drained. Should sprout in a month or two. Protect from freezing. In about 50 years or so, your grandchildren will bless you.

Incidentally, a great way to combine dates is to mix them whole or chopped with rolled oats. Then just soak in milk or fruit juice for a breakfast of great value.

CARS

Most American cars are built to last about five or six years at the most. This is evident when you talk to auto repair people. They will tell you that if a car is that old, it would cost more to repair it than to buy another one of comparable age and make in good running condition. I once saw a garage full of older American cars that had bills of 500 dollars and up for relatively minor repairs. You could have bought almost any of them in operating condition for 500 dollars or less!

So, the point is this; don't buy an American car unless you like to throw your money away. Is this unpatriotic? No, we the consumers must teach our own car industry to convert to methods and materials used by competitors overseas. We can do this by voting "no" to throwaway cars with our refusal to buy them, new or used.

I have owned perhaps three dozen cars in my life and now drive a 1970 Volvo station wagon, 145S. No American car that I have owned has ever come close to the Volvo in terms of performance, reliability, economy, comfort and looks. I hope to keep it indefinitely.

My is plan to write about this subject in updates of this manual, but for now, just take my advice and limit your review of cars that are built to last—like Volvos, BMW's and older bugs. Do not buy fuel injected cars as they are expensive to repair. Stay out of Japanese cars—it's their way of getting back at us for beating them in WWII. And be sure and stay out of small Italian cars and jeeps.

I often visualize an older woman in a Ford on a dark and stormy night on the L.A. freeway and the dumb thing dies in the fast lane. That's why I have no respect for what I call FIX OFTEN REPAIR DAILY.

BUGS

I have had a lot of experience with bugs—the VW beetle I believe is the best small car ever built. Although dangerous because of its small size, the same characteristic makes it a smaller target and able to get through holes in traffic that would smash a larger vehicle. I have owned perhaps half dozen of them and was pleased with them all. Ruth still drives one and will apparently not give it up, even for a big, safe Volvo.

To me, the bug beats all others in terms speed, economy, upkeep, ease of maintenance and so forth. However, I am referring to the old VW's because apparently something happened in the 70's. Someone evidently made a decision to stop production of this little jewel and start building an American-style throwaway junk like the highly-touted Rabbit.

In a recent issue of a local paper there is conclusive evidence of how people regard the new and old VW product. A 1972 bug was offered for 2,700 dollars while a 1980 Rabbit was 2,000 dollars or best offer. My theory is this—the bug simply lasted too long and there was a need to convert VW addicts to a car that would require a lot of expensive parts and labor and would go belly up in five or six years. So, they did it, the rats!

But there's a way out. Buy a pre-1972 VW bug with a good body and frame and rebuild it with new engine, tires and such. What you will end up with is a NEW VW bug and it will be better in almost every way than any of the new VW models now being hawked out of showrooms worldwide. And another plus is that you can always find VW parts, new or used, in any town on earth. After all, they built millions of them and I predict that millions of them will still be running well into the 21st century.

SOAP

Lauryl sulfate is the major detergent ingredient. No matter what they add to it in the way of colors and perfumes and other additives, all brands are basically the same. You get it when you buy Lux or Tide or the generics. So save your money, seniors. Just get the low-cost box.

Another tip is to test effectiveness by soiling a rag, tear it in half and then see how little soap will clean it in two separate washes. Most people use too much soap for the work to be done and it often does not rinse out completely.

HYDROGEN PEROXIDE

Loss of teeth is a serious matter for seniors and most teeth are lost due to gum disease rather than cavities. So try this inexpensive method to keep your teeth. Rinse your mouth. Then brush and/or floss to clean out the major debris. Then take a tablespoon or so of three percent hydrogen peroxide in your mouth and swish it around and let it do its work. It will scavenge any harmful bacteria and bits of food that were missed by your brush.

You'll be surprised how clean your mouth feels and what an invigorated set of gums you'll have. Repeat as often as you wish. Peroxide is not hazardous in such weak solutions.

SARDINES

I recently read of a method to arrest and even reverse the aging process. You simply eat at least three small cans (about four ounces) of sardines each week. You can also use any cold-water fish like salmon, tuna or herring. The mechanism is the presence of nucleic acid which is important to cell integrity and rejuvenation. If you don't like fish, then disguise them in a salad or loaf—sardine salad or salmon loaf or creamed tuna. Personally, I think this works because since I have upped my intake of fish, my ability to write has improved greatly. Also, I have more energy.

Try it and see if it doesn't help you in many ways. Sardines are cheap compared to other protein and they sure are handy to carry around for a quick snack.

Incidentally, we haven't talked much about longevity in this book, but I am working on a chapter which will be included in the next edition. In the meantime, if you are interested in the latest advances in adding healthful years to your life, just go to your library and ask for the latest books on the subject.

BIKES

You loved them as a child, why not now? You'll love them more. Forget your car for most errands and leap on your bike since you'll go faster in the long run, get some exercise, have plenty of parking spaces and save lots of money. I once road a motorcycle everywhere, but admit I feel much more delighted on a trusty three-speed.

INDIAN FLOUR

Caught out camping with no flour for pancakes? Do what the Indians have done and are still doing—gather wild seeds such as oats or sunflower and grind them between two stones. You will be surprised how quickly you can make a coarse but healthy flour. It will be a 1,000 percent better than anything you can buy in a supermarket. And it's free!

Tip: if the seeds have whiskers, just pass them quickly over an open flame. Hulls? Just grind them up to as they provide fiber.

THE SAME OLD SONG

My oldest daughter Wendy is most perceptive about me. After all, she's known me for her entire life. She once said that I write the same book over and over and it's true. My goal is to make that same book better each time. How does this relate to your goals in life?

SENIOR PERFORMERS

No one is too old to be an actor or actress, witness the many Hollywood stars now in their 80's and 90's (George Burns, for one) who are as active as ever. Here is a publication of a Bay Area group which could be the model for a group of players in your own area. Write them for more information.

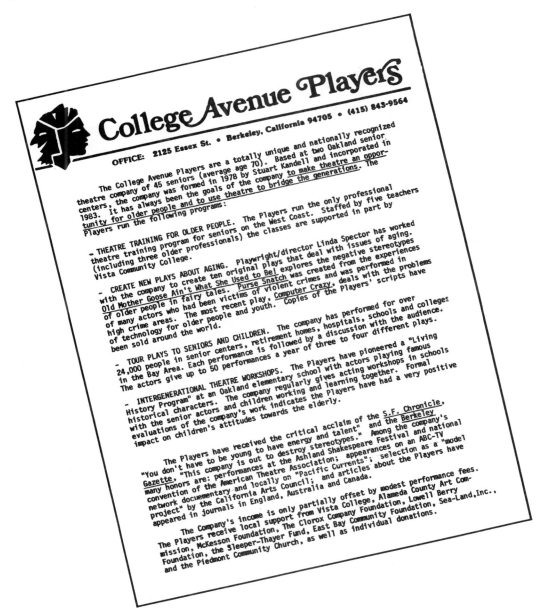

College Avenue Players

OFFICE: 2125 Essex St. • Berkeley, California 94705 • (415) 843-9564

The College Avenue Players are a totally unique and nationally recognized theatre company of 45 seniors (average age 70). Based at two Oakland senior centers, the company was formed in 1978 by Stuart Kandell and incorporated in 1983. It has always been the goals of the company to make theatre an opportunity for older people and to use theatre to bridge the generations. The Players run the following programs:

- THEATRE TRAINING FOR OLDER PEOPLE. The Players run the only professional theatre training program for seniors on the West Coast. Staffed by five teachers (including three older professionals) the classes are supported in part by Vista Community College.

- CREATE NEW PLAYS ABOUT AGING. Playwright/director Linda Spector has worked with the company to create ten original plays that deal with issues of aging. Old Mother Goose Ain't What She Used to Bel explores the negative stereotypes of older people in fairy tales. Purse Snatch was created from the experiences of many actors who had been victims of violent crimes. The most recent play, Computer Crazy, deals with the problems high crime areas. The most recent play, Computer Crazy, deals with the problems of technology for older people and youth. Copies of the Players' scripts have been sold around the world.

- TOUR PLAYS TO SENIORS AND CHILDREN. The company has performed for over 24,000 people in senior centers, retirement homes, hospitals, schools and colleges in the Bay Area. Each performance is followed by a discussion with the audience. The actors give up to 50 performances a year of three to four different plays.

- INTERGENERATIONAL THEATRE WORKSHOPS. The Players have pioneered a "Living History Program" at an Oakland elementary school with actors playing famous historical characters. The company regularly gives acting workshops in schools with the senior actors and children working and learning together. Formal evaluations of the company's work indicates the Players have had a very positive impact on children's attitudes towards the elderly.

The Players have received the critical acclaim of the S.F. Chronicle, "You don't have to be young to have energy and talent" and the Berkeley Gazette, "This company is out to destroy stereotypes." Among the company's many honors are: performances at the Ashland Shakespeare Festival and national convention of the American Theatre Association; appearances on an ABC-TV network documentary and locally on "Pacific Currents"; selection as a "model project" by the California Arts Council; and articles about the Players have appeared in journals in England, Australia and Canada.

The Company's income is only partially offset by modest performance fees. The Players receive local support from Vista College, Alameda County Art Commission, McKesson Foundation, The Clorox Company Foundation, Lowell Berry Foundation, the Sleeper-Thayer Fund, East Bay Community Foundation, Sea-Land,Inc., and the Piedmont Community Church, as well as individual donations.

ANN KEY

An old friend from our Delta boating days, Ann is one of those delightful senior women who can do just about anything, and do it well.

If you have this kind of talent, then share it with others. I was blessed with a word sense so if I can help any reader make a start in writing, just send me a note in care of the publisher.

Artist to display paintings

by Mimi Peck

Artist Ann Key recently returned to Bethel Island for a visit and is making plans to display some of her paintings in a soon-to-be opened shop.

Ann is well known to many residents as the person who opened the Artist's Table restaurant, where many of her works are still featured. She is also responsible for the Duck Crossing signs on Dutch Slough Road, along with a watercolor print of the scene on a Bethel Island postcard.

The silver-haired woman is not only an artist. She is talented in a number of fields including the graphic arts, candlemaking, and writing. She has written a book on wines.

The duck crossing signs, along with camel crossing signs she did for the Virginia City Camel Races, are some of the examples of her work as a graphic artist. She also designed the t-shirts with the personalized map of the Island on them.

Her candle-making talent extends to candles she has patented, some of which have been bought by such companies as Hallmark and Disneyland. She has also done some custom candle work for friends.

As with the Duck Crossing signs, much of her work is done on a whim. While at the Artist's Table she wanted to have information on wines available for customers, so she wrote a book about it.

Her artistry has taken her many places. As a young woman she came to the Island with her father and while he fished, she painted.

"Bethel Island has it's own independence and own feeling," she commented. Many of the paintings she will soon display here will hood scenes from the area, some that are no longer around.

Ann's favorite place she has been was a castle in France. She was invited to spend some time there and paint, which she did.

"It was like one of those fairy-tale castles I dreamed about when I was young," she reminisced, "and one of the most wonderful experiences of my life."

Most of the very popular castle paintings have been sold and the few that are left she has kept for herself, memories of one of the highest points in her life.

Ann has spent recent years at her latest gallery in Gold Hill Nevada, in a building that is complimentary to her work. A few years ago she chanced upon the lease to the First California Bank of Nevada, built in 1862. She renovated the historical landmark, making it her home and gallery. Possibly it lead to some of her inspirations as some of the trappers shacks and old barges have inspired some of the paintings she will be displaying here.

Ann will be visiting the Island soon as she will honor the grand opening of the Something Special shop with her paintings and presence.

SENIOR TAXES

Fortunately, as you grow older, the necessity for handing over a lot of your income to the IRS diminishes. However, some seniors do have tax problems related to income, property, inheritance and so forth. Personally, I like the stance of J. Pierpont Morgan who said,

> *"Anybody has a right to avoid taxes if he can. No citizen has a moral obligation to assist in maintaining the government. If Congress insists on making stupid mistakes and passes foolish tax laws, citizens should not be condemned if they take advantage of them."*

INCOME TAXES

My good friend Bill Greene has developed a system for avoiding all income taxes, whether withheld from your pay (if you are working) or otherwise. It is so easy you'll wonder why you didn't think of it yourself.

All you have to do is buy some low-cost rental units—even one would do. As Bill points out, there are so many valid tax deductions allowable when you are a landlord that you probably won't have to pay a cent. And if one unit won't quite give you enough deductions, then buy more.

Greene has written several books on legal tax avoidance and they are not only completely relevant, they are fun to read. His best is, *Winning Your Personal Tax Freedom* and if you don't find a copy in your library, write to *Harbor Publishing, 1668 Lombard St., San Francisco, CA 94123.*

Incidentally, if you would rather not own rental property, then consider going into a small business of your own. Keep it simple, low-overhead and you can still have a generous number of tax deductions—probably enough to cancel out any tax liability. I know that I have had no legal tax obligations for many years because as a freelance writer, almost everything I do is a tax writeoff. You can do the same.

PROPERTY TAXES

These are hard to escape, but there are some new plans to make it possible to keep your home no matter what the taxes are. You can sell it and lease it back, enroll in a program whereby you pay no taxes until the house is sold after your death. Another option is to have your kids stay in your home.

If none of the above are suitable to you, sell it and buy a motorhome and join me on the road—taxes are quite low on rolling stock. Or if you like the water, buy a boat and I'll see you afloat!

INHERITANCE TAXES

These are easy to avoid. Just put your assets into a trust and when you die they will be passed on to your heirs with no taxes due since they will already have possession through the trust. One of the best sources of information on this subject may be obtained from Dr. Martin Larson, *PO 15059, Phoenix, AZ 85060*. When you write to him about trusts, mention my name and also ask for a copy of his catalogue. He has written some excellent books on taxation and related subjects.

In summary, I have always believed that a senior should not have a large tax liability. But if the government won't arrange that happy state of affairs, just do it yourself.

AND A WORD FROM THOREAU

*"Public opinion is a weak tyrant compared with private opinion.
What a man thinks of himself, that is what determines
or rather dictates his fate."*

— *Henry D. Thoreau*

CHAPTER FIFTEEN
ENERGY

NEW SOURCES

Most of us seniors have become accustomed to a certain level of comfort and convenience. When we flip the switch, we expect light to flood the room. When we turn on the faucet, a stream of clean warm water is supposed to gush from the shower. Until now, these amenities have been the work of utility companies. However, in the last ten or 15 years, new methods of providing energy and utilities have emerged. These include:

- Photo-Voltaic Electrical Power Generation

- Small-Scale Hydroelectric Power

- Solar Water Heating

- Low-Voltage Systems Allowing Self-Generated Power

- Appliances for Lower Voltage Systems

What these systems yield is the opportunity for a completely new way of life for everyone, seniors as well as younger people. For example, 20 years ago it would have been difficult and expensive to enjoy urban comforts in a remote cabin. Today you can have stereo music, hot and cold running water, heating and lighting, TV and VCR's and all operated with self-contained systems that have no connection whatever with utility companies!

Now, many pieces of otherwise unsalable and unusable property become practical places to settle. Furthermore, you can live comfortably on a boat, an RV or even a sturdy tent pitched in a lovely forest. In short, the new technology of energy generation has liberated us from the tentacles of the power monopoly. No longer are we constrained by wires and pipes from some central location. We can tap into the power of the sun directly from any location on earth and after the equipment is paid for, the power is free!

We can also harvest the wind and water energy in rural or even wilderness regions. And best of all, this technology is becoming more efficient, sophisticated and cheaper every day.

Here, from a valuable catalogue by *Jade Mountain*, are some samples of what you can obtain to make yourself energy-sufficient anywhere you please.

Incidentally, if you want to see this concept in action, I recommend that you take a trip to Mendocino or Humboldt Counties in northwest California. Here, thousands of happy people have created their own fiefdoms with equipment as described in the following pages.

Alternate Energy Applications

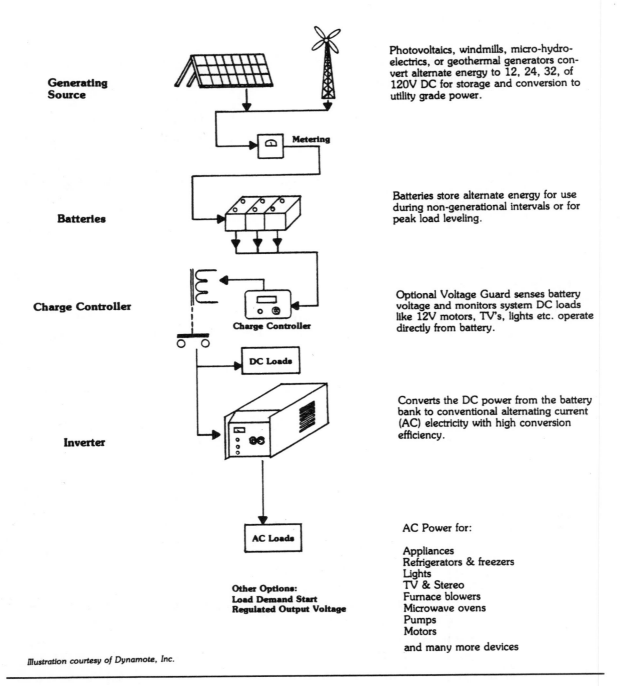

Generating Source

Photovoltaics, windmills, micro-hydro-electrics, or geothermal generators convert alternate energy to 12, 24, 32, of 120V DC for storage and conversion to utility grade power.

Metering

Batteries

Batteries store alternate energy for use during non-generational intervals or for peak load leveling.

Charge Controller

Optional Voltage Guard senses battery voltage and monitors system DC loads like 12V motors, TV's, lights etc. operate directly from battery.

DC Loads

Inverter

Converts the DC power from the battery bank to conventional alternating current (AC) electricity with high conversion efficiency.

AC Loads

AC Power for:

Appliances
Refrigerators & freezers
Lights
TV & Stereo
Furnace blowers
Microwave ovens
Pumps
Motors

and many more devices

Other Options:
Load Demand Start
Regulated Output Voltage

Illustration courtesy of Dynamote, Inc.

Photovoltaics

Solar Electric Generation

Sunlight is a kind of energy that is permanent, free and universally available. The sun is really a nuclear power plant that generates radiant energy at an enormously high kilowatt (kW) rate estimated to be a staggering 110-trillion kW. Even though less than one billionth of this energy is intercepted by the earth, every 10 sq. feet of the earth's surface facing the sun is estimated to receive about 1000 watts at mid-day.

A photovoltaic device or silicon solar cell converts light into DC (direct current) electricity. It does not use heat from the sun as does thermal solar hot water. In fact, the higher the ambient temperature, the less efficient a solar electric cell becomes. The most common commercially available solar cell is a small wafer or ribbon of semiconductor material, usually silicon. One side of the semiconductor material is positive (+) and the other side is negative (−). When light strikes the positive side of the solar cell, the negative electrons are activated and produce a tiny unit of electrical current.

When a group of solar cells are connected or the semiconductor ribbon material is applied to a predetermined surface area, a solar module is created. Quantitative electrical output is determined by the number of cells or ribbon material connected together within the module and then further determined by the number of modules connected together. More than one module connected together is called a solar array.

A properly planned photovoltaic system consists of the simple components described in the introduction. They are: (A) A system based on the number of Kwh you will use each day, with back-up or secondary generator (wind, hydro, etc.) (B) The choice of a roof, ground, pole or

passive tracker mounting. (C) A charge controller system.[1] (D) Metering Panel. (E) Battery Storage. (F) Inverter (if desired.)

A battery storage system is necessary to act as a buffer between the solar array and your home on nights and sunless days. Although a solar array will generate some electricity on cloudy days and even under a full moon, the output will vary greatly on both a daily and seasonal basis. A battery system smoothes out some of the variation.

There are exceptions to the need for a battery storage system for solar electric power generation. Some appliances and equipment run directly from the power produced from one or more solar modules. These are called "sunsynchronous" devices. You will find some of them listed in the Cooling section of the catalog featuring solar powered fans and evaporative coolers, others in the Water Pumping section featuring solar powered water pumps and in the Solar Hot Water section featuring sun-powered solar hot water pumping.

On the following pages you will find a selection of photovoltaic modules by different manufacturers, most of whom we have worked with for many years. These modules are highly reliable and warrantied by their respective manufacturers for five years; however you can expect a twenty year life span or more with a possible power degradation of between 10% and 20% over that time, according to a study presented to the 1982 IEEE photovoltaic conference in San Diego, California. There are no residential systems that have been in service for twenty years, so we really can't say for sure just how long a module will last but it looks like the life expectancy is substantial.

CHAPTER SIXTEEN
ABOUT THE AUTHOR

I was born in Chicago in 1922, but I didn't stay there long. My parents moved me and my older brother to South Pasadena to escape Illinois and its impossible climate. South Passassadena, as my Dad pronounced it, was a great improvement. I enjoyed a modified Tom Sawyer/Huck Finn type of lifestyle, complete with wanderings in the Arroyo Seco with my raft, and such fun times as the Fourth of July, the day that school let out, and Christmas. All in all, I have no complaints about growing up, although my father died when I was nine. From that time on, I was almost completely on my own; my mother had other interests and my older brother was light years from me in every way. This early independence was a valuable training period for later life. I have always delighted in cultivating self-reliance in all aspects of living.

As an example, I developed a business of my own when I was about six. I would take my little red wagon and go down to the local ice company (yes, refrigerators were not in common use in 1928) and collect the chips and cuttings that were sawn from 200 pound blocks of ice. These piles of manufactured "snow" were sold for a nickel a load to people too poor to buy ice. Later, when the Great Depression hit, my business boomed as even more people became dreadfully poor.

Like many other children of my generation, I had a number of ways of earning money, including a paper route, magazine sales on street corners, collecting deposit bottles and saving the lead foil from tobacco cans. All of this activity netted very little cash but great rewards in feeling confident and capable of handling my own affairs, regardless of circumstances.

In looking backward, it is clear that the real key to being your own man or woman stems from an early indoctrination in standing on your own two feet. On the other hand, I have always believed that it is never too late to make a change in your life. After all, Grandma Moses is often cited as having taken up her successful career as a painter when she was 70!

School was always a pain in the neck for me. I hated the regimentation, the emphasis on learning ONLY what was taught, and the habit of the clock in my 6th grade class to run backwards at times. I can recall several years passing as the clock tried to lift the big hand from 2:30 p.m. to 3 p.m. What I loved most of all was the freedom of all non-school times and summers were all too short for me. I know that I learned much more from my free time than I did in school. Here are some examples:

- How to make a fine gun from a stick, a clothespin and a discarded inner tube.

- Where to buy hamburger for ten cents a pound and how to cook it over an open fire in a remote canyon.

- The design and construction of a scooter from an apple box, a short length of 2 x 4 and one roller skate. Lost my front tooth with a fast model of this unit.

- How to build a playhouse with nothing but empty cardboard boxes and also build caves with a hole in the ground and some old boards.

- Where to find delicious food for free...from behind grocery stores and on apricot, plum and peach trees that no one watched closely during harvest season.

- That nature was the best classroom of all and an afternoon spent high in a leafy tree gave one the equivalent of a Ph.D. in botany as well as complete spiritual rejuvenation.

The years wheeled by, some fast, others slow, as I tried to find a balance between the life I saw in the movies and real life. My real education in how to think about our American culture actually came from films; I was a serious and dedicated student. I saw virtually every film that came to the Rialto Theater. Among the things I learned and had to unlearn later were the following:

1. If you go to war and kill a lot of people you will get a chestful of medals and get to kiss your girl in front of the entire regiment. You will then be considered a wonderful hero for the rest of your life.

2. Crime does pay; if not in money then in excitement. Also you can wear dark blue shirts with yellow ties and get away with it. Furthermore, guns are exciting toys that every he-man needs to own. Those that shoot more than one cartridge with a single trigger pull or machine guns are the most exciting of all.

3. Romantic love is the ultimate goal of every man and woman, and in a good marriage there is no chance for boredom, straying or harsh words.

4. Money and possessions are the prime objectives, especially large homes with white bedrooms and a Rolls Royce parked in front.

5. A perfect role model would be someone like Humphrey Bogart who can handle a dame as well as a machine gun and finds great pleasure in using both. Also, he can confront authority with impunity since he has that .38 tucked away in his belt. Finally, he can use a cigarette as a dramatic prop in any given situation.

6. Fast cars, big yachts, trips to Porto Fino, gambling in Vegas, pretty show girls are what life really should consist of, or else you're wasting your time. Never mind going to college, except if Jack Oakie and Arline Judge are registered and you have the money to buy a raccoon coat.

7. Pay no attention to your immortal soul or its salvation.

In addition to the above, I learned that if you see a number in a pay station phone directory, rip out the entire page and take it with you. Also, when you toss your hat towards a hat rack you had better not miss or your gum-chewing, wise-cracking secretary will laugh at you.

Somehow, the deceit of film fun came through, despite spending many hours watching Joan Crawford dance and Clark Gable spit in the eye of a Chinese pirate. I recall leaving the theater after a matinee, noting the littered streets, the harsh light of late afternoon and having a blinding headache in my cranium while thinking that if movies were mirrors of reality, then this horror could not, dare not exist. A quandary presented itself that is hardly reconciled to this day.

One afternoon I found a book titled, *Our Movie-Made Children*. It described how films influenced children to the point of taking over their lives. I believed the book, and proof was demonstrated when I started smoking in the Bogart manner—letting the smoke get into my eyes and then grimacing in a menacing way.

Once out of high school I got a job in a furniture factory making tubular furniture. One week at two dollars/day was enough to satisfy my needs for steady employment. The following Monday I headed for San Pedro where I was lucky to get a job on a fishing boat at five dollars a week plus food and a bunk up forward. In time I became the youngest pilot to handle a charter boat solo. The sea, how I loved it, and still do. Huge, timeless, immutable and with no two days alike. The giant rolling billows were beautiful beyond any words and the flight of gulls was like a manifestation of God's aerial designs at the their best. I was fortunate to spend many days enjoying the marine world and even if I didn't often collect that five dollars, I would still opt for a life afloat.

One afternoon I was watching a large Japanese freighter leave the harbor without its usual cargo of scrap iron. A friend turned to me and said, "Mark my words, we'll have a war with the Japs before the end of the year."

It was January 1941.

Prior to World War II, I had read a lot about World War I. I had no illusions; wars were created to make big profits for the arms makers. As a result, I could muster no hatred for either Japanese or Germans. After all, they were caught up in the same Catch-22 as I was. Fortunately, my naval duties during World War II did not involve harming anyone directly. In fact, towards the end of the war, I was selected to become an officer for the planned invasion of Japan in the Fall of 1945. And, as we all know, that didn't come off as planned.

With the end of the war, I had to evaluate what I would do with the rest of my life. A wise old personnel manager at a large plant advised me to get a college education as did my older brother. So I started studying English Literature at the University of Redlands with modest diligence and finally ended up with a Bachelor of Arts from a bigger institution, USC in Los Angeles.

Now what?

Yes, indeed, now what?

What could I do with a B.A. in English Literature in the L.A. market place? What else but a job as an insurance claims examiner, a task that had me climbing the walls with frustration and anger within months. I found that working with my hands was far more satisfying so I became a cabinetmaker. At least until one day when my daughter asked me to move to a locale where there were sidewalks; she wanted to skate. To obtain a sidewalk I needed a new house and this required a better paying job. So I returned to my professional training and became a technical writer for a large aerospace firm in the San Fernando Valley. Again, frustration and lack of fulfillment, but the needs (or what I had been programmed to believe were needs) of my family took precedence and I stuck out a long seven years at a test lab in Simi Hills.

One day I took a good look at my future in the persona of my boss. He was fat, grumpy, harried and never seemed to smile. Since I didn't want to have those characteristics in another ten or 20 years, I quit my job, bought a trailer and set out to seek my fortune. My oldest daughter was 14, my youngest, 9. That was my turning point!

In looking back at that juncture in my life, it was clear that I was making what Carol Sheehy would call a "passage," an evolutionary transformation based on the realization that the real onward was UPWARD! Certainly it required some sacrifices, but then doesn't all change? I know that before I left the corporation I had this vision: I saw most workers as farmers who had been given a 52-acre plot and were cultivating 50 acres for the landlord and using only two for themselves. The 52 acres were, of course, the 52 weeks of the year. Why should a good farmer want to give away the bulk of his life, his sustenance for a fraction of it back? No reason that I could see. I decided to plow the 52 acres/weeks and plant my own idea seeds, and that is exactly what I did after June of 1963.

Again, looking back, did I make the right decision? I am confident that I did or else I would not be capable of writing this book that I know will be of benefit to others. All I can say is, hallelujah!

The years following my resignation from Rocketdyne were not all easy ones. I had to start my earning pattern anew and many times felt discouraged. But at no time was I inclined to go backwards, to return to my old job as some naysayers had predicted. Instead I began exploring new methods of earning money for my family and at the same time learning how to conserve money. I am certain of this fact: it is much easier in America to save a unit of money than it is to earn it!

Among the many avenues that I pursued were the following:

- Sales of products door-to-door in the business area
- Sales of advertising to the same market
- Marketing counsel based on the premise that any business could use more customers no matter what they were selling
- Technical writing on a freelance basis
- Freelance writing for magazines
- Mail order marketing for manufacturers

Not all of my ventures worked well, but enough of them did so that my family lacked for little. In fact, it turned out that while some of my daughter's friends overdosed on drugs because they had unlimited funds, my own children did not suffer the misfortune simply because we had no extra money for drugs. It was about this time that I realized that too much money is like too much food; it produces a spiritual indigestion unless great restraint is practiced. Sound old-fashioned? No more so in my book, than the law of gravity.

After nearly four years of exploration into alternative ways of earning money and living, I had the call to freelance on a full time basis. As Thoreau says,

> *"If one advances confidently in the direction of his dreams and endeavors to live the life which he has imagined, he will meet with a success unexpected in common hours."*

This is exactly what occurred. I happened to write a letter to a newly-formed publishing company sponsored by *Rolling Stone* magazine. At first the response was negative, but suddenly and unexpectedly I was offered the opportunity to write a 350-page book on farming for novices, as long as I could complete it in about a month. Since I had been blessed with the capability to wield a "fast pen," I accepted. The book was my first and greatest success, selling some 50,000 copies all over the world.

From that point on, my career was established and many more books were written and published including:

- *How To Live In The New America*
- *The Robin Hood Handbook*
- *Great Hot Springs Of The West*
- *Eat Well On A Dollar A Day*
- *The Dollar A Day Cookbook*
- *Tax Wars*
- *We Never Went To The Moon*
- *A Piece Of The Action*
- *Independent Business Guides*
- *Privacy*
- *Bill Kaysing's Freedom Guide*
- *Great Hideouts Of The West*
- *How To Prevent And Cure Aids The Natural Way*

and many other short books, ghost written works, columns for newspapers, magazine articles, speeches and so forth.

Despite many hours at the IBM, I managed to find a lot of time to play, explore, travel and just plain HAVE FUN! My philosophy has always been to enjoy this life and be concerned about other things on a secondary or tertiary basis. In fact, I intend to write a book called *Invest In Fun*. It will advise people to forget gold and silver, stocks and bonds, and especially the often highly-painful real estate, and to simply invest your time and money in the enjoyment of yourself, your friends and Mother Nature—otherwise known as God's beautiful world. I know that this has worked for me as the following story will illustrate.

I received a phone call from Hank Greenspun who owns the *Las Vegas Sun*. He had read my book, *Tax Wars*, and asked me to write a series of columns for his paper on that subject. I did them, collected my fee and took off for a wonderful tour of southern Nevada. I had my trusty GMC camper, food and water and set out to get close to Mother Nature's wonders.

There is a little-known area about a hundred miles northeast of Las Vegas called the Pahranagat Valley—an Indian name of course. The Pan-American Highway, 93, bisects it. Here I found thousands of acres of desert producing a healthy crop of fragrant chaparral and other plants, despite the scanty rainfall. On the western side are the Sheep Range mountains, rugged and beautiful and seldom visited. Despite some snow and slippery, rocky roads, I was able to ascend this alpine range and enjoy fantastic views in all directions—one could see 80 or 90 miles on a clear day. In the light snow I found the tracks of many wild animals including deer, bear, rabbit, cougar and raccoon. Here and there were springs of clear water. It was a magical place, totally unknown to me and evidently to most everyone else in the U.S. I didn't see a single person or vehicle the entire time I was there. Eventually, I descended to the valley floor again probing here and there by foot and wheel and simply looking at the unique features of this silent, pristine and isolated area.

One night I built a campfire and for hours watched the dancing flames of orange, red and every shade of blue. Later, a small desert fox crept up behind me to see what was going on. I tossed him a bit of bread and he came closer, seemingly unafraid of this odd visitor and the colorful display of flames. The moon rose in the east and the earth slowly revolved beneath me and for the first time in my life I was aware of the majestic motions of the entire universe.

Here I was, little Willy from South Pasadena, living in the desert and learning some timeless truths. It became clear to me during this time period that:

- We are evolving with the universe.

- We can participate in its evolution.

- The universe is aware of us and welcomes our assistance.

- The major problem of man is boredom, but this can be remedied by simply becoming interested in anything and everything.

I curled up in my sleeping bag and fell into a deep sleep. The next morning I watched the moon set and the sun rise and it became so wonderfully evident how we are linked to the cycles of time. As I walked later along a massive escarpment of solid stone, I seemed to receive a message.

"As you are now, so once were we. And as time passes, you will become as we are and so on...on and on endlessly since time is infinite and so is space."

Our immortality became so clear to me—minerals of the earth become the essential building blocks of our bodies. And then, in time, these minerals become great stone bluffs! Obviously, there is no death, only transfiguration, change and evolution to some, always higher and higher to more wondrous levels.

Later I began to consider some of these revelations, especially the one about boredom being the major problem of man. I recalled Norman Mailer's great WWII novel, *The Naked and the Dead,* in which he makes it clear that men often go to war because they are stupefied by the sterility of their lives. They want activity and excitement and war is one way to have it. But, as I thought, why not channel this desire into more productive avenues such as research, helping the less fortunate, self-discovery. And this, I believe, is now what is happening despite the many brush-fire wars that afflict our planet. I also recalled Marilyn Ferguson's classic work, *The Aquarian Conspiracy,* in which she offers such telling proof that we are now in the throes of a great spiritual transformation, the paradigm of our cultural beliefs is being wrenched into new forms and no one can prevent it.

Until I went into the desert, there were many unanswered questions in my life. And well, there might be since I had never really taken the time to sit down undistracted and really try to think things through. My life, like so many of my contemporaries, was caught up in the perpetual rat race of getting and spending, being the "prosmers"—producer/consumers that Toffler referred to in his book, *The Third Wave.*

Today, I often wonder how much anguish could be eliminated if people simply went off by themselves for a while to examine who they are, what they are doing and why. Another quote from the great lover of solitude, Thoreau, is appropriate here:

"I went to the woods because I wished to live deliberately, to front only the essential facts of life and see if I could not learn what it had to teach and not, when I came to die, discover that I had not lived."

It is interesting that this observation is a bridge to one by Henry James, in his play *The Ambassadors:*

"Live all you can; it's a mistake not to. It doesn't matter what you do in particular, so long as you have had your life. If you haven't had that, what HAVE you had? What one loses, one loses, make no mistake about that. The right time is any time that one is still so lucky as to have... LIVE!"

Oddly, these profound observations appear in comic form in the children's classic, *The Wind in the Willows:*

"Believe me, my young friend, there is NOTHING, absolutely nothing half so much worth doing as simply messing about in boats. Simply messing...about in boats —or with boats. In or out of them, it doesn't matter. Nothing seems really to matter, that's the charm of it. Whether you get away or whether you don't; whether you arrive at your destination or whether you reach somewhere else, or whether you get anywhere at all, you're always busy and you never do anything in particular, and when you've done it, there's always something else to do and you can do it if you like but you'd much better not. Look here, if you've nothing else on hand this morning, supposing we drop down to the river together and have a long day of it?"

— Kenneth Grahame

My life was transformed by the desert experience. I am convinced that we all need some alone-time to find ourselves. Interestingly, as the time to move on came, I simply asked out loud what I should do with the rest of my life. I was referred to Matthew 10:8 in which these three words appear:

HEAL THE SICK

My interpretation of this was that most people on this planet have some sickness, whether it's physical or mental or spiritual. So, within 24 hours I was heavily involved with the distribution of DMSO which is discussed elsewhere in this book. One evening, I received a call from a man at the Sahara Casino. He had to leave early in the morning and wanted to take some DMSO home to his arthritic wife. When I went to his room to deliver a bottle he said, "I prayed that something would come along to help her."

It's a great feeling to be the answer to someone's prayer and that incident was all I needed to give my full energies to the DMSO project.

Where am I now as I wind up this monologue? At 65, I feel more like 25 in every way. I can fly a plane, operate any kind of boat from a dinghy to a twin-engine cruiser, ride any make of motorcycle and race them, build a house, write a book, travel the world over with joy and curiosity, tangle with the establishment, hike in the High Sierras and smell the roses with deep appreciation for every moment I am alive. As to goals, I have three major ones at present:

1. To disseminate practical knowledge to those who need it, thus this book.

2. To educate people about Kaysite, the boat restoration method so that boats can be restored and used, especially in poor countries.

3. Prove that the U.S. Government is public enemy number one and is not to be trusted under any circumstances. After this was written, the extreme corruption of our current administration corroborated the above statement.
   Wish me luck!

CHAPTER SEVENTEEN
SOURCES

Here, in my findings, are what I feel to be great sources of information. Many are little-known and rare. It is both surprising and exciting to begin using a network of information sources. You will soon come to realize that the more you use them, the more accessible you become in seeking all the data you need to accomplish anything you wish.

Our categories are:

- Directories • Catalogues • Books • Publications • Organizations

DIRECTORIES

Have you ever seen the *Directory of Directories*? It will show you where all the hidden philanthropists are housed and where they hold 3,500 trade shows a year in the U.S. Or, if you have a computer, how would you like to know every firm that provides a data base?

All of this information and much more is available from *Gale Research, Book Tower, Detroit, MI 48226*. Just send them a postcard and ask for their latest catalogue of *Gale Reference Books*. I know that you'll be amazed at the wealth of basic information.

Just two directories can open up a whole new world of ideas and opportunities for any senior. These are the *Directory of Directories* and the *Encyclopedia of Associations*.

The first one lists ten thousand directories on virtually every conceivable subject. No matter what interests you, you'll find a directory to help you get more information.

Interested in boats? Then you will find a directory for every type of boat supply and service. Food and cooking your specialties? Then check out the endless possibilities by reviewing the pages presenting these subjects. What is so amazing is that once you find the right directory for your proposed project or study area, it will lead you to other sources and on and on.

Would you like to know more about the health benefits of garlic, where to buy the giant variety, how to grow it? Then what you can do is find the corresponding association which is devoted to that subject. Just check out Gale's *Encyclopedia of Associations*. I have found it invaluable—being able to obtain the exact, detailed, up-to-date information I need to write a book or an article, for example.

In summary, virtually everything you need to know, from acupuncture to zebras, is on one or more of the pages in Gale's many reference books. Get to know them well and open up some new worlds for yourself.

International Directory of Alternative Cancer Tests and Therapies, RFD 1, Box 411, Mashpee, MA 02649. About 1,000 Americans die of cancer daily. 55,000,000 Americans will eventually get the Big C. If you want to be prepared with some options to cut burn and poison (the latter is called chemo-euthanasia by some wry physicians) then send for this catalogue. A donation of ten dollars is suggested but I have the feeling that they will accept any donation. The information could not only save your life, it could prevent you from a lot of needless suffering through the CB and P modalities (surgery, radiation and chemotherapy).

CATALOGUES

My reference library is strong on catalogues. I find them absolutely essential to my work, which is of course, compiling and updating relevant information to seniors and others. For the price of a postcard to *Aurora Book Companions, PO 5852, Denver, CO 80217*, you will receive a marvelous catalogue, arranged by subject, on health and fitness books. Here's a sample page:

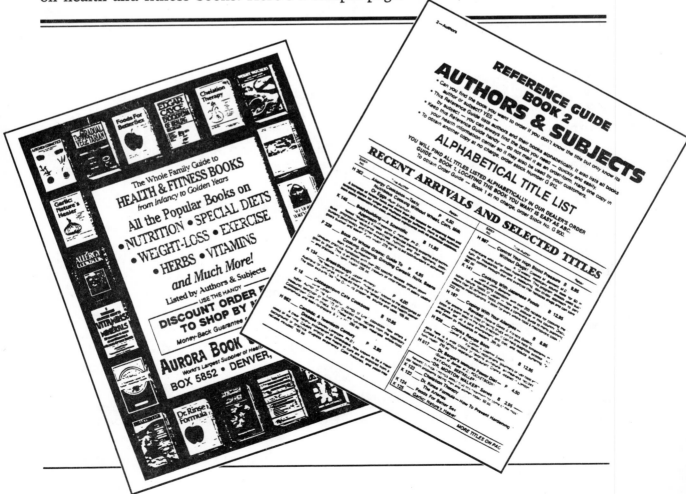

There is no lack of vital information in various forms and from different standpoints. Any one of these books could mean the difference between disease and boundless health.

Here are some of my favorite catalogues:

Loompanics, PO 1197, Port Townsend, WA 98368. Make available books that you search for and never find—unusual and innovative titles like *Great Hideouts of the West* and *The Paper Trip*.

Eden Press, PO 8410, Fountain Valley, CA 92728. Good selection of alternative-type books such as *How to Live in the New America*.

Bellwether Productions, 321 Hampton, Ste. 106, Venice, CA 90291. A new publisher with some innovative titles like Dr. Nittler's *Optimal Guide to Nutritional Health*.

Nolo Press, PO 544, Occidental, CA 94565. Many "fight for your rights" titles just great for self-reliant seniors.

University of Alaska Cooperative Extension Service, Publications, Fairbanks, AK 99701. Want to know how to build a log cabin or keep bees? Then send for this free catalogue. Many of the booklets are also free.

Vita or *Volunteers in Technical Assistance*, 80 S. Early St., Alexandria, VA 22304. As eclectic as the preceding one, but more Third World oriented with such titles as *Six Simple Pumps*, *Village Texturizers*, *Radios That Work for Free* and *Introduction to Soap Making*. I am particularly fond of *Village Sailwing Windmill*. They charge for the booklets, but much valuable information is there.

Holy Terra Publications, PO 1845, Carmel Valley, CA 93924. Some interesting books on how to win your case against the Internal Revenue Service.

Aspen Cabin, PO 712, Prescott, AZ 86302. This mail order book company sells wilderness titles such as *Tan Your Hide*, *The Sourdough Book* and *One Acre and Security*. I have always enjoyed dealing with a bookseller who could mix *25 Kites That Fly* with the *Fighting Knife*. You just know that these people have diverse interests.

> *"I do not know any reading more easy, fascinating*
> *and delightful than a catalogue."*
>
> — Anatole France

Triess Sciences, Inc., 622 Colorado St., Glendale, CA 91204. Need a little manganese dioxide, nitric acid, pure cotton or a 1,000 cc flask, some anatomical charts or modeling tools for your research projects? This is the outfit for you; they deal with a lot of unusual and hard-to-find items.

San Francisco Herb Co., 250 14th St., S.F., CA 94103. Buy your spices and herbs wholesale in quantity by mail and you are guaranteed a huge savings. Join with others in a big order so you can get the lowest prices. Minimum order is 35 dollars, but where else can you get red clover seed for sprouting or growing your own for just $1.80 a pound? Red clover is known to be cancer fighter when joined with desert chaparral.

Bronson, 4526 Rinetti Lane, La Canada, CA 91011. A man who wins two Nobel prizes deserves an attentive ear. So Linus Pauling is probably right when he says that some of our ailments stem from a lack of vitamin C, the only vitamin that the body cannot synthesize. Where to get this in pure form at a low price. Try Bronson's. Very satisfactory service and the prices are a fraction of what you pay in a drugstore.

Abco Inc., *2377 Stanwell Drive, Concord, CA 94520*. I know these people quite well and can vouch for the purity of their many products. You can buy many basic commodities in bulk form. Send for their catalogue and tell Bill that Wild Bill Kaysing sent you. If this sounds like a commercial, it is, since quality is hard to find at fair prices.

Cross Organic Seeds and Grains, *HC69 Box 2, Bunker Hill, KS 67626*. Parrots eat nothing but sunflower seeds and water and live to be a hundred or more. You can do the same outside of a cage if you get your sunflower seeds from an organization devoted to organics. And as of this writing, they are only $1.50 a pound hulled. This drops to $1.20 a pound if you buy 50 lbs. or more. They have all the grains, sprouting seeds and beans and just about everything that a health-aware senior would want in his or her pantry.

E.C. Kraus, *PO 7850, Independence, MO 64053*. They have all the equipment and supplies you need to make homemade wine. Few people know that you can make wine from many fruits like pomegranate, chokecherry, rhubarb, persimmon, prickly pear, watermelon and so on. A glass of wine with meals is supposed to aid digestion and it can certainly modify the behavior of a grouch. But in my own personal life, there is no space for alcohol.

Glen Boat Building and Marine Supplies, *9152 Rosecrans Blvd., Bellflower, CA 90706*. Lots of items that you'll need to build or restore a vessel. Also provides fine plans including one for the 40-foot houseboat, Mark Twain.

Sierra Club Books, *Distribution Center, Random House, Westminster, MD 21157*. If you would like the be-all, end-all guide book to the deserts of the Southwest, then try the Sierra Club versions—maps, photos, plants and animal directories—in short, the works in great detail. Many books on the outdoors and how to live there joyfully.

Harian Publications, *1 Vernon Ave., Floral Park, NY 11011*. I have always loved this company's books—*Formula for Long Life*, *Off the Beaten Path*, *All About the Southwest*, *America by Car*, *Florida at Affordable Prices* and *Where to Retire on a Small Income*. If you are oriented towards far-off places, buy their *Retirement Paradises of the World*; it describes Spain, Majorca, the Bahamas and other great places for seniors to live. Best of all, the books are quite inexpensive.

Samuel Weister Books, *PO 612, York Beach, ME 03910*. If you hae been looking for that obscure book titled *Grass Mountain, A Seven Day Intensive in Ch'an Training* or the *Ritual Book of Magic*, then this catalogue of books on higher consciousness is for you.

Cornell Maritime Press, *PO 456, Centreville, MD 21617*. If your senior group is planning to take a restored liner around the world, then you need books from this esteemed maritime publisher and bookseller. Titles read like a shipboard library: *American Merchant Seaman's Manual*, *Celestial Navigation* and the *Marine Engine Blue Book*.

International Marine Books, 21 Elm St., Camden, ME 04843. Get on their mailing list and you're almost sure to find something you want in one of their monthly catalogues. If you are a boating buff, then you would want to read Hiscock's *Cruising Under Sail* or *Want to be Comfortable at Sea?*.

The Burke Company, PO 5818, San Mateo, CA 94402. If you get serious about doing a boat with the Kaysite process, you'll need Burke's catalogue on concrete additives.

The Boater's Friend, 1822 Second St., Berkeley, CA 94402. Catalogue is one dollar and shows lots of used and new items for your liveaboard boat. Just bought a fine anchor and chain there that is holding my sloop nicely.

The Great American Houseboat, 1-800-262-BOAT. This organization provides houseboats in various areas. Try the waterborne life first before you invest.

Back to Basics Products, 11660 S. State St., Sandy, UT 84070. The best way to describe this catalogue is to show a sample page. If you are going to be your own food processor and I heartily recommend it, then you will need this type of equipment. I know that it will pay for itself in terms of better health and savings on groceries. After all, it's well proven that most people in the world live on food costing less than 25 cents a day and that they are healthier than most Americans with their fat and sugar-loaded diet.

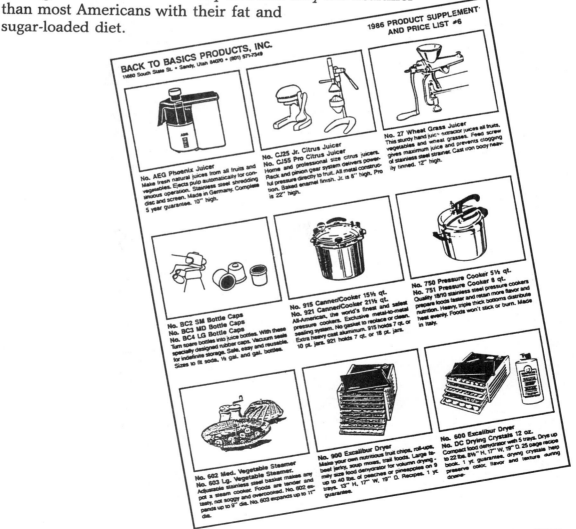

Cumberland General Store, RT 3, Box 479, Crossville, TN 38555. Want a buggy or a halter for your horse. Then this is the source. Great survival equipment that our forefathers used and brand new.

Memphis Net and Twine Co., PO 8331, Memphis, TN 38108. Great source book for any kind of fishing enterprise. Browsing through it gives you lots of ideas on how you can become more self-sufficient.

Trulock Video, 98 Main St., Tiburon, CA 94920. Videotapes on subjects such as gardening, building, cooking. They seem to be somewhat pricey, but like everything else in electronics, they'll come down. After all, many libraries are now beginning to offer video tapes on a loan basis just like books.

Illustrated List of Plans for Houses, Cooperative Farm Building Plan Exchange, *Agricultural Engineering Dept. of University of Maryland,* College Park, MD 20742. Exactly what it says.

Harris Moran Seed Company, 1155 Harkins Rd., Salinas, CA 93901. If you plan to grown large quantities of food, then this no-nonsense catalogue is for you. Beautifully illustrated with color photos of fine vegetables.

Sea Eagle Inflatables, PO 944, Smithtown, NY 11787. If you own a boat or are near the water, then you need this catalogue.

Boaterhome, PO 9100, Nampa, ID 93652. The ultimate combination boat and motorhome. See it to believe it. Free color brochure. I would love to play around with one of these; you drive it around and then launch the boat segment in any lake or the sea itself. Thus, no part of the world would be safe from your exploration.

Bear Tribe, PO 9167, Spokane, WA 99209. Books and other items reflecting an Indian culture. Highly recommended.

Impact 2000, 60 Irons St., Toms River, NJ 08753. A great selection of high tech items to make your senior life exciting.

Information Unlimited, PO 716, Amherst, NH 03031 provides an extensive array of unique and innovative plans for all kinds of electronic and related goodies. For example, want to get rid of rats without poison? They have a device that disorients the little critters so they leave and go live with your pesky neighbor down the street.

Whole Earth Catalogue, 558 Santa Cruz Ave., Menlo Park, CA 94025. The grandaddy of catalogues with many imitators and descendants. There are many issues that can often be found in used bookstores.

Floating Through Europe, 271 Madison Ave., NY, NY 10016. This is one of those wish books that could be reality for the more affluent senior. Stunning photos of cruises on the canals and rivers of many European countries.

Play Mate Resort Marinas, 730 Cypress, La Habra, CA 90631-6886. If floating through spectacular landscapes around Lake Mead, Shasta or the California Delta would make you happy, then send for this striking color catalogue.

William Mitchell College of Law Bookstore, 40 N. Milton St., St. Paul, MN 55105. Just a page from this catalogue will be an adequate alert as to the importance of this book vendor. As he says, "history shows us that freedom is obtained and retained by the most powerful weapon of all, KNOWLEDGE."

Self-Help, Valley of the Sun Publishing, PO 2010, Malibu, CA 90265. If you're into reincarnation, the spiritual aspects of this life and related subjects. I like his book, *The Master of Life Manual*, for its forthright statements about human relationships. They cut through the hype of our cultural constraints with the sharp blade of truth.

Paladin Press, PO 1307, Boulder, CO 80306. Good old Paladin. You can count on them for books about ACTION.

Institute of Human Development, PO 1616, Ojai, CA 93023. About 180 degrees from Paladin, with mostly tapes, but very VERY interesting. Their list includes a tape on health imaging. For those troubled with chronic or acute diseases, these may be very helpful.

Barnes and Noble, 126 Fifth Ave., NY, NY 10011. Books, tapes, and many other items in many categories. If you don't have a bookstore in your community, then let B and N take care of you. Extensive free catalogue.

Encore, 1400 Fruitridge Ave., Terre Haute, IN 47811. A fun catalogue filled with music and laughs from a vast number of songs by a vast number of recording artists. Send for this free fun catalogue.

Shelter Institute, 38 Center St., Bath, ME 04530. Want to build a house of your own for two thousand dollars? Then send for the catalogue of plans and training that this organization offers. They have a wide selection of books and if you can't go to their location for training, then get the video cassettes. A very heads-up group that can help put a roof over your grizzled head before winter snows flurry around it.

Paneling by Weldwood. This is a small brochure/catalogue that is available free from many lumberyards or from *Champion International Corp*. Call them free at 1-800-828-7879.
1-800-828-7879.

Shelter Kit Inc., 22 Mill St., PO 1, Tilden, NH 03276. Many ideas and kits for low cost housing.

Dovetail Press Ltd, PO 1496, Boulder, CO 80306. They offer information on a tankless water heater which is a must for those small, compact senior dwellings. It's easy to install.

East West Design Inc., Box 6022, Madison, WI 53716. Starplates can make building a snap. These stamped metal brackets allow the easy connection of basic timbers and the resultant erection of almost any kind of structure. You then cover with plywood, canvas or whatever and have an instant shelter.

Container Storage Inc., 23 Maine Ave., Richmond, CA 94804. We've all seen those huge steel containers that are used to ship goods overseas. When they get banged up a bit, they're sold to companies like this. And then you can acquire them outright or rent them and do just about anything in the shelter line from making a small home from them to creating a shop or business. I have one myself that's used for storage, but plan to turn it into an emergency shelter soon.

Here are addresses of several fine seed companies for your garden projects. All catalogues are free:

Henry Fields, Shenandoah, IA 51602

Johnny's Seeds, Albion, ME 04910

Mellingers, 2310 W S. Range Rd., North Lima, OH 44452

Stark Bros., Louisiana, MO 63353-0010. They are THE tree people with a great variety of other horticultural items inlcuding grapes, berries, and nuts. Wonderful catalogue.

Yellowstone Basin Properties, 1119 N. 7th Ave., PO 3027, Bozeman, MT 59772. Most urban dwellers dream of tall mountains crested by conifers with bubbling brooks and languid rivers. You can get 20 acres of pristine land for as little as 7,000 dollars with 150 dollars down and about 100 dollars a month. Definitely worth sending for this well-planned catalogue and its completely free.

United National Real Estate, 4700 Bellview, Kansas City, MO 64112. A big, thick illustrated wish book of properties nationwide. I have been studying it for years and once bought a fine property through this organization with no problems.

American Marine Electronics and Supply Inc., 5725 Oleander Dr., Wilmington, NC 28403. If there is one field where electronics has made life easier and safer, it's in the marine world. So send for this catalogue if you plan to go to sea seriously.

Jabsco, 1485 Dale Way, Costa Mesa, CA 92626. Heavy on marine pumps, this catalogue also features marine sanitation equipment that you might need on your freedom afloat project.

Modern Farm, 1825 Big Horn Ave., Cody, WY 92414. Love this type of catalogue with its emphasis on living outdoors. Lots of fine gear for the lady or gentleman farmer.

Northern Hydraulics, PO 1499, Burnsville, MN 55337. All kinds of interesting gadgets and surplus for the inventor/craftsman/do-it-yourselfer.

Work Shops, PO 28114, Warrensville Hts., OH 44128. For the man or woman who wants to review every conceivable tool for home or business. Several items would permit setting up a home business, like a wet grinding wheel for sharpening knives and scissors and such.

Lawn and Garden, Montgomery Ward, 2825 E. 14th St., Oakland, CA 94616. If there's no Ward's store in your area, then buy by mail. This catalogue is full of barbed wire, riding tractors and other goodies to make your home, garden or small farm productive and prosperous.

Marshall Tool and Supply Corp., 2850 E.Olympic Blvd., LA, CA 90023. Just about everything for the home mechanic and artisan, from digital micrometers to production lathes and mills. Easy to run a home business with this kind of quality equipment.

Nasco Farm and Ranch, 901 Janesville Ave., Fort Atkinson, WI 53538. Here's an·end-all catalogue for all you farmers to-be. Professional equipment and supplies for practically every type of farm and ranch. You'll get an education just reading this catalogue.

Keene Engineering, *9330 Corbin Ave., Northridge, CA 91324.* If you plan to operate a mining claim, then this is one of the best supply centers. Almost every small mine item in addition to a generous supply of books on the subject.

Burden's Surplus Center, *PO 92209, Lincoln, NE 68501.* I love catalogues like this because they are really dream books. You can visualize all kinds of unique and esoteric devices being built from these government surplus items that sell for a fraction of their cost to the taxpayers. Love that hydraulic pump that works on 12 volts. Can see a lot of uses for it.

Everett Marine and Fishing Supplies, *1220 80th SW, Everett, WA 98203.* You would expect the Seattle area to have one of the largest suppliers of marine hardware and so it is. Pumps, rope, life jackets, plus a lot of interesting gadgets that would make life at sea a delight. If you plan to fish, it's all here.

Synchronics, *Bldg. 42, Hanover, PA 17333.* We all love gadgets and this is what this firm offers in abundance.

Radio Shack, *500 One Tandy Center, Ft. Worth, TX 76102.* There are these chain stores in almost every city but if you don't find one, then you can order their catalogue.

Heathkit, *Benton Harbor, MI 49022.* Long known for its kits, Heath has expanded to offer many new items for the computer world. Keep up to date with this innovative catalogue.

Mailer-Frey Inc., *631 Fourth St., Santa Rosa, CA 95402* has a catalogue of kerosene heaters. They are illegal in some areas because they have the tendency to asphyxiate their users if not properly vented. However, they are used successfully in many parts of the world and have been for many years. All you must do is to vent them and to turn them off at night. A major distribution outlet on the east coast is in Kent, CT 06757.

Komfort Industries, *PO 4698, Riverside, CA 92514.* They offer a marvelous free color brochure showing the most exquisite RV's you've ever seen. Having always had gypsy blood in my veins, the very sight of these handsome, well-furnished travel rigs makes my heart pound for the open road. See if you don't agree.

Homestead Design, *PO 430, Langley, WA 98260.* This catalogue is so close to my own visions of low cost, comfortable senior homes that I feel a strong kinship with Craig Wallin, the designer.

Kountry Style, *Newmar Corp., PO 30, Nappanee, IN 46650.* This color catalogue will stimulate anyone housebound to go out and travel. Many warm, cozy interiors of motorhomes, campers and trailers are shown.

Owner Builder, *1516 Fifth St., Berkeley, CA 94710.* Also a publication, but partly a catalogue of what they offer to do-it-yourself home builders. A most valuable resource.

Airstream Inc., *Jackson Center, OH 45334.* This is THE classic trailer and you should see it and the real thing before you make your final decision on your Rocinante. Incidentally, Airstreams are noted for their ability to withstand the rigors of worldwide travel. They are often transported on ships or by rail to penetrate the most remote wilderness. Also, Airstream owners are fiercely loyal to the make and often gather in huge enclaves to celebrate their choice.

BOOKS

What follows are brief reviews of books that have been important in shaping this book. After all, there is really nothing new under the sun—all writers get their inspiration from other writers, at least in part.

If you can't find these in your local library or used bookstore, get in touch with me through the publisher and I'll try to help locate a copy. I have been considering creating a lending library by mail for books that are hard to find.

How To Quit the Rat Race, by J.F. Edwards. This is my favorite subject, since I was able to get off the track myself almost 25 years ago. This book provides basic counsel in a well-organized form. It is realistic, practical and authentic, as Edwards practices what he preaches. It is a valuable guide for pre-seniors reading this book who wish to enjoy more years of freedom.

The Best Investment, Land in a Loving Community, by D.W. Felder. "Just by living in a land co-op, a person is contributing toward change because intentional communities are experimental communities."

This would be the handbook that I would recommend to a group of seniors intending to create a communal living facility. Authentic because Felder actually did it in Florida. Well-written and with the kind of details you need to actually start a commune with an account of people who are doing what others merely talk about.

One Acre and Security, by Brad Angier. Good old Angie—he writes with such joy and enthusiasm. An inveterate dropout, he spends a lot of time in the wilds of northern British Columbia. Here, talking self-sufficiency, he is at his absolute best.

Guerrilla Capitalism. I am very fond of iconoclastic, exciting, thought-provoking, anti-authoritarian books like this one. A typical *Loompanics*, publication. The author points out that a feudal slave only had to donate 25 percent of his labor to the lord of the manor; today the average worker has to fork over about 50 percent of his total income to the bureaucrats and tax collectors. But it does not have to be that way Cash tells us. You and anyone else can easily create an enterprise that totally eliminates the need to give any money to those avaricious bandits. And just think, no more of your money will go to buy superfluous arms. After all, we now have enough weapons to kill everyone on earth 16 times over!

Author's Note: Here are two of the best books every published on the subject of taxes. I feel honored that I know both authors quite well. There are no greater true patriots of the genre of Washington, Jefferson and Paine than my friends, Dr. Martin Larson and Bill Greene.

Tax Revolt, by Dr. Martin Larson. In 1975, I checked out a book from the Antioch Library, *Tax Rebellion USA*, by Larson. After reading it, I was never the same. He proved to me beyond any doubt whatsoever that we have been manipulated by money managers since about 1913 when both the Federal Reserve and the income tax took power over American money. Larson's twenty books are meticulously researched books. He is the manifestation of the best of Jefferson, his hero, and Thomas Paine. I cannot recommend him enough to all Americans.

Dr. Larson's influence on me was powerful. For years I could think of nothing else but his stunning truths about how our country has been misused and mismanaged by men whose greed is beyond comprehension. I immediately began writing tax revolt books of my own including *Tax Wars* and *Tax Relief*.

Today, Dr. Larson has an updated version, *Tax Revolt, the Battle for the Constitution*. This book reviews the entire tax rebellion to date, cites cases of both victories and defeats and describes just how you can not only cope with the IRS but fight back successfully.

Dr. Larson is the dean of tax rebels in the U.S., but this accomplishment is but one of many. He is a true scholar and renaissance man and I predict that historians will rank him with Jefferson and other giants of the age. For a catalogue of his books write to *Dr. Martin Larson, PO 15059, Phoenix, AZ 85060*.

Win Your Personal Tax Revolt, by Bill Greene. Funny, enigmatic, colorful, courageous, outrageous, successful—you could heap the adjectives on Bill and never quite define his unique personality. Once he dressed up as Don Quixote and rode a white horse down Market Street in San Francisco to demonstrate his contempt for the Internal Revenue Service. He has been super-successful in teaching people how to keep their hard-earned money away from the IRS and into useful, productive pursuits.

The Natural Foods Cookbook, by B.T. Hunter. It's understandable why this book sold millions of copies—it's the best one on making tasty dishes from natural foods.

Recipes for a Small Planet, by E. Ewald. Meatless cooking that still affords good protein rations.

Passport to Survival, by E. Dickey. The author selects four foods—wheat, honey, powdered milk and salt (mainly as a preservative) as the chief foods in a food storage and survival program. She makes a good case and provides many recipes which are unique and very creative. Also included is a section on other aspects of survival. All in all, a definitive and relevant book for seniors.

Let's Get Well, by Adelle Davis. As she says, lecithin is a powerful emulsifying agent and for this reason is important in preventing and correcting athersclorosis, a disease prevalent among seniors. Thus, Ms. Davis, rest her sweet soul, proceeds to provide some of the most relevant data on food, nutrition and health that you could possibly read. Typical of her best-selling books, this one is basic and a must for anyone over 55 who wants to enjoy the delights of well-being.

Food is Your Best Medicine, by Henry G. Bieler, M.D. Today this is a much-reprinted classic and deservedly so. Dr. Bieler was a physician to the Hollywood stars and makes a powerful case for eschewing drugs in favor of good food. He cites actual cases to make his points and the proof will be your own good health if you take his advice. A don't-miss type of book for seniors.

The Food Conspiracy Cookbook, by L. Wickstrom. How to form your own food cooperative and then prepare the food you acquire.

A New Breed of Doctor, by A.H. Nittler, M.D. Alan followed Bieler's advice and became a famous nutritional advocate and brought enlightenment to millions of suffering people. Another absolutely MUST book if you are to have a complete understanding of the importance of food to health.

Freedom From Cancer, by M.L. Culbert. "Cancer is essentially a disease of civilization; its incidence is high in 'civilized' countries and diminishes as people decline on the 'civilization' scale." As Culbert points out, the primary variable in cancer is diet. Specifically, it is, like scurvy and rickets, a deficiency disease and the vitamin lack is B-17. It is worth anyone's effort to avoid cancer, and if it means just eating more apricots and other sources of B-17, I say, why not!

The book points out a salient fact: if you receive conventional treatment for cancer, you will die a bit quicker than if you had received no treatment at all!

International Protocols in Cancer Management, by R. Bradford, M. Culbert and H. Allen. If I had cancer, I would rather have a copy of this book than treatment from the best orthodox cancer cure center in the U.S. Both this and the above book may be obtained from *Bradford Foundation, PO 1003, Los Altos, CA 94022.*

Natural Sources: Vitamin B-17/Laetrile, by M. Timms and Z. Zar. Did you know that the Taos Indians of New Mexico have no cancer and that their favorite drink is made from the ground kernels of apricots? The authors of this *avant garde*, but practical guide add a long list of evidence that cancer may well be caused by a lack of proper nutrition. It might well be worth your life to read it.

The Practical Encyclopedia of Natural Healing, by Mark Bricklin. This is a landmark book on health without synthetic drugs and operations. My good friend Gene Schwartz, a mail order expert, had no trouble selling about 40,000,000 dollars worth of this important book. If that alone indicated its worth, it would be wise to buy it. And as you read, remember that most of the world depends on natural healing.

World Without Cancer, by G. E. Griffin. THE definitive work on how cancer has become a big and protected business in the United States.

DMSO, The Pain Killer, by B. Tarshis. An excellent review of the best arthritis relief around; one with no side effects. Get in touch with me in care of the publisher if you can't find DMSO.

Back to Eden, by Jethro Kloss. This author is one of the timeless breed who has created an old-fashioned book that you should keep on your shelf as long as you live. Healing herbs are described, home remedies are outlined and the message is that a good diet can produce good health. It's that simple and straightforward and I know you'll love it.

Health Secrets from Europe, by Paavo Airola, M.D. It's no secret that the Europeans are far beyond us in sophisticated medical practice. They have spas, much purer food, muesli, GH-3 and the methods to calm jangled nerves as we've never heard on this side of the Atlantic. But you can learn a lot from this best-seller written by the late and missed Airola.

I especially treasure his cogent explanations of such diseases as arthritis being a systemic ailment and not just something that appears in a joint. He also provides a nutritional solution for hair loss. It's a fact-filled book that you will read and re-read with your grateful friends.

The Best Health Ideas I Know, by Robert Rodale. Bob has been around for a long time doing good works; this book is no exception with something over 100,000 copies in print. He subtitles it, *My Personal Plan for Living* and from his appearance, he must be on the right track.

Robert calls health a talent and emphasizes that like any talent, it can be developed. He cites some simple rules: no rich foods, work up a sweat once a day, do things in moderation and get plenty of rest. He cites the following as true components of health:

- Greater personal efficiency
- A better mental situation
- A slower aging process
- Physical fitness
- Resistance to infection
- Beauty
- Sexual vitality
- Continuous challenge

On the latter, he points out that there is no limit to how healthy you can become at any age.

"Now learn what and how great benefits a temperate diet will bring along with it.

In the first place you will enjoy good health."
— *Horace, 65 B.C.*

Nutrition Scoreboard, Your Guide to Better Eating, by M. Jacobson, Ph.D. A little over 100 pages of relevant data on what you should eat and not eat. An excellent summary for those who want their information in compact form.

Commercial Foods Exposed, by G. D. Horsley. One of my favorite books and one much thumbed-over the years. Gaye has done an admirable job of research denouncing such accepted foods as margarine (it turns out to be close to plastic and little short of lethal). In addition to some great whistle-blowing on the merciless American food industry, she provides some fine recipes using whole, natural and real food!

Note: If you are interested in this subject, ask a local food processor for his copy of *Food Technology*, a magazine that reveals how bad American food has become. All about phoney tomato paste, cheese made from oil and chocolate that never saw a cocoa bean. If you can't find a copy locally, try a nearby university. Very tough to find this publication and when you read it, you'll understand why.

Backyard Bonanza, Editors, Rodale Press. This is a booklet only 48 pages long filled with the basics on how to grow your own delicious fresh vegetables in even a small back yard. It's all here in compact form—you'll hardly need any other book.

Planning for Wellness, by D. Ardell and M. Trager. If I could take only one book with me in my intergalactic spaceship, it would be this one. It is obvious that the authors have spent much time planning this book. For example, their list of the eight areas of life that should be considered in organizing a complete wellness plan include:

- Physical fitness
- Psychological/Spiritual health
- Stress management
- Leisure time
- Job satisfaction
- Relationships
- Family life
- Nutrition

This list is corroborated in a subjective manner. I once concluded that you could dine on the best foods nature provides, but if you had to work with impossible people on the job, all those vitamins and minerals would be for nothing.

This is a book in which you can participate actively and also one that many younger people will use and enjoy.

Physicians Desk Reference. This giant book is available at most library reference desks. Check the side effects of the drugs you are taking. A guaranteed and powerful reference book.

Shelter, by Lloyd Kahn. Probably one of the best books on alternative housing ever published. Many illustrations and infinite ideas for a roof over your head.

Commonsense Architecture, by J.S. Taylor. A cross-cultural survey of practical housing with an abundance of fine drawings revealing how people have responded to the need for shelter. Throw away *House Beautiful* and buy this book.

An Old Guy Who Feels Good, by W. McDonald. The autobiography of a free-spirited working man. Well worth reading for the data on SAGE (Senior Actualization and Growth Exploration). The author's son is the famous musician, Country Joe.

Home is Where You Park It, by Kay Peterson. A no-nonsense guide to living on wheels by a woman who has done it successfully for years. She also publishes a bi-monthly newsletter full of valuable information. For the book and newsletter write, *Kay Peterson, PO 2870, Estes Park, CO 80517.*

The Aquarian Conspiracy, by Marilyn Ferguson. In my opinion, the most important book written in the 80's. Ferguson, who writes as though she were a combination of Shakespeare and Einstein, brings it all together neatly, lucidly and with such great and entertaining style. Don't miss this book even if you miss all the others. And especially don't miss page 183.

The Illuminati Papers, by Robert Anton Wilson. Jesus said, "You are Gods." Sarfatti said, "...we are the hidden variable." A connection? More data than you can assimilate in a year. Much of it relates directly to seniors, such as "survival is assured by forming communes of shared voluntary frugality."

The Mystic Path to Cosmic Power, by Vernon Howard. "Happiness is a state of psychic understanding not of emotional feeling. Real happiness never changes; regardless of exterior conditions, it just IS!" My copy of this great book is well-annotated. I have found it to be the most comprehensive and concise interpretation of the wisdom of the ages. Nothing really new here and nothing you don't already know, but when you read, study and then practice what the book advocates, your life changes miraculously for the better. Here's an example of its beguiling simplicity:

"To live the way you want, just stop living the way you don't want."

Note: If this type of book interests you, then send one dollar for a catalogue of similar books to *DeVorss and Company, PO 550, Marina Del Rey, CA 90294-0550*. One of the best sources of books on raising your consciousness.

Passages, by Carol Sheehy. A best-seller and deservedly so; it identifies a predicament of life that most seniors have experienced. That was the time when we were around 40 or so and began to evaluate who we were and what we were doing with our lives and why. If we made the "passage" to a life that matched our real desires for self-fulfillment, then we are probably quite happy. If not, the reader can answer that for him or herself.

The Third Wave, by Alvin Toffler. By the author of the blockbusting *Future Shock*, this is also a remarkable book in that it describes what we all sense but seldom voice; the fact that we, as seniors, have been programmed from childhood to be good "prosumers," Toffler's term for producer-consumers.

Toffler reveals that our programming began in school when were overtly taught reading, writing and arithmetic but covertly made to be obedient, prompt and capable of withstanding boredom. Look back on your grammar school years and see if you don't agree that our schooling always directed us toward conformity and acquiescence. Much to learn about why we are the way we are.

PUBLICATIONS

We have all read *Time* and *Newsweek* and the daily newspapers. But how many people know *Spotlight* or *Freedom* or have even heard of *Rebel* or *Scanlan's*? Despite our touted freedom of the press, most people are unaware of what is really going on in the world. Here are some alternative publications.

Health Freedom News, PO 688, Monrovia, CA 91016. Official magazine of the *National Health Federation*. Suggest you join it and they'll send the magazine free. A most worthwhile organization that is into helping everyone, but has a lot to say about and for seniors.

Whole Life Times, 18 Shepard St., Brighton, MA 02135. Found free in many health food stores, this is worth a subscription if you can't find it. Recent articles discussed diet, complications of calcium (important with respect to our bone integrity) and poking around salad bars. Many worthwhile products advertised.

Mother Earth News, PO 70, Hendersonville, NC 28793. One of the oldest of the back-to-the-land periodicals. The early issues have the most basic data and you can find them in used book and magazine stores.

Shotgun News, PO 669, Hastings, NE 68901. All ads, no editorial, but it arms the second amendment in a pragmatic way. Send three dollars for a sample copy.

Utopian Classroom, 543 Frederick St., S.F., CA 94117. A most unusual publication backed by an *avant garde* group with some very unique ideas. Send for sample but enclose something for postage to aid this non-profit organization.

Boats and Harbors, Crossville, TN 38555. I can go through this newspaper of pure boating ads for hours and dream about casting off for far-off places. It is the best source I know of commercial boats. Many super-bargains in small freighters that would be ideal floating communes for senior adventurers. Also lots of marine equipment ads. Altogether, a publication with sea gulls crying and salt-spray flying.

Latitude 38, PO 1678, Sausalito, CA 94966. Huge free magazine stuffed with ads and great data on boats and boating. Entirely up-to-date with no misnomers about the romance of sea trips. In the section called "Changes in Latitude," there consists fun, first-person narratives of adventures on boats in far-off places. Not particularly for rag sailors, but with some ads and data on stinkpots. Rag sailors use sails; stinkpotters are engine lovers.

Trailer Life. The bible of all those who make trailers their home, whether for a weekend or a lifetime. Authoritative with ads that tell you what's new and vital. They also publish magazines on motorhomes and houseboats, in addition to many directories and buyers' guides. A must if you have gypsy blood.

Horticulture, the Magazine of American Gardening, PO 2595, Boulder, CO 80323. The ads are often more relevant than the articles, since they point you to the sources of all the seeds and tools you'll need to grow all of your own food. However, the data is pertinent and you'll enjoy the lovely color photos and drawings.

Health Food Business, 567 Morris Ave., Elizabeth, NJ 07208. This is a large trade magazine for the health food industry; if you can't afford a subscription, then ask your local health food store to save you their old copies. They are packed with trendy information lists of health food manufacturers and brokers. A valuable source of information for all seniors into natural food.

Common Ground, Mono Ave., Fairfax, CA 94930. Copies are free around San Francisco, but are three dollars by mail. A handsomely produced directory on a quarterly basis presenting new age resources—psychic arts, intuitive science, spiritual practices, healing, conferences and festivals. Most pertain to the San Francisco Bay area, but you'll learn a lot about what is new countrywide in terms of higher consciousness. And that, we all know, can strongly affect our total lives. Tell Sherman that Wild Bill sent you.

New Shelter, 33 E. Minor St., Emmaus, PA 18049. Fine collection of ideas on how to build or remodel a home. Rodale is the publisher; when you write, ask for a complete catalogue of all that they produce. Much of it is highly relevant to senior life. You can also obtain another magazine from this address titled, *The New Farm Magazine of Regenerative Agriculture.* Lots of tips on natural methods of farming. Good for the home gardener as well as the senior farm manager.

Communities, a Journal of Cooperation, Community Publications Cooperative, 126 Sun St., Stelle, IL 60919. This lists many intentional communities which invite people to come and look for possible long-term stays. I know of one in central California that I would like to try—Harbin Hot Springs near Middletown. The cost of the directory is five dollars.

Staking a Claim on Federal Land is neither a book nor a publication, but a hybrid from the *U.S. Dept. of the Interior, BLM, Washington, D.C. 20240-0001.* It will explain how you can obtain 20 acres of federal land as a mining claim as long as you are a citizen and the land has mineral possibilities (not just gold, but any mineral). Relatively few people are aware that this is a possibility to have the use of land and also earn a living. To learn more about this, write to *Keene Engineering, 9330 Corbin Ave., Northridge, CA 91324* and ask for their catalogue. They have all the equipment that a miner would need in addition to an extensive book list. We intend to cover this as a complete chapter in an update of this book because we feel it is important for seniors to know of all alternatives. In the meantime, pursue this on your own and good luck!

Freedom, 1301 N. Catalina, LA, CA 90027. It is rare to find an American magazine with such titles as: *Inside a an American Gulag* by George Hansen, *The Dump Truck Economy* and *The Erosion of National Sovereignty.*

ORGANIZATIONS and MANUFACTURERS

Harvest Trails is an organization typical of those which encourage the sale of produce direct from the farm to the consumer. They publish a handsome guide for the central California area. If you plan to be there, write for a free copy, *765 Main St., Half Moon Bay, CA 94019.*

No matter where you live, there are possibilities of buying fresh from the farmer. And if there isn't a guide, why not start one yourself?

The Stelle Group offers a complete town in which to live on a cooperative basis. They also publish the best I have found on the subject of intentional communities. Write *PO 75, Quinlan, TX 75474.*

Walpole Woodworkers makes kits that can be erected into charming little garden houses, patio cabanas, wilderness cabins and so forth. Even if you don't buy a kit, their literature will give you a lot of ideas on small-scale housing. Walpole was a major inspiration for the microhouses that I helped build in central California. Send one dollar to cover mailing costs to *767 E. St., Walpole, MA 02081.*

SUMMARY

In hopes that you are pleased with *Sources*; it has been challenging and entertaining to seek out the non-linear data bases. Please feel free to comment and to send your own favorite information source in care of the publisher.

McDonald's Ingredient Information

NUTRITION INFORMATION PER SERVING - SANDWICHES

ITEM	Hamburger Amount	%USRDA	Cheeseburger Amount	%USRDA	Quarter Pounder Amount	%USRDA	Quarter Pounder w/cheese Amount	%USRDA	Big Mac Amount	%USRDA	Filet-O-Fish Amount	%USRDA	McD.L.T. Amount	%USRDA
Serving Size (g)	100.		114.		160.		186.		200.		143.		254.	
Calories	263.		318.		427.		525.		570.		435.		680.	
Protein (g)	12.4	19.	15.	23.2	24.6	37.9	29.6	45.5	24.6	37.9	14.7	22.7	30.	45
Carbohydrate (g)	28.3		28.5		29.3		30.5		39.2		35.9		40.	
Fat (g)*	11.3		16.		23.5		31.6		35.		25.7		44.	
Mono-unsaturated fatty acids (g)	5.07		6.12		10.7		12.4		12.7		8.64		15.9	
Poly-unsaturated fatty acids (g)	0.98		1.09		1.72		1.86		7.6		9.45		9.55	
Saturated fatty acids (g)	4.43		6.66		9.11		12.8		11.5		5.56		14.8	
Cholesterol (mg)	29.1		40.6		81.		107.		83.		46.6		101.	
Sodium (mg)	506.		743.		718.		1220.		979.		799.		1030.	
Vitamin A Activity (IU)	100.	2.	353.	7.1	128.	2.6	614.	12.3	380.	7.6	186.	3.7	508.	10
Vitamin C (mg)	1.79	3.	2.05	3.4	2.56	4.3	2.79	4.7	3.	5.	< 2.15	—	8.	15
Thiamin (mg)	0.31	20.6	0.30	19.8	0.35	23.5	0.37	24.8	0.48	32.	0.36	23.8	0.56	35
Riboflavin (mg)	0.22	12.9	0.24	14.1	0.32	18.8	0.41	24.1	0.38	22.4	0.23	13.5	0.46	25
Niacin (mg)	4.08	20.4	4.33	21.7	7.20	36.	7.07	35.3	7.20	36.	3.	15.	8.	40
Calcium (mg)	84.	8.4	169.	16.9	98.	9.8	255.	25.5	203.	20.3	133.	13.3	250.	25
Iron (mg)	2.85	15.8	2.84	15.8	4.3	23.9	4.84	26.9	4.90	27.2	2.47	13.7	6.6	35

*In addition to the "fatty acid" values listed here, "fat" also includes glycerine, fat soluble vitamins and other fat soluble components.

NUTRITION INFORMATION PER SERVING - CHICKEN McNUGGETS AND SAUCES

ITEM	Chicken McNuggets Amount	%USRDA	Hot Mustard Sauce Amount	%USRDA	Barbeque Sauce Amount	%USRDA	Sweet & Sour Sauce Amount	%USRDA	Honey Amount	%USRDA
Serving Size (g)	109.		30.		32.		32.		14.	
Calories	323.		63.		60.		64.		50.	
Protein (g)	19.1	29.4	0.6	0.9	0.4	0.6	0.2	0.3	0.04	0.1
Carbohydrate (g)	14.7		10.5		13.7		15.		12.4	
Fat (g)*	20.2		2.1		0.4		0.3		0.04	
Mono-unsaturated fatty acids (g)	10.8		0.61		0.06		0.05		< 0.01	
Poly-unsaturated fatty acids (g)	1.99		1.42		0.18		0.14		< 0.01	
Saturated fatty acids (g)	5.1		0.47		0.03		0.03		< 0.01	
Cholesterol (mg)	62.5		2.7		< 0.3		< 0.1		< 0.1	
Sodium (mg)	512.		259.		309.		186.		2.	
Vitamin A Activity (IU)	<109.	—	9.	0.2	45.	0.9	200.	4.	<14.2	—
Vitamin C (mg)	2.07	3.5	< 0.3	—	< 0.64	< 1.1	< 0.3	—	< 0.15	—
Thiamin (mg)	0.16	10.9	0.01	0.8	0.01	0.9	0.01	0.4	0.002	—
Riboflavin (mg)	0.14	8.3	0.003	0.2	0.01	0.6	< 0.01	—	0.003	0.2
Niacin (mg)	7.52	37.6	0.08	0.4	0.08	0.5	0.07	0.4	0.03	0.1
Calcium (mg)	11.	1.1	8.	0.8	4.	0.4	2.	0.2	1.	0.1
Iron (mg)	1.25	7.	0.17	0.9	0.12	0.7	0.08	0.5	0.02	0.1

*In addition to the "fatty acid" values listed here, "fat" also includes glycerine, fat soluble vitamins and other fat soluble components.

McDonald's also offers carbonated and noncarbonated soft drinks. The food value in these products consists almost entirely of carbohydrates - a source of energy. The nutritional value of these beverages is listed below:

Soft Drinks   Per 12 Fl. Oz. serving with ice

	Coca-Cola Classic	Orange Drink	Sprite	Diet Coke
Carbohydrate (g)	32.	33.	36.	0.4
Calories	129.	133.	143.	2.
Sodium (mg)	6.	10.	45.	18.

APPENDIX A

NUTRITION INFORMATION PER SERVING - OTHER ITEMS

ITEM	French Fries Amount	%USRDA	Apple Pie Amount	%USRDA	Vanilla Milk Shake Amount	%USRDA	Chocolate Milk Shake Amount	%USRDA	Strawberry Milk Shake Amount	%USRDA
Serving Size (g)	68.		85.		291.		291.		290.	
Calories	220.		253.		352.		383.		362.	
Protein (g)	3.	4.6	1.87	2.9	9.3	20.7	9.9	22.	9.	20.
Carbohydrate (g)	26.1		29.3		59.6		65.5		62.1	
Fat (g)*	11.5		14.		8.4		9.		8.7	
Mono-unsaturated fatty acids (g)	4.37		6.48		2.5		2.48		2.51	
Poly-unsaturated fatty acids (g)	0.57		0.75		0.37		0.4		0.41	
Saturated fatty acids (g)	4.61		4.73		4.13		4.15		4.14	
Cholesterol (mg)	8.57		7.2		30.6		29.7		32.2	
Sodium (mg)	109.		398.		201.		300.		207.	
Vitamin A Activity (IU)	< 17.	—	< 34.	—	349.	7.	349.	7.	377.	7.5
Vitamin C (mg)	12.53	20.9	< 0.85	—	3.2	5.3	< 2.91	—	4.06	6.8
Thiamin (mg)	0.12	7.7	0.02	1.3	0.12	7.7	0.12	7.7	0.12	7.7
Riboflavin (mg)	0.02	1.2	0.02	1.2	0.70	41.1	0.44	25.7	0.44	25.6
Niacin (mg)	2.26	11.3	0.19	0.9	0.35	1.7	0.50	2.5	0.35	1.7
Calcium (mg)	9.	0.9	14.	1.4	329.	32.9	320.	32.	322.	32.2
Iron (mg)	0.61	3.4	0.62	3.5	0.18	1.	0.84	4.7	0.17	1.

*In addition to the "fatty acid" values listed here, "fat" also includes glycerine, fat soluble vitamins and other fat soluble components.

NUTRITION INFORMATION PER SERVING - OTHER ITEMS (cont'd.)

ITEM	Soft Serve and Cones Amount	%USRDA	Strawberry Sundae Amount	%USRDA	Hot Fudge Sundae Amount	%USRDA	Hot Caramel Sundae Amount	%USRDA	McDonaldland Cookies Amount	%USRDA	Chocolaty Chip Cookies Amount	%USRDA
Serving Size (g)	115.		164.		164.		165.		67.		69.	
Calories	189.		320.		357.		361.		308.		342.	
Protein (g)	4.3	6.6	6.	10.1	7.	10.8	7.2	11.1	4.2	6.5	4.2	6.5
Carbohydrate (g)	31.2		54.		58.		60.8		48.7		44.8	
Fat (g)*	5.2		8.7		10.8		10.		10.8		16.3	
Mono-unsaturated fatty acids (g)	1.29		2.81		2.88		2.71		4.72		6.48	
Poly-unsaturated fatty acids (g)	0.25		1.11		1.		0.91		1.33		0.93	
Saturated fatty acids (g)	2.24		3.18		5.42		3.47		4.18		8.19	
Cholesterol (mg)	23.5		24.6		26.6		31.4		10.2		17.7	
Sodium (mg)	109.		90.		170.		145.		358.		313.	
Vitamin A Activity (IU)	218.	4.4	230.	5.5	230.	4.6	279.	5.6	< 26.8	—	75.9	1.5
Vitamin C (mg)	< 1.15	—	2.79	4.7	2.46	4.1	3.61	6.	< 0.94	1.6	1.04	1.7
Thiamin (mg)	0.06	3.8	0.07	4.4	0.07	4.4	0.07	4.4	0.23	15.2	0.12	8.3
Riboflavin (mg)	0.36	21.	0.30	17.4	0.31	18.4	0.31	18.4	0.23	13.5	0.21	12.4
Niacin (mg)	0.44	2.2	1.03	5.2	1.12	5.6	1.01	5.	2.85	14.3	1.7	8.5
Calcium (mg)	183.	18.3	174.	17.4	215.	21.5	200.	20.	12.	1.2	29.	2.9
Iron (mg)	0.12	0.6	0.38	2.1	0.61	3.4	0.23	1.3	1.47	8.2	1.56	8.7

*In addition to the "fatty acid" values listed here, "fat" also includes glycerine, fat soluble vitamins and other fat soluble components.

NUTRITION INFORMATION PER SERVING - BREAKFAST ITEMS

ITEM	Egg McMuffin Amount	%USRDA	Hotcakes w/butter Syrup Amount	%USRDA	Scrambled Eggs Amount	%USRDA	Pork Sausage Amount	%USRDA	English Muffin w/butter Amount	%USRDA	Hashbrown Potatoes Amount	%USRDA
Serving Size (g)	138.		214.		98.		53.		63.		55.	
Calories	340.		500.		180.		210.		186.		144.	
Protein (g)	18.5	28.5	7.9	12.2	13.2	29.4	9.8	19.5	5.	7.7	1.4	2.5
Carbohydrate (g)	31.		93.9		2.5		0.6		29.5		14.6	
Fat (g)*	15.8		10.3		13.		18.6		5.3		8.9	
Mono-unsaturated fatty acids (g)	4.99		3.7		5.12		8.69		1.51		5.3	
Poly-unsaturated fatty acids (g)	1.52		1.14		1.69		2.38		0.6		0.63	
Saturated fatty acids (g)	5.87		3.78		5.1		7.03		2.32		2.94	
Cholesterol (mg)	259.		47.1		514.2		38.8		15.4		3.6	
Sodium (mg)	885.		1070.		205.		423.		310.		325.	
Vitamin A Activity (IU)	591.	11.8	257.	5.1	652.	13.	< 31.8	—	164.	3.3	< 13.75	—
Vitamin C (mg)	< 1.38	—	4.71	7.9	1.18	2.	< 0.53	—	0.82	1.4	4.14	6.9
Thiamin (mg)	0.47	31.3	0.26	17.1	0.08	5.2	0.27	18.	0.28	18.9	0.06	4.
Riboflavin (mg)	0.44	26.	0.36	21.4	0.47	27.7	0.11	6.2	0.49	28.9	< 0.01	—
Niacin (mg)	3.77	18.8	2.27	11.3	0.20	1.	2.07	10.4	2.61	13.1	0.82	4.1
Calcium (mg)	226.	22.6	103.	10.3	61.	6.1	16.	1.6	117.	11.7	5.33	0.5
Iron (mg)	2.93	16.3	2.23	12.4	2.53	14.1	0.82	4.6	1.51	8.4	0.40	2.2

*In addition to the "fatty acid" values listed here, "fat" also includes glycerine, fat soluble vitamins and other fat soluble components.

BISCUIT SPREAD (10 calories)
Ingredient List: Partially hydrogenated soybean oil, lecithin, artificial flavor, TBHQ (a preservative), artificial color, methylsilicone. (Used to prepare buttermilk biscuits)
Supplier: Hunt-Wesson Foods, Inc.

CAKE CONES (40 calories)
Ingredient List: Flour, sugar, starch, partially hydrogenated vegetable shortening (may contain one or more of the following oils: soybean, cottonseed or palm), salt, baking soda, annatto extract, vanillin.
Suppliers: Sweetheart Cones, Keebler Cookies.

CANADIAN STYLE BACON (33 calories)
Ingredient List: Sliced Canadian style bacon with natural juices, fully cooked, smoked, cured with water, salt, dextrose, corn syrup, sodium phosphate, sodium erythorbate, sodium nitrite.
Suppliers: Anderson Meat and Provisions, Inc., Rose Packing Company Inc.

CHEESE (55 calories)
Ingredient List: American cheese, water, milkfat, sodium citrate, kasal, salt, sodium phosphate, sorbic acid as a preservative.
Suppliers: Kraft Inc., Schreiber Foods, Inc.

CHICKEN McNUGGETS (1 piece: 54 calories)
Ingredient List: Chicken (white meat, dark meat, skin, salt, sodium phosphate) breaded with water, enriched wheat flour {with niacin (a "B" vitamin), iron, thiamine mononitrate (vitamin B1), riboflavin (vitamin B2)}, corn flour, modified corn starch, salt, leavening (bicarbonate of soda, sodium acid pyrophosphate, sodium aluminum phosphate, monocalcium phosphate, calcium lactate), spices, whey, wheat starch, monosodium glutamate. Cooked in 100% Vegetable Shortening.
Suppliers: Keystone Foods, Tyson's Chicken.

CHOCOLATY CHIP COOKIES (342 calories)
Ingredient List: Enriched wheat flour {with niacin (a "B" vitamin), reduced iron, thiamine mononitrate (vitamin B1), and riboflavin (vitamin B2)}, sugar, animal and/or vegetable shortening, (beef fat and/or partially hydrogenated soybean, coconut, palm kernel and/or palm oils), sweet chocolate (with lecithin and vanillin), butter, whey, molasses, cocoa, salt, leavening (sodium bicarbonate, sodium acid pyrophosphate, monocalcium phosphate), emulsifiers (lecithin, sorbitan monostearate, polysorbate 60), cocoa (processed with alkali), dextrose and artificial flavor.
Supplier: Keebler Company.

CHOCOLATE FLAVORED SYRUP (For a complete chocolate milkshake, 383 calories)
Ingredient List: Corn syrup, water, cocoa, sugar, malt, salt, sodium benzoate or potassium sorbate as a preservative, citric acid and vanillin.
Suppliers: Richardson Food Corporation, Golden State Foods Corporation, R. W. Snyder Company Inc.

COCA-COLA® Classic (12 calories per fluid ounce)
Ingredient List: Carbonated water, high fructose corn syrup and/or sucrose, caramel color, phosphoric acid, natural flavors, caffeine.
Supplier: Coca-Cola U.S.A.

MAYONNAISE (136 calories)
Ingredient List: Soybean oil, whole eggs, egg yolks, vinegar, water, salt, sugar, lemon juice, and natural flavors. EDTA added to protect flavor.
Suppliers: McCormick and Co., Kraft Inc., Golden State Foods Corporation.

McDONALDLAND COOKIES (308 calories)
Ingredient List: Enriched wheat flour {with niacin (a "B" vitamin), reduced iron, thiamine mononitrate (Vitamin B1), and riboflavin (Vitamin B2)}, sugar, animal and/or vegetable shortening (beef fat and/or lard and/or partially hydrogenated soybean oil), corn syrup, salt, leavening (sodium bicarbonate, sodium acid pyrophosphate, monocalcium phosphate), lecithin and artificial flavor.
Supplier: Keebler Company.

MILKSHAKE MIX (Including chocolate or vanilla or strawberry syrup, 352-383 calories)
Ingredient List: Whole milk, sucrose, non-fat milk solids, corn syrup solids, cream, guar gum, dextrose, sodium hexametaphosphate, carrageenan, vanillin, cellulose gum.
Suppliers: Borden's, Meadow Gold, Carnation, H.P. Hood, Associated Dairies, Atlanta Dairies, Barber Pure Milk, Byrne Dairy, C.F. Burger, Cumberland Dairy, Dairy Farm Products, Dairy Mix, Dairylea Cooperative, Elgin-Honeyhill, Flav-O-Rich, Foremost Foods, Gallicker Dairy, Golden State Foods Corporation, Harbin Mix, Knudsen, Kohler Mix Specialities, Lambert Ice Cream, Maui Soda and Ice Works, Midwest Farms, Model Dairy, Prairie Farms

Ingredient List (100% Vegetable Shortening for Chicken McNuggets, Filet-O-Fish, Hashbrowns, Hot Pie Desserts): Partially hydrogenated corn oil, cottonseed oil, hydrogenated cottonseed oil, monoglyceride citrate and propyl gallate added to protect flavor. (This shortening is 75% unsaturated.)
Supplier: Interstate Foods.

SOFT SERVE MIX (150 calories)
Ingredient List: Whole milk, sucrose, cream, nonfat milk solids, corn syrup solids, mono and diglycerides, guar gum, vanillin, carrageenan, cellulose gum, annatto extract.
Suppliers: Meadow Gold, Borden's, Carnation, H.P. Hood, Associated Dairies, Atlanta Dairies, Barber Pure Milk, Byrne Dairy, C.F. Burger, Cumberland Dairy, Dairy Farm Products, Dairy Mix, Dairylea Cooperative, Elgin-Honeyhill, Flav-O-Rich, Foremost Foods, Gallicker Dairy, Golden State Foods Corporation, Harbin Mix, Knudsen, Kohler Mix Specialities, Lambert Ice Cream, Maui Soda and Ice Works, Midwest Farms, Model Dairy, Prairie Farms Dairy, Roberts Dairy, Russell's Ice Cream, Shenandoahs Pride Dairy, Southeastern Dairies, Taylor Milk, Tres Monjitas, Watts-Hardy, Wayne Dairy Products.

SPRITE® (12 calories per fluid ounce)
Ingredient List: Carbonated water, high fructose corn syrup and/or sucrose, citric acid, natural lemon and lime flavors, sodium citrate, sodium benzoate (preservative), salt.
Supplier: Coca-Cola U.S.A.

STRAWBERRY PRESERVES (37 calories)
Ingredient List: Sugar, strawberries, pectin, and citric acid.
Suppliers: Kraft Inc., McCormick and Co., Golden State Foods Corporation, Serv-A-Portion, Sigma Quality Foods.

STRAWBERRY SUNDAE TOPPING (61 calories)
Ingredient List: Strawberries, sugar, water, natural flavors, corn syrup, citric acid, pectin, locust bean gum, sodium benzoate or potassium sorbate as a preservative, artificial color and calcium chloride.
Suppliers: Johnston's, Golden State Foods Corporation, R. W. Snyder Company Inc.

ORANGE DRINK (13.6 calories per fluid ounce)
Ingredient List: Water, corn sweetener, sugar, citric acid, concentrated orange juice, natural and artificial flavors, glyceryl abietate, vegetable gum, processed vegetable oil, glycerine, artificial color, preserved with sodium benzoate.
Suppliers: Golden State Foods Corporation, R. W. Snyder Company Inc., Richardson Food Corporation.

ORANGE JUICE (80 calories per 6 oz. serving)
Ingredient List: 100% pure reconstituted orange juice from concentrate — no sugar added.
Supplier: H. P. Hood Inc.

PORK SAUSAGE (210 calories)
Ingredient List: Pork, water, salt, spices, corn syrup, dextrose, MSG, BHA, propyl gallate and citric acid.
Suppliers: Rudy's Farm Company, Anderson Meat and Provisions, Inc., North Side Packing Company, Brooks Sausage Company.

SHORTENING BLENDS
Ingredient List (For French Fries): Selected blend of beef shortening and vegetable shortening (cottonseed oil), monoglyceride citrate, propyl gallate added to protect flavor. (This shortening is 57% unsaturated.)
Supplier: Interstate Foods.

DIET COKE® (0.1 calories per fluid ounce)
Ingredient List: Carbonated water, caramel color, phosphoric acid, sodium saccharin, potassium benzoate (preservative), natural flavors, citric acid, caffeine, potassium citrate, aspartame (NutraSweet brand), dimethylpolysiloxane. Diet Coke is sweetened with a blend of saccharin and NutraSweet (a registered trademark of the NutraSweet Co).
Saccharin: Use of saccharin in this Coca-Cola product may be hazardous to your health. This ingredient has been determined to cause cancer in laboratory animals.
NutraSweet: Phenylketonurics: contains phenylalanine.
Supplier: Coca-Cola U.S.A.

DILL PICKLE SLICES (5 calories)
Ingredient List: Cucumbers, water, salt, vinegar, sodium benzoate as a preservative, natural flavoring, alum, polysorbate 80, and turmeric.
Suppliers: Vlasic Foods, Heinz, Atkins Pickle Company, Bluhill, Chas. F. Cates & Sons Inc., M. A. Gedney Company, Nalley's Fine Foods, Green Bay Foods.

EGGS (90 calories)
Ingredient List: USDA Grade A Large Shell Eggs.
Suppliers: From chickens around the U.S.A., collected by the farmers of Agway Egg Marketing, Cargill, Crystal Foods, Jersey Coast Eggs, Krasno Eggs, Inc., Mendleson Egg Company, Midwest Poultry Services, Inc., Morning Fresh Farms, Mountain Valley, National Foods, Olson Farms, Oskaloosa Foods, Seaboard, Southern New England Egg, Sunny Fresh Farms, Inc., Weaver Brothers, Inc., and Zephyr Egg Company.

Prime Timer
by Bill Kaysing

Prosumers

In his latest book, *The Third Wave*, Alvin Toffler presents some stunning insights into life as it is lived in the Industrial Age. He points out, for example, that compulsory education was designed to make people prompt, obedient and willing to endure boredom. In short, going to school was a prerequisite to going to a factory or office. (Ever notice the astonishing resemblance of most schools to factory compounds?)

Later he discusses what he calls the producer-consumer (prosumer), the average industrial age citizen who produces some gimcracks or veeblefetzers and then proceeds to consume them. Our entire international business complex revolves around this simple principle...keep everyone busy either producing or consuming 24 hours a day.

You see, if you're either making or breaking, you don't have too much time to reflect on the inherent unpleasantness and dissatisfaction of your life. What most people have done is exchanged the possibility of dying of hunger for the probability of dying of boredom. FROM A NEW ZEALAND PUBLICATION: "To make sure the people remained in a situation of simple control it was advisable to restrict the content and volume of information that was available. It was ideal that they were subjected to enormous quantities of trivial and irrelevant data. If they could be preoccupied with the ideas of fashion, of status, of titillation, they would fail to notice that they were being deprived

of information that did affect themselves and their environment. This filtering of the news that allowed only the most trivial to reach the masses was also an aid to their continuing production and consumption."

About twenty years ago I decided to let someone else win the rat race and I became a freelance writer. What I did, in effect, was exchange the assurance of a life of boredom (my job was aerospace technical writer) for the possibility of dying of hunger. Well, the latter hasn't happened YET. And I must admit that I have more fun in one day than I used to have in a year. Ruth, my faithful co-writer and playmate, says I'm not alone.

Golf, Shuffleboard and Bingo...Are they enough? (by Ruth Kaysing)

Starting a new career after retirement is a challenge more and more of us are taking up. Awareness of good health practices enables us to continue being active, and as the rocking-chair-and-TV stereotype fades, we feel a new surge of ambition. Even better, for perhaps the first time in our long working careers, we have the freedom to choose doing the kind of work we truly enjoy.

Such, for example, is the case with Sam McKeever. After many years as an auditor for both San Bernardino and Santa Cruz counties, Sam retired. But trailering and playing golf weren't enough to occupy Sam's restless brain. He began getting involved in the issues affecting him as a mobile home

park resident and was soon chairing meetings and giving talks. Now he has assumed a new role, that of Director for GSMOL's (Golden State Mobilehome Owners League) 10th district. With a mind geared to retaining facts and figures and a natural bent toward leadership, Sam seems ideally suited to his new senior career.

Anne Zauss is another example. Even though past retirement age, Anne wasn't ready to discontinue using the polished skills acquired over many years of secretarial work. Anne is a rare bird... she really loves to type. Moving to Santa Cruz provided the incentive to start a new career, her own secretarial service, with the very important addition of a sophisticated computer. She is presently mastering the intricacies of this modern-day equipment with an ease we might expect from a far younger neophyte. Watch for her shingle.

In my own case, sharing the hosting of a radio program for seniors has proven the perfect outlet for my gift of gab. Talking has always come easy for me. Although most of my working years were spent as a secretary, occasionally I had a chance to give a lecture and always found it a heady experience. Last summer when KUSP's program director asked me to share the hosting for the new *Prime Time* program, I agreed enthusiastically. Finding interesting individuals to interview weekly is as challenging as the live interview itself is exciting.

In summary, finding a new career can mean simply being open to trying something new. The main thing is to jump in and get involved, for as Thomas Henry Huxley said, "The great end of life is not knowledge but action."

Supplemental Incomes

Many retired people find living on SS and small pensions a real drag — there's never

enough money to finance the little pleasures that make life more livable. So here are a couple of suggestions on how people of ANY age can acquire a little extra cash without making a large capital investment.

Cookies are increasingly popular as a snack and we find cooky bakeries springing up all over. If you love to bake, here's my suggestion. Work up a truly delicious cooky ... perhaps a variation on the ever-popular oatmeal-raisin-nut variety. Bake up a batch and wrap them in clear plastic with a colorful label. Delivered to various outlets, sales are almost assured since few people can resist fresh, homemade cookies.

I know a woman in her thirties in the Carmel valley who has built a prosperous business from cookies alone. She can hardly keep up with the demand. Oh yes, check with the powers-that-be regarding sanitation, licenses, etc. To avoid hassles, you could use a facility that is already approved. Just trade those yummy cookies for a few hours use each day (or evening).

Hot and cold snacks such as rye-cheese-olive canapes are served free with drinks in many bars during happy hour. I knew a couple in Santa Barbara who built a successful business providing elegant, colorful, appealing trays of these items for bars and lounges in that city. It's easy to do, there are books in abundance on how and I'm almost certain that many cocktail places would welcome something new and different each day. Again, check with those who govern this work but always consider a joint venture with a caterer or small restaurant that's already approved.

In future columns we'll have more spare-time income ideas and you are most welcome to contribute any of your own.

©1984 Bill Kaysing

Prime Timer
by Bill Kaysing

The Marx Brothers were ahead of their time

Seniors will recall growing up with the Marx Brothers. Such films as *Coconuts, Horsefeathers, A Night at the Opera* and *Duck Soup* made even the grimmest of depressions a little easier to handle.

Over the years, I've given a lot of thought to the Brothers Marx and have decided that they were well ahead of their time. For example, in *Duck Soup* there's a scene where they are fighting a pitched battle. Huge shells are drifting through their redoubt amidst the smoke and noise of combat. A bemedaled general turns to Chico and says, "I want that machine gun nest cleaned out right away." Chico, deadpan, replies,

"I'll get the janitor on it right away."

Thus, I suggest that instead of peacekeeping forces in belligerent areas, we send old Marx Brothers films. In that way, the antagonists can, perhaps, see the absurdity of war.

Incidentally, Groucho was once asked which jokes got the biggest laughs when they were in vaudeville. He cited these:

ZEPPO: Dad, the garbage man is outside.
GROUCHO: Tell him we don't want any.

CHICO: I'd just like to say goodbye to your wife.
GROUCHO: So would I.

This brings me to the subject of humor as a health aid. There are few things in life that cannot be improved with a laugh or two. Fun makes good times better, the bad times easier to bear. That's why Ruth and I are working on a new booklet titled, *Health is a Laughing Matter.*

There's plenty of proof that people who laugh a lot have far fewer ailments. Norman Cousins cited funny films as a major therapy in his recovery from what might have been a terminal disease. Physiologically, endorphins circulate when you are laughing and having fun, and they create a state of good feelings and even euphoria. Psychologically, here are two short analyses:

"The biggest laughs are based on the biggest disappointments and the biggest fears."

—Kurt Vonnegut, Jr.

"A man sufficiently gifted with humor is in small danger of succumbing to flattering delusions about himself because he cannot help perceiving what a pompous ass he would become if he did."

—Konrad Lorenz

Homes for the Homeless

That's the title of a new booklet soon to be published by HOLY TERRA BOOKS. Contents will consist of:

MOVE IN NOW: Instant housing for the person with little or no money.

COMMUNES AND CO-OPS: Popular with older people, it works at any age.

NOMADS: Millions of Americans now live "on the road" for fun and adventure plus great economy.

RECYCLED HOUSING: All about converting old buildings from churches and schools to gas stations to comfortable dwellings.

BUILD IT YOURSELF: In Mendocino County there are houses built complete for less than a payment on a crackerbox.

SQUATTING: It's legal and here are the parameters.

FREEDOM AFLOAT: With more than 3/5ths of the earth water, a floating home makes good sense.

Short, concise and loaded with tips for those 3 million Americans who have no address, this booklet will fill a great need. For more information, drop a postcard to HOLY TERRA BOOKS, 2932 Old San Jose Road, Soquel 95073.

Boat fever

That time is coming soon. A good source of information on boats of all description can be obtained from *Boats and Harbors*, Crossvill Tenn. 38555. Write for free sample copy.

The stress of the IRS

Have you ever thought about how much pressure this one bureaucracy puts on citizens. While doing a series for a Nevada newspaper, I learned that many people have become ill just thinking about the tax collector and their often unconstitutional methods of operation. But there's lots of good information around from some very learned people. If you want to reduce the stress of the IRS, drop a card to my good friend Dr. Martin Larson, a really genuine Ph.D. who has devoted the last 35 years to a study of what the IRS can and cannot do under our protective constitutional shield. His address is PO 15059, Phoenix, AZ, 85060. His book list includes such gems as *Tax Rebellion USA*, and *The Middle Class vs. the IRS*. He has others that will give you the information you need to enjoy the rights to which you are entitled. I personally guarantee it.

Wise men

Two philosophers who lived centuries apart defined the term: Confucius said that "a wise man has no foregone conclusions, no arbitrary predeterminations, no obstinacy and no egoism." Cervantes was briefer. He said that "he who lives well, preaches well."

© Bill Kaysing 1984

Prime Timer
by Bill Kaysing

The Wizard of IRS

THE IRS AND FRANK MORGAN

There's a marvelous scene in *The Wizard of Oz* when Dorothy and her friends finally discover the Wizard's hideout and see him in action. Instead of a powerful, formidable adversary, they learn that the Wizard is really a fearful pipsqueak equipped with a lot of noise and smoke-making machinery.

A distinct parallel may be drawn between the IRS and Frank Morgan's portrayal of the Wizard of Oz. The IRS consists of about 30,000 pale and spiritually-anemic, indoor bureaucrats. Like Frank, they use all kinds of smoke and noise to strike fear into the hearts of American taxpayers. For example, right around April 15th, articles will begin appearing in big-city papers concerning this or that taxpayer who is going to jail or who got a big fine or assessment. By squashing one or two, usually, high-profile tax rebels, the IRS is able to bamboozle and intimidate the majority of all taxpayers into thinking it's all-powerful.

In reality, *it's not powerful at all* and will *back down* like a *schoolyard bully* if you show even a small amount of backbone. Take my own case. In 1977 I wrote a book titled *Tax Wars* which advocated tax rebellion by various means. The book was so fiery and convincing that even I took its advice and stopped paying all income taxes. Naturally, the IRS responded to my Fifth Amendment return by asserting that it was "not proper." I wrote back and asked the *name and address* of the specific IRS agent who defined my return as "not proper." And do you know, I have NEVER HEARD FROM THE IRS SINCE!! Not a postcard, not a phone call, absolutely NOTHING!!! I can only presume that the IRS Wizard in Washington decided to go on to sheep that could be more easily sheared.

Last April 15th, (1983) I stood on the steps of the Santa Cruz County Building and tore up a 1040 form in view of TV cameras and a small audience. The deed was duly reported in print and on KMST TV. It's reasonably certain that the IRS caught my act but again...I HAVE NOT HEARD ONE WORD FROM THE IRS!!

Now what can we learn from this personal experience? I know that it generated lots of energy and several people decided to join me in tax resistance. Furthermore, it motivated me to write up a PERSONAL DECLARATION OF TAX INDEPENDENCE. This document is similar to the famous DECLARATION OF INDEPENDENCE but only requires one signature, *yours*. Send a SASE to 2932 Old San Jose Road, Soquel, CA 95073 for your copy or check with the Unitarian Fellowship (684-0506) since I'll be speaking there and handing out copies free in the near future.

Incidentally, *this is my personal invitation* to *all* local *IRS agents* to attend the Unitarian meeting. I would like to help them obtain *honest employment*, at no charge or obligation.

THE AA TEAM

Recently I read a science fiction story about America in 1990. It seems that a fleet of space ships lands in the U.S. and out step the "AVENGING ANGELS." They line everyone up and ask if they did or didn't pay income taxes. Those that say they *did* are immediately vaporized, the non-payers are set free. Apparently the AA Team is operating on the basis of the Nuremberg Principle. As you recall, this was established by American courts after WWII and resulted in the execution of several war criminals. The contention of this justice system was that if you obeyed a law that was inhuman or contrary to a higher morality, you were guilty of a crime against humanity.

The story concluded by pointing out that if you now contribute your tax money for the establishment of ruthless dictatorships in Chile or the Phillipines (and many other places), the purchase of weapons that virtually assure international suicide or otherwise support evil, you had better hide when the AA Team arrives.

EASTERN PHILOSOPHY

Oriental culture is the oldest on this planet. The lovers of raw fish and chop suey have had lots of time to think things over and condense their knowledge. It is appropriate that we conclude this brief dissertation on countering the stress of the IRS with some of their profundities:

"We are not punished for our sins but by them."
　　　　　Buddhist saying

"To win one hundred victories in one hundred battles is not the highest skill. To subdue the enemy without fighting is the highest skill."
　　　　　Sun-Tzu

"Softness triumphs over hardness, feebleness over strength. What is more malleable is always superior over that which is immovable."
　　　　　Lao-Tzu

PS: To the friends of "THE NEMESIS OF THE IRS", Paul Bell; please write him at 3600 Guard Road, Lompoc, CA 93436.
　　　　　©1984 Bill Kaysing

Send your letters to *The News* to PO Box 327, Aptos 95003. Letters must be signed and include an address in order to be printed.

Prime Timer
by Bill Kaysing

"Allowing for inflation, wheat now sells for less than in 1932."

Can you *really* eat well for one dollar a day?
Several years ago, Ruth and I appeared on a number of TV talk shows to publicize our book *Eat Well On A Dollar A Day.* The host would often be polite during the show and listen to our presentation. But afterwards, they would take us aside and say,

"C'mon now, level with me. You can't *really* eat on a dollar a day. You're just saying that to sell the book, aren't you?"

Our response to that was the same then as it is now...you *really* can enjoy a good, nutritious and delicious diet for just one dollar a day *if* you know how.

Here's proof, three different ways.

Proof Number One
The average person on this planet has a very low income. About one fourth of the world's population is living in abject poverty. They don't *have* a dollar to spend. The World Health Organization estimates that the average

person lives on about 20 cents worth of food a day. It may not be the best and most interesting diet in the world but it gets them through the day.

In Africa, a popular menu consists of millet in many forms and yams or sweet potatoes which are easy to grow and quite prolific. These items plus some fruits, vegetables, and perhaps a little meat, are sufficient to maintain good health at well below 50 cents per day. And it is worthwhile to point out that this diet virtually eliminates the problem of internal cancer. The food has so much roughage that it scours the colon clean with each meal. An English doctor made this discovery several years ago and his research triggered the present-day popularity of bran as an internal broom.

So, not only do these Africans eat cheap, they die of something besides cancer of the digestive tract.

Proof Number Two
The average human being eats about six times his own body weight per year. If you weigh 150 pounds, you'll pro-

bably eat 1000 pounds of food per year or about three pounds per day. Those pounds include the water content of food.

As this is being written, a local feed and seed store is selling whole grain wheat for human use for $12 per hundred pounds. If you bought it in bulk from a wholesaler in Stockton, you would probably pay only $8 or so. But let's be generous and stick to the $12 per hundred-pound figure. Wheat, when made into cereal, bread, or other edible goodies, gains about three times in weight. Thus, cooked to your taste, this $12 sack of wheat produces 100 lb. × 3 = 300 pounds! Now we're getting somewhere. Dividing 300 pounds into $12 yields 4 cents per pound for healthful, nutritious, freshly-prepared food.

Now let's say that you are a whole wheat nut: you eat nothing but bread, biscuits, hot cereal, pancakes, muffins and cookies for breakfast, lunch and dinner. At 4 cents a pound for your basic food, you would be spending on 12 cents a day! Just three sacks of whole wheat grain at $12 each would provide you with virtually your entire year's supply of food! Think of it; less than $40 for a whole year!

Now it's obvious that few people will live on just one commodity unless, like the 19th century Irish with potatoes, they have to. But our point is clear. If you base

your diet around whole grains, beans, vegetables, seeds and such, you'll spend lots less than a dollar day for food.

Proof Number Three
If you come and visit me sometime I will treat you to a dollar a day menu. We'd start out with a big steaming bowl of oatmeal with some sunflower seeds and raisins plus a little skim milk. That and an apple or orange is it for breakfast. Total cost; perhaps 20 cents. For lunch, a salad of greens, a little grated cheese, half of a hard-cooked egg and a chunk of sourdough bread. Another apple. Cost...maybe 35 cents.

For dinner, we'd live it up. Tacos a la Wild Willy. I buy tortillas for 25 cents a dozen at a Mexican tortillaria. We cook up some pinto beans with a little oil and lots of onions and cumin and just maybe, a few shreds of chicken or other meat. Fill the heated tortilla with the thickened beans, add shredded cabbage (hangs in there better than lettuce), a bit of grated raw onion, slivers of tomato and whatever else is handy. Top with hot sauce and we'll all enjoy. Total cost for three or four generous homemade tacos? Not over 45 cents. So, .20 + .35 + .45 = One dollar even!

Reprise
So there are three distinct and different proofs that we've all been conned into thinking that food has to cost a lot of money. Not only can you spend a lot less, you'll enjoy better health. That old guy with the grey hair zipping around on an ancient Honda in Soquel is me! Questions on this? Write to me c/o *The News.*

© 1984 Bill Kaysing

INDEX